DATE DUE

			PRINTED IN U.S.A.

Japan's Foreign Aid to Thailand and the Philippines

David M. Potter

St. Martin's Press
New York

For Yumiko and Micah

Library of Congress Cataloging-in-Publication Data

Potter, David M., 1961-
   Japan's foreign aid to Thailand and the Philippines / David M.
Potter.
      p. cm.
   Includes bibliographical references and index.
   ISBN 0-312-12563-1
   1. Economic assistance, Japanese—Thailand. 2. Economic
assistance, Japanese—Philippines. I. Title.
HC445.P644 1996
338.9'1520593—dc20   95-50658
                                                       CIP

Book Design by Acme Art, Inc.

First Edition: July 1996
10 9 8 7 6 5 4 3 2 1

Table of Contents

List of Tables and Figures iv

List of Abbreviations v

Foreword vii

Introduction ix

1 Overview of Japan's Aid Program 1

2 Overview of Japan's Foreign Aid to Thailand
    and the Philippines 23

3 Japan's Aid and Thai Development 41

4 Japan's Foreign Aid and Philippine Development 69

5 Accommodation of Interests in the Aid Relationships 101

6 Case Studies in the Accommodation of Interests 127

7 Conclusion 153

Notes 163

Bibliography 189

Appendix: Interviews and Assistance 201

Index 203

List of Tables and Figures

Table 2.1   Japan's Official Development Assistance to Thailand,
               1967–93 25

Table 2.2   Sectoral Distribution of Japan's Loan Aid to Thailand 26

Table 2.3   Sectoral Distribution of Japan's Grant Aid to Thailand 27

Table 2.4   Regional Distribution of Japan's Loan Aid to Thailand 29

Table 2.5   Regional Distribution of Japan's Grant Aid to Thailand 30

Table 2.6   Terms of Japan's Loan Aid to Thailand 31

Table 2.7   Japan's ODA to the Philippines, 1968–93 33

Table 2.8   Sectoral Distribution of Japan's Loan Aid to the Philippines 34

Table 2.9   Sectoral Distribution of Japan's Grant Aid to the Philippines 35

Table 2.10   Regional Distribution of Japan's Loan Aid to the Philippines 36

Table 2.11   Regional Distribution of Japan's Grant Aid to the Philippines 37

Table 2.12   Terms of Japan's Project Loans to the Philippines 38

Table 2.13   Terms of Japan's Non–Project Loans to the Philippines 39

Figure 3.1   Sectoral Distribution of Second Plan Development Budget 44

Figure 3.2   Sectoral Distribution of Third Plan Development Budget 47

Figure 3.3   Sectoral Distribution of Fourth Plan Development Budget 52

Figure 3.4   Sectoral Distribution of the National Budget, 1984–86 56

Figure 3.5   Sectoral Distribution of the National Budget, 1987–90 63

Figure 4.1   Sectoral Distribution of FY 1971–74 Plan 71

Figure 4.2   Sectoral Distribution of 1974–77 Plan 75

Figure 4.2A   Sectoral Distribution of Foreign Aid, 1974–77 76

Figure 4.3   Sectoral Distribution of 1978–82 Philippine Plan 80

Figure 4.4   Sectoral Distribution of 1983–87 Plan 84

Figure 4.5   Sectoral Distribution of 1987–92 Plan 89

List of Abbreviations

ADB	Asian Development Bank
AID	Asian Industrial Development Plan
AJDF	ASEAN-Japan Development Fund
ASA	Association of Siamese Architects
ASEAN	Association of Southeast Asian Nations
BAAC	Bank for Agriculture and Agricultural Cooperatives
CAID	Countryside Agro-Industrial Development Plan
CARL	Comprehensive Agrarian Reform Law
CARP	Comprehensive Agrarian Reform Program
CCPAP	Coordinating Council for the Philippine Assistance Program
CODA	Committee on Official Development Assistance
DAC	Development Assistance Committee
DAR	Department of Agrarian Reform
DTEC	Department of Technical and Economic Cooperation
ECFA	Engineering Consulting Firms Association
EPA	Economic Planning Agency
ESDP	Eastern Seaboard Development Plan
FESAR	Fund for External Support of Agrarian Reform
IFCT	Industrial Finance Corporation of Thailand
IMF	International Monetary Fund
JAIDO	Japan-Asia Industrial Development Organization
JEMIS	Japan Emigration Service
JETRO	Japan External Trade Organization
JICA	Japan International Cooperation Agency
JOCV	Japan Overseas Cooperation Volunteers
LDC	Less Developed Country

MAFF	Ministry of Agriculture, Forestry and Fisheries
MAI	Multilateral Assistance Initiative
MFA	Ministry of Foreign Affairs
MITI	Ministry of International Trade and Industry
MOF	Ministry of Finance
MPWH	Ministry of Public Works and Highways
MTPIP	Medium-Term Philippine Investment Program
NEDA	National Economic and Development Authority
NESDB	National Economic and Social Development Board
NGO	Nongovernmental Organization
NMP	National Maritime Polytechnic
OCAJI	Overseas Construction Association of Japan, Inc.
ODA	Official Development Assistance
OECD	Organization for Economic Cooperation and Development
OECF	Overseas Economic Cooperation Fund
OTCA	Overseas Technical Cooperation Agency
PFC	Project Facilitation Committee
UNDP	United Nations Development Program
USAID	United States Agency for International Development

Foreword

When I first got the beginnings of the idea for this book some years ago at the University of California at Santa Barbara, the topic of Japan's foreign aid was practically untouched. Alan Rix and Dennis Yasutomo had written a book apiece on the subject, and William Brooks and Robert Orr had done a useful but brief article on it. Today, Japan's foreign aid has become something of a growth industry, not only for Japanese companies and aspiring career bureaucrats, but for academics as well. Despite the proliferation of work on this topic, however, the original question that drove this research has remained unanswered. Amidst the wealth of writing one set of actors remains unaccounted for: aid recipients. This is puzzling, since foreign aid involves transactions between donor and recipient and would therefore appear to require analyses of both sets of players. Without recipients, discussions of aid policy remain limited.

The question of recipient interest is not only academic. As the Japanese aid program has expanded around the world the beneficiaries of that assistance now include practically every nation with a reasonable claim to being a developing country. As concessional economic resource transfers to the developing world have declined in real terms in recent years, the question of who continues to give aid has become increasingly important to those nations. This book is an attempt to examine Japanese aid from that uninspected angle.

Over time, the work has undergone a series of changes small and large. Along the way I have had valuable comments and insights from Haruhiro Fukui, Michael Gordon, John Woolley, Steve Jackson, Simon Reich, Andy Kipnis and Gary Hawes. I am grateful, as well, to those people who granted me interviews, and provided me with information and other assistance during the fieldwork. Many requested anonymity so I do not include their names here. A number of people—Elizabeth Zagorodney, Leighton Armitage, Deborah Baker, Richard Whirty, and Bunji Sawanobori—provided moral and emotional support while this project was in progress. My thanks also to Mike Thomson for valuable technical assistance with the manuscript.

Foreign aid begins with institutions that give money and other support. Like the aid recipients in this book, I found myself facing the classic two gap dilemma: inadequate domestic savings and considerable fieldwork and writing expenditures. I am grateful to the following for providing financial support to cover those gaps: the Japan Ministry of Education, the University of California at Santa Barbara, the Association for Asian Studies, and Northern Kentucky University. I am likewise indebted to the Tohoku University faculty of law and Gifu University for providing me with facilities at which to conduct research.

Introduction

In 1983 the Japan International Cooperation Agency (JICA) made a grant of medical equipment for the Chiang Mai University medical faculty in northern Thailand. It furnished the university's hospital with three radiology machines and a radiation meter for treatment of cancer patients. The Japanese Foreign Ministry's evaluation shows that the grant had all the features of a technology-intensive project: the project needed more computer and other technicians as well as continued aftercare by Japan for the equipment. Most important, because it had the new equipment, the hospital accorded preference to cancer patients at the expense of others, even though basic care remained a critical need in the area.[1] The grant fits a pattern of provision of high technology equipment beyond the capabilities of endusers to maintain, a phenomenon that critics of Japan's aid contend is rampant.

That same year Philippines President Ferdinand Marcos requested a commodity loan to support the flagging copper smelting industry in that country. At that time, copper was an important Philippine export to Japan. From the Japanese perspective a loan would seem to guarantee an important source of the metal for its industries, clearly a prime consideration for its vaunted resource diplomacy. Yet the latter government politely rebuffed Marcos' request, suggesting that copper exports to Japan were a matter best left to the private sector.

Did Thailand get what it wanted from Japan's aid program? Why didn't the Philippine government get the aid it wanted in this case? This book examines Japan's aid program in Thailand and the Philippines in light of these questions. It will focus on the period from 1970 to 1993, and will assess Japan's aid in terms of the development priorities set by the Thai and Philippine governments. It argues that Thailand and the Philippines get much, but not all, of what they want because their aid priorities, and the way they pursue them, can accommodate the interests of the other major actors in the bilateral aid relationship.

The study of Japan's aid to date can be divided into two literatures. The first studies Japanese aid policymaking, and has shed considerable light on how aid policy gets made in Tokyo. Alan Rix and Robert Orr characterize the policymaking process as at once centralized and fragmented. While decisionmaking is confined almost exclusively to the aid bureaucracy in Tokyo, it is divided among four agencies: the Ministries of Finance (MOF), Foreign Affairs (MFA), International Trade and Industry (MITI) and the Economic Planning Agency (EPA). There is a great deal of competition between the four agencies for influence in aid policymaking. Although the MFA has gradually asserted its control over policymaking in the 1980s, all retain power in the decisionmaking process because they participate in joint consultation on loan packages and other matters of policy. Policy innovations proposed by one must be accepted by the others. This system results in policies based on the least common denominator. Aid policy is also reactive because Japan will not initiate aid projects and will respond only to aid requests made by recipient governments through formal diplomatic channels. The implementing agencies are characterized as weak because they are captured by officials seconded from the policymaking agencies and the private sector on which they rely for technical expertise. The purpose of aid policy, therefore, tends to be ambiguous. Japan lacks a basic aid law, and specific policies will tend to reflect the perspective of whichever ministry has the most influence. Aid policy decisions tend to be incremental and formalistic with little room for innovation and planning.[2]

A subtheme of this literature discusses those foreign policy goals aid is intended to serve. Throughout most of the Japanese aid program's history, the distinction between aid and other economic activity has been ambiguous. Aid has tended to be lumped in with other private sector activity such as overseas investment. The most explicit Japanese government statement of this approach developed in the 1970s under the rubric of resource diplomacy, in which aid and other resources were to be given to countries possessing resources vital to Japanese industrialization.[3] Dennis Yasutomo, Robert Orr, and others have discussed Japan's aid-giving in terms of strategic interest and attempts to help stabilize friendly governments.[4] Various studies also assess the contribution of Japan's aid in maintaining the international economic and political system.[5] A subset of the latter is a growing interest in Japan-United States aid relations and its effect on overall bilateral alliance management.[6]

A second kind of literature, much of it in Japanese, takes a more critical look at Japan's aid. It shares a common perspective with the first literature in that it sees the institutional weakness in the aid system. The second literature usually portrays Japan's foreign aid as a tool for the advancement of narrow economic interests, in particular the expansion of both private sector export and overseas investment.[7] This view tends to be taken as an article of faith among critics in Japan, especially since the revelations of private sector misconduct in the aid program to the Philippines during the Marcos administration. The Japanese literature's underlying thrust is ideological; it assumes a priori that Japanese aid is bad, and looks about for evidence to support that view. Much of it is also prescriptive, and argues that Japan should improve its aid program. This literature's evidence also tends to be episodic, focusing on case studies drawn from a wide variety of countries, and so neither provides an understanding of aid to particular countries nor allows us to understand typical processes in the aid program.[8]

Most important for this study, neither of these bodies of work systematically considers the priorities of the recipient governments and the strategies they employ to achieve them. The first literature focuses on Tokyo, and uses cases to highlight aspects of policymaking in the Japanese bureaucracy. It therefore reduces the aid interactions of sovereign nations with potentially divergent goals to a policy problem for the Japanese government. The second literature either ignores the recipient governments by examining the grassroots effects of aid or assumes that they behave as compradors acting against the interests of their citizens. Both are inadequate.

This study contends that the preferences of recipient governments matter in the process of aid giving. In the general literature on foreign aid, there has been an increasing awareness since the 1970s that recipient and donor interests differ.[9] It is also apparent that donor interests cannot completely explain global aid flows, but that recipient needs and humanitarian and cooperative efforts to maintain the international order are equally important.[10] As will be discussed in later chapters, recipient governments do have aid priorities. This study argues the significance of those priorities.

Recipient governments have aid priorities that they articulate in their relationships with Japan. If Japan's aid program is request-based, then we would expect recipient priorities to affect the composition of Japan's aid. This could happen in two ways, through changes in overall Japanese policy or changes in specific aid packages. This study also argues that the latter is more likely to happen because the recipient has more control over the latter than the former.

There are several reasons for believing that an aid recipient can affect the kind of aid it gets. Although the general literature on foreign aid deals overwhelmingly with what donors do to recipients, some research suggests that recipients do have some control over the aid they receive. Leon Gordenker found a relationship of mutual influence in the interactions between the United Nations Development Program (UNDP) and three East African nations.[11] Work of more recent vintage by Paul Mosley suggests that recipient priorities will be best represented in sectoral and regional allocations of aid.[12] Robert Cassen and Anne Kreuger, Constantin Michalopolus and Vernon Ruttan, while dealing almost exclusively with the tools of donor influence such as policy dialogue and leverage, nevertheless find that those tools work best when applied to policy changes the recipient wants to make anyway.[13] Indeed, John White as well as Keith Jay and Constantin Michalopoulos argue that recipients will often accept aid conditions from donors because those conditions do not conflict with the recipients' own objectives, and frequently involve reforms they would have undertaken anyway.[14] Mosley, Jane Harrigan, and John Toye, followed by Howard Lehman, argue that there is "slippage" between World Bank conditionality and the actual economic reforms undertaken by recipient governments. While this is due in some cases to developing governments' inability to overcome opposition from domestic actors, in some cases slippage is a deliberate strategy pursued by those governments.[15]

This is not to say that I expect that the governments of Thailand and the Philippines will always get what they want from Japan, or that they will always be able to articulate their aid priorities consistently. No government can achieve that, and most students of comparative politics would agree that the governments of developing societies face special problems in that regard. Moreover, the ability to formulate priorities does not say anything about how to get a donor to follow them. One study, looking over thirty years of international aid experience, concluded that a major constraint on the effective use of aid is that recipients very often do not understand donor aid procedures and decisionmaking processes.[16]

This book investigates the preferences of the recipient governments, their abilities to articulate them, and the ways in which they go about trying to get the aid they want from Japan. This exercise is significant because it alerts us to recipient perceptions of their development needs and how they see Japan's role in satisfying them, a perspective heretofore lacking in the study of Japan's aid. It also alerts us to the fact that aid is the result of negotiation between national governments and not simply the result of policy decisions made in the donor's capital.

Repeated interaction is a significant feature of the aid relationships. Japan and the two recipients discussed in this study interact constantly. Since the late 1970s, the principals in the aid relationships have consulted on aid packages almost every year. Chapter Two notes the continuity of projects between aid packages. The aid relationships are complex, and consultation and negotiation go on at a number of levels and stages.

Repetition in aid negotiations is important because it allows for learning as players interact with one another over a series of negotiations. They become able to forecast their counterparts' priorities and capabilities and to adjust their strategies accordingly. There is evidence that aid recipients worldwide do this.[17] The hypothesis in this study is that the governments of Thailand and the Philippines, specifically their economic planning agencies, can do it as well.

How well recipients forecast donor priorities and capabilities, and whether key actors in those governments can act on those forecasts, is another matter. Neither donor nor recipient can be considered unitary actors. The Japanese aid bureaucracy is composed of competing ministries and agencies. The recipient governments are equally pluralistic. To begin with, aid negotiators in the recipient government are different from the aid users. That is to say, the former are the planning and budgeting authorities and the latter are the implementing agencies. Their differing missions and perceptions of aid potentially creates conflict within the recipient governments themselves. Moreover, because aid enables the implementation of programs in the developing countries, it also attracts the attention of political leaders who seek to harness it to their political agendas.[18] Those agendas may well differ from those of the aid negotiators.

The management of a bilateral aid program from the recipient's perspective can be seen as two sets of related principal-agent relationships. In the first set, the aid planners can be understood as the aid program's principals and the implementing agencies their agents. While the planners are responsible for screening projects in light of development plans and negotiating with donors for aid for suitable projects, they depend on the implementing agencies for projects in the first place. This first set is complicated by several factors. First, the aid planners and negotiators are the agents of the country's political executives—presidents, prime ministers, and their cabinets. While they may wish to control the course of development plans and their implementation, they can be overridden by their principals. Second, the whole process of development planning is subject to a great deal of slack. Developing country governments face very real obstacles in their attempts to identify and assess development priorities and to link them with the necessary implementing measures.[19] Implementing agencies have their own interests. Planners may not have sufficient assessment and enforcement capabilities. They also may not know what kinds of aid donors are willing to give.

The second set of relationships is fraught with greater difficulties. In fact, it may even appear absurd to speak of donor governments as the agents of developing country governments. Principal-agent problems are usually studied in the context of superior-subordinate relationships within organizations.[20] Foreign aid involves the interactions between independent sovereign states. Donor governments are independent of their aid recipients. Recipients have no legal right to aid from developed countries, and even their moral claim to it is attenuated by other political and economic factors. The economic, and consequently political, power that donors have over their developing counterparts is in many cases not inconsiderable, and would seem to demonstrate their superiority. Conditionality, the practice of attaching economic policy requirements to the provision of aid, would seem to suggest that donors are principals and recipients are their agents.

Formally, however, donors are agents. Consider the intent of aid: developed countries have agreed to put some of their resources at the disposal of developing countries in order to support their economic development. In Japan's case, its role as an agent is formalized by its insistence on funding only formal requests from recipient governments. In effect, the donor promises to subordinate its resources to the recipient's development goals. The role of an agent played by donors, then, is voluntary but real.

That stated, we must turn to the very real problem of agency slack. First, donors have their own interests: other recipients, support of domestic contractors, preferences for certain kinds of aid, and biases in technical expertise. Second, they force the recipient to try to narrow the gap between its goals-development plans and debt policies-and available aid. Third, they force the structuring of project priorities back on the recipient governments, in effect requiring them to control the slack between the distribution of power at home and donor preferences and capabilities. Conditions placed on aid may interfere with recipient objectives. Fourth, because principal and agent are sovereign nations it is practically impossible for the recipient to force compliance with its development objectives. The potential for agency slack is built into the aid relationship. Because transactions are voluntary the donor can discontinue its agency role. As we will see, Japan has suspended its agency role for brief periods in the case of the Multilateral Assistance Initiative (MAI) in the Philippines and unilaterally changed the nature of its agency role in Thailand by "graduating" it out of grant aid eligibility in the early 1990s.

The request-based organization of the Japanese aid program tends to make the principal-agent problem more difficult for the recipient. Consider aid from donors like the United States. Because of its proactive stance, the United States Agency for International Development (USAID) initiates project identification. It may be that recipient implementating agencies lobby USAID as vigorously as they do any donor agency, but USAID takes a formal and overt role in structuring the hierarchy of projects it funds. Preliminary review is shared by the Washington office and the recipient's planning authority. Project formulation is well underway before the implementing agencies take a formal role in the aid process. In contrast, in the Japanese case the recipient implementing agencies have a formal role in the initiation of project requests. The structuring process falls on the recipient planning agencies. While in theory this gives the recipient government autonomy from donor interference, in fact it means that the planning agencies are forced to choose among implementing agency projects. This forces them to control, or not, the slack between development plans and individual projects.

Finally, the agency problem is exacerbated by the fact that the donor has its own agents. The Japanese aid bureaucracy relies heavily on private firms at all stages of the aid process from project identification to implementation. They are the donor's agents. As such, they are indispensable to the Japanese aid program. They also create potential slack problems because they have their own interests, profit being the most important. Because oversight by aid officials is weak, if not supplanted by overt promotion, companies can often act independently within the Japanese aid bureaucracy. Oversight by recipient planners is equally weak, despite suspicion of foreign company motives, meaning that they operate equally independently within the recipient environment. Chapter Six discusses a particularly severe problem of agency slack in regard to Japanese contractors.

This study argues that recipients get the kind of aid they request from Japan, but that they get it because their requests can accommodate the interests of the major actors involved. Those actors-the recipient governments, Japan's aid bureaucracy and the Japanese companies that play a crucial intermediary role between the first two-have potentially divergent goals in the aid program.)The recipient governments want projects that simultaneously meet the overall development plan goals and the particular concerns of the implementing agencies, which may not be complementary. The Japanese aid bureaucracy wants requests that meet its preference for capital-intensive infrastructure projects and support of Japanese business, and the Japanese consulting firms and trading companies want projects that provide short-term profits to them.

The formulation, negotiation, and implementation of Japan's aid program in each country would be impossible without the participation of these three sets of actors. Therein lies the problem for the recipient. Thai and Philippine planners cannot get aid from Japan without meeting Japanese aid criteria, both formal and informal. The recipient implementing agencies cannot get aid for projects unless they have project proposals, for which they must often rely on Japanese companies. Moreover, their proposals must meet the planners' priorities if they are to be accepted for request to Japan. The need to find proposals that meet all of these preferences frames the interactions between recipient and donor.

Cooperation in this context is likely to be limited by that need. I use the word "accommodation" advisedly because it describes the basic dilemma faced by the recipient's aid planners: they must balance their own preferences with calculations of what is acceptable to their own ministries and to the donor. The recipient negotiators, therefore, tend to make their requests fit those of the donor agency. The recipient implementing ministries in turn will tend to make their proposals fit the preferences of the planning authorities who actually negotiate with Japan. The implementing agencies are on good ground here because they often rely on Japanese companies for project formulation, which in turn know what Japan's aid criteria are. In any case, the interactions of the major players can be seen as a series of adjustments to one another's priorities. If anything, this process will reinforce the tendency for suboptimal outcomes already found in the bureaucratic politics model.

The recipient accommodates the interests of the donor because of the nature of the power relationship between them. The kind of power the Japanese aid bureaucracy exercises over its counterparts in the Thai and Philippine governments has been described by Bachrach and Baratz as the "second face of power."[21] While we find cases of the overt use of influence over the recipient by Japan in aid disputes, the more common kind of power advantage that Japan enjoys is the ability to keep some kinds of discussions about aid off the bilateral agenda. Japan can simply refuse to entertain certain aid proposals from the recipient. We will find this the case most often in discussions of aid terms, but such refusal can include types and amounts of aid as well. In short, Japan can define the playing field on which the aid game is played.

The phenomenon of learning, the adjustment of behavior in light of experience, is an important element in this study because it allows recipients to increase their ability to get their preferred projects onto annual bilateral aid agendas. Agendas are important to recipients since they constitute the list of key subjects requiring attention by policymakers. In this study, the agenda is defined as the list of projects included in the recipients' development plans that are considered plausible for request to the Japanese aid authorities. Because of the repetitive nature of aid relations in the two cases presented here, it is expected that the negotiators will have a reasonably good idea of how their counterparts will behave. Prenegotiation takes place in the aid relationships studied here in the form of anticipatory bargaining. This is a two-level process by which recipients attempt to improve the chances of getting aid that meets their priorities by requesting from Japan those projects that best fit the preferences and organizational profile of Japan's aid program. Anticipatory bargaining is therefore a form of agenda setting by the recipient.

Anticipatory bargaining should be seen as an adaptation to the donor's power advantage, mentioned above. Anticipatory bargaining would fall under what Bachrach and Baratz call the law of anticipated reactions.[22] The recipient cannot define the playing field; it succumbs to the second face of power by not proposing those projects it knows Japan cannot or will not fund. Rather, it limits its proposals to those projects likely to be funded. Yet, the responsibility for making aid proposals, thereby setting specific agendas, lies with the recipient because Japan adheres to the principle of request-based aid. At this level, the recipient does have power, if only in the choice of tactics for playing on the field chosen by the donor.

Thailand and the Philippines have been chosen as cases for this study for several reasons. First, as Southeast Asian countries they are perceived by Japan to be within its sphere of vital interests.[23] As such, Japan sees aid as an instrument of foreign policy designed, *inter alia,* to promote good political and economic relations with them. Second, they are two of the top ten recipients of Japan's aid for the period under study, and generally in the top five. In some years, each has been the recipient of Japan's largest aid commitment. In both cases that donor's assistance has accounted for between ten and twenty percent of their public investment in key infrastructure sectors. As such, Japan's aid matters a great deal to these two recipients. Third, the two recipient governments have had repeated interactions with Japan in the aid field since the 1970s. Thus, there is sufficient data on the aid program to allow us to observe the changes in interactions over time and to generate conclusions about the nature of those interactions more accurately than if recipient and donor interacted only once or infrequently. Finally, both recipients have been the beneficiaries of important innovations in Japan's aid policy. Thailand benefited from the new emphasis on strategic aid in the late 1970s and early 1980s, and the Philippines has benefited from new modes of aid-giving within the framework of the

MAI since 1989. We can therefore examine the adjustment of donor and recipient preferences in these contexts.

The work is divided into three parts. Chapter One examines Japan's aid program as the starting point in understanding the recipient's external environment. The chapter provides an overview of the development of Japan's aid program, its organizational character, and motivations. Chapter Two considers the two bilateral aid relationships. It examines the origins and development of Japan's aid programs in Thailand and the Philippines, then turns its attention to the sectoral and regional distributions and terms of that aid within each country.

Chapters Three and Four examine the aid preferences of the governments of Thailand and the Philippines, respectively. In both chapters, aid priorities are measured by examining statements on both aid policy and sectoral and regional development priority contained in the medium-term development plans since 1970. These statements are supplemented where possible and relevant by other government statements of priority. The development plans are not treated as blueprints for the aid program; rather, they are seen as statements of political and economic priorities that influence the governments' decisions about aid allocations. Following the criteria set out in Chapter Two, these two chapters consider the governments' sectoral, regional and aid priorities in each development plan period, then compare those priorities to the actual allocations of Japan's aid during those periods.

Chapters Five and Six move the analysis to the level of individual projects. The chapters analyze the ways in which the recipients request individual projects for assistance from Japan. Beginning with the premise that the aid relationships can be seen as iterated games of cooperation, they discuss the interactions of the major players in the aid relationships, and the ways those interactions affect the recipients' establishment of an aid agenda. The chapters argue that in environments of bureaucratic politics the major actors interact under conditions of bounded rationality. The ability to cooperate is limited by the need to accommodate the potentially divergent interests of the players. The accommodation of interests therefore provides a framework in which the potential of cooperation is limited by the institutional capabilities of the key actors. The chapters also discuss the role that learning plays in the recipients' abilities to calculate the kinds of aid Japan is most likely to give, and therefore their assessments of what to ask for. Each chapter concludes with case studies of individual project negotiations, which examine the ways in which divergent interests were resolved. Finally, Chapter Seven refines the idea of accommodation and sums up the findings of the research.

1

Overview of Japan's Aid Program

Introduction

It is not only possible but probable that donors' motivations, interests, and methods of aid allocation will differ from the interests and developmental goals of aid seekers. In the aid relationship, the recipient can try to manipulate the form and quantity of aid to its advantage, but faces difficulties in its attempts to maximize its benefits. Donor and recipient abilities to alter their external environments differ. Donors are donors because they are perceived to be in a position of economic power that allows them the luxury to help their poorer counterparts. Economic power enables them to alter their environments in their favor. This is not the case for aid recipients. At the intergovernmental level, the recipient finds it impossible to manipulate a significant part of its external environment: the donor government's aid organization. Recipients can choose among donors and strategies to attract aid, but they cannot change the character of a donor's aid agency and its aid process.[1] This chapter examines this limitation on recipient power in the aid relationship by outlining the characteristics of Japanese aid. It will outline the volume and direction of Japanese official development assistance (ODA), the nature of its aid administration, and the reasons the Japanese government gives aid.

The International Context

Japan is, as two scholars have termed it, a "donor of consequence."[2] It is not, however, the only one. Indeed, given its reluctance to define a leadership role in the international aid community, it may not even be the most important one. Important forces outside of Japan have shaped the boundaries of Japan's aid program. An important consideration in the interactions between Japan and its aid recipients is the existence of what Robert Wood calls the international aid regime. This aid regime is not as well defined as some other regimes, but its informal norms guide the actions of donor and recipient alike in the provision of aid worldwide. Wood avers that the aid regime has four broad components: bilateralism, in which the interactions of donors and recipients are structured through channels between individual donors and individual recipients; strategic nonlending, in which donors agree to withhold aid for projects deemed appropriate for private sector investment; institutionalized noncompetition, in which donors agree that the aid terms of the qualified lender that most closely approximate the market's should provide aid for a requested project; and conditionality.[3]

An important component of donor-recipient interactions is the shared view of the proper use of foreign aid: aid is for public investment, such as infrastructure development, which the private sector cannot handle. Why do donor and recipient share this point of view? From the Japanese perspective, this point of view grew out of its own development experience. The Philippines and Thailand have internalized the lessons of Western development, at least as ideals. These lessons include the importance of providing public investment that does not crowd out private sector initiatives, and are reinforced by the international aid regime.

The aid regime bounds but does not determine donor programs. Indeed, given the fact that there are more than two dozen official aid agencies operating internationally, the problem for a donor is how to distinguish itself from the rest of the pack. Donors often duplicate aid efforts. Even so, the creation of specialized programs, or niches, by individual donors is a constant in the aid field. Japan has established niches because it finds itself in limited competition with other donors: by the time Japan seriously got into the aid business in the early 1970s there were already a number of donors with active aid programs in Thailand and the Philippines. In Thailand the World Bank, USAID, and West Germany were major donors, with the UN, Australia, and other Colombo Plan donors providing grant aid.[4] The World Bank, USAID, and Australia were also major donors in the Philippines and have continued to play a larger role there than they have in Thailand. For Japan, as for any donor, the problem is how to develop comparative advantage in order to secure a part of the aid market.

Donor competition would seem to enhance the ability of recipients to get the best deal possible in this area. We should remember that recipient planners no more see a donor in isolation from other donors than aid donors see individual recipients in isolation from other recipients. The recipient is presented with a menu of potential project and program capabilities and terms. The decision to approach Japan will be made in light of what other donors can give. While the aid regime tends to keep aid negotiations bilateral, those negotiations are not completely isolated.

Development of Japan's Aid Program

Although the origins of Japan's aid lay in the war reparations program, the aid program per se began in the early 1960s.[5] In 1960 Japan was admitted to the Development Assistance Committee (DAC) of the OECD. In so doing it entered the circle of "developed nations," and assured itself it would not be isolated from the rest of the developed world. It also agreed to accept the responsibilities of membership, one of which was provision of foreign aid. How it fulfilled its responsibilities was another matter. For example, Japan has never agreed to the international ideal that one percent of each member's GNP be spent on foreign aid. Rix notes that throughout the early period of Japan's membership the government was concerned that it be able to set its own aid levels. Nevertheless, membership made Japan aware of its aid responsibility. It also clarified the government's distinction between "aid" and "economic cooperation", a distinction it had not made before then.

Japan's role in the DAC aid debate was limited by the relative hardness of its aid terms and its poor aid performance. Perceptions of the merits of DAC positions varied within the Japanese government. While the Ministry of Foreign Affairs (MFA) was generally positive toward DAC pronouncements, and often used the DAC as a support for its preferences against the other ministries, the Ministry of Finance (MOF) preferred to isolate Japan's aid administration from DAC policies. In any event, the DAC did constitute an external prod to Japanese aid efforts and throughout the 1960s and 1970s it criticized Japan's aid giving.[6]

Concurrent with rapid economic development, in the 1960s Japan increased its foreign aid disbursements. Yet aid remained a small part of its foreign economic policy. Total foreign aid flows increased from $246 million in 1960 to $1.8 billion in 1970, and to $5.8 billion in 1973. ODA disbursements as a percentage of GNP rose from 0.14 percent in 1960 to about 0.25 percent in the early 1970s. By the early 1980s the percentage had risen to roughly 0.30 percent, and has stabilized at about that level.[7] ODA, which excludes private economic flows and other official flows such as export credits and Export-Import Bank lending, rose from $305 million in

1965-67 to $1.1 billion in 1976. During the same period, Japan became the DAC's fourth largest aid donor, trailing only the United States.[8]

Japan's aid program moved to international prominence beginning in the late 1970s. From the recipient's perspective, a notable feature of Japan's aid program since then has been the continuous growth in aid volume. The Japanese government expressed its commitment to increasing the quantity of its aid by implementing a series of medium-term aid targets through the mid-1990s. In 1978, the government pledged to double ODA flows from the 1977 level of $1.4 billion by 1980 under the First Medium-Term Target. In 1980 ODA disbursement reached its highest level yet at $3.3 billion. Japan then announced its Second Medium-Term Target, intended to double the 1976-80 ODA level to $21.4 billion by 1985: in dollar terms it achieved only 85 percent by the target date, although the plan was successful in yen terms. In 1985, the government announced its intention to double its 1985 ODA level to $7.6 billion by 1992. In 1988, the government promised to disburse more than $50 million in its five-year program to 1992, a target that it moved up in 1990 following the rapid appreciation of the yen.[9] In 1994 it announced its fifth medium-term aid plan in which it pledged efforts to provide $70 to 75 billion from 1993 to 1997.[10] Since 1992, Japan has been the largest aid donor in the world.

Remarkably, this dramatic increase in foreign aid expenditures occurred in an era of budgetary restraint. In the 1980s outside of foreign aid only defense received large budget increases. While the foreign aid budget increased 31.5 percent from 1981 to 1985, other government budgets stagnated.[11] The trend continued through the late 1980s, with foreign aid and defense budgets increasing by about 8 percent each year. With the end of the Cold War, even defense budgets have stagnated, leaving ODA as the leader in budgetary increases, albeit at about 4 to 5 percent per year.

Types of Aid

Japan disburses three types of aid: loans, grants and technical assistance. It also contributes to multilateral aid agencies. The bilateral program, composed of loans and grants, has continued to dominate the program; multilateral aid volume did not reach parity with the bilateral aid programs until the late 1980s. In 1992, for example, multilateral aid comprised one-quarter of total aid compared to 41 percent for loan aid and just over 34 percent for grants and technical assistance combined.[12]

Since the inception of the Japanese aid program, loans have dominated aid giving. Japan gives three kinds of loan aid: project loans, commodity loans, and program lending. Project loans are the most common form of aid lending, although commodity loans and program lending increased in importance in the 1980s. Loans emphasize economic infrastructure development, which is also true of overall aid policy. In that sense, the Japanese loan aid program resembles the World Bank more than other bilaterals. Unlike the multilaterals, however, Japan favors the continued provision of loan aid to medium-income countries that are deemed to have developed to the point that they no longer need aid. ODA allocations for energy, transportation, and public utilities have dominated loan aid allocations. In the 1970s Japan favored large yen loan-funded infrastructure development projects. In the 1980s, however, Japan moved away from the large-scale development aid projects of the 1970s. The success rate with such projects was low, and they tended to accentuate the gap between rich and poor. Instead, Japan moved toward support of economic infrastructure and agriculture development in recipient countries.

Grants, unlike loans, are given without expectation of repayment. Japanese capital grants are generally used for social infrastructure development in such areas as housing, medicine, research, and education, as well as agriculture and marine projects, and emergency aid. Grant aid is the sole source of funding for building construction in Japan's aid program and as such is avidly sought by recipient government agencies for smaller facilities' construction projects. Grants are also given for cultural activities. While grants are made to developing countries according to DAC guidelines, they are also given to middle-income countries based on the criteria of demonstrated need, inappropriateness of loans, and friendly relations with Japan.

Technical assistance is the third kind of Japanese aid. Despite the fact that the Japanese aid bureaucracy considers technical expertise to be one of Japan's strengths, several factors have hampered efforts to implement this kind of assistance. Language barriers have limited Japanese experts' efforts abroad: JICA has provided language training programs for key recipient countries only since the 1980s. Since most technical experts are recruited from the private sector for short term assignments, however, language training remains incomplete. Training of foreign nationals in Japan has increased over the years, but language and other difficulties remain. In some cases recipients have complained of the inflated cost of experts. These problems remain despite attempts to improve and expand the technical assistance program. Although Japan now gives more technical assistance in dollar terms than almost all other DAC donors, technical assistance comprises a small portion of the aid budget. In 1986, the share of technical assistance of the total ODA budget was just 11 percent, compared to 38 percent in France, 30 percent in West Germany, and 22 percent in England. By 1993, it had risen to just under 23 percent.[13]

Project aid has comprised the bulk of Japan's program. Project aid gives the donor more control than program aid over how the aid is used, and Japan continued to emphasize it after other DAC donors moved toward provision of program aid and structural adjustment aid in the early 1980s. In recent years Japan has followed suit by extending structural adjustment loans in conjunction with the multilateral banks. Unlike the World Bank, which conditions this type of lending on improvements in the recipient's macro-economic management, Japan as a bilateral donor is not in a position to condition its structural adjustment loans. This type of lending can be quickly disbursed, an advantage given Japan's cumbersome aid policy process.[14]

Japan has gradually expanded its aid to multilateral institutions since the 1960s. It has been a supporter of multilateral aid and, in contrast to its performance in other areas, its contributions to multilateral institutions are better than the DAC average. Since 1984 Japan has been the second largest shareholder with corresponding voting rights at the World Bank, although the relatively small number of Japanese personnel and an increasingly divergent view of the role of government in economic development have limited its role there. Japan contributes to several multilateral financial institutions as well as a number of United Nations agencies. Japanese contributions to United Nations aid agencies has fit well with Japan's postwar foreign policy goals, and contributions to other multilateral aid donors enjoy the advantages of political neutrality and efficient use by aid specialists. The Asian Development Bank (ADB), established in 1965, has been the favored institution for multilateral aid activities. Since its establishment, its presidents have been Japanese. Japan is the Bank's major financial contributor, and holds a greater voting share than any other member nation. Japan does not dominate the ADB, given its position in the Bank's bureaucratic structure and the short-term nature of Japanese bureaucrats' appointments in it, but its profile is higher there than in any other multilateral.[15]

Concessionality

Despite quantitative improvements in aid outlays, Japan has been criticized repeatedly for the low concessionality of its aid. Early loans were tied to the procurement of Japanese goods and services. In 1977 the government began to untie official loans. Yet, the levelling of tied versus untied aid resulted mostly from an increase in multilateral ODA flows; bilateral ODA continued to have a proportionately higher tied aid component.

In the 1980s and early 1990s, the government has taken care to point out its efforts to untie its ODA. In 1985 the MFA reported that 61 percent of its bilateral loans were untied, down from 70 percent in 1984, and 63 percent in 1983. Another 35 percent in 1985, 28 percent in 1984, and 34 percent in 1983 was partially untied. West Germany was the only country with a comparably-sized economy with a higher untied aid ratio.[16] Yet complaints continue that Japan's choice of projects favors Japanese procurement, resulting in de facto tying. Consultancy terms have been "LDC-untied," which means that only companies from Japan and less developed countries (LDCs) can tender bids. Critics in the OECD and developing nations alike accuse Japanese consultants of favoring Japanese goods and services. Beginning in 1988, Japan announced that it would untie the consultancy portion of its aid to selected countries in Southeast Asia.[17] Diplomats in Tokyo argue that despite formal untying, four-fifths of Japan's ODA is spent on Japanese goods and services anyway.

Despite the growth of Japan's aid program in the 1970s and 1980s, aid as a proportion of both GNP and the general account budget has remained modest. As mentioned above, ODA as a percentage of GNP now hovers around 0.3 percent: Japan has consistently ranked near the bottom of DAC donors since the OECD began measuring it in the 1970s. Similarly, ODA as a percentage of the government budget has remained small, 1 percent or less, ranking at the bottom of the DAC donors. Moreover, the grant element of Japan's ODA is lower than most other donors. In the 1960s and 1970s Japanese loans were given at near-commercial rates. Even in the late 1980s loans were given on harder terms than most other DAC donors.[18]

The appreciation of the yen since 1985 has had two consequences for Japanese aid. On the one hand, it has inflated the amount of aid Japan gives. Japan's ascension to the position of largest aid donor in the 1990s is due in no small part to the measurement of its contribution in dollars. On the other, recipient currencies have depreciated against the yen, making it harder for them to repay loans. In effect, Japan's loan aid has become less concessional because it must be repaid with inflated yen. Oddly, despite the appreciation of the yen, Japanese yen loans in the late 1980s still remained more concessional than multilateral loans. The sharp appreciation of the yen against the dollar in early 1995 prompted requests by China and Indonesia to help them alleviate their increased debt burden, overtures to which the government of

Japan at first demurred, before announcing a modest decrease in interest rates on loan aid in mid-year.[19]

Geographical Distribution of Japanese Aid

Japan's aid program now includes countries all over the world. By 1988 Japan was providing aid to 134 countries. By 1990, it was the leading donor in twenty-eight.[20] The bulk of Japanese aid, however, has been given to Asian nations since the program's inception. In the early 1970s, Asia accounted for almost 80 percent of Japanese aid. That bias changed slowly. In the course of the 1970s a loose 70-10-10-10 formula for aid disbursement to the above-mentioned regions took shape. It continued in the 1980s, with Asia receiving about 65 percent of Japan's bilateral ODA, Southeast Asia receiving 35 percent, and the Middle East, Africa, and Latin America about 10 percent each. The Association of Southeast Asian Nations' (ASEAN) share fluctuated from about 30 percent to 23 percent, depending upon the year. In 1982 China became the largest recipient of Japanese ODA. In turn with Thailand, Indonesia, and the Philippines, it has rotated as the largest recipient in any given year since then. The MFA defended its record by arguing that Japan has a close relationship with Asian nations, and that the Middle Income Economies, especially ASEAN, still need ODA loans to further their economic development.

The aid-trade nexus has also been strong in Japan's relations with Southeast Asia. The nations of that region, with which Japan concluded reparations agreements, were the focus of Japan's export drive in the 1960s. By the 1970s Japan and the United States were the two largest investors in ASEAN. Japanese investment in raw materials production and extraction increased in the 1970s and, coincident with the shift by Asian countries toward export promotion and the offshore movement of the Japanese manufacturing sector. Southeast Asia remains a favored site for plant transfers as successive rises in the value of the yen force Japanese manufacturers offshore. In the 1980s and 1990s the region has been the site of government attempts to augment official aid efforts with private capital through the mechanisms of the Japan Industrial Development Organization (JAIDO), the ASEAN-Japan Development Fund (AJDF), and most recently a proposed Asian investment fund to be administered by the Export-Import Bank.[21]

Japanese assistance to ASEAN has been consistent with Japan's perception of the importance of trade and investment with that region, although its emphasis on infrastructure development means that aid and trade have complementary rather than overlapping functions. In the 1960s Japanese net official bilateral assistance to Southeast Asia trailed only that of the United States.[22] Between 1969 and 1973 Southeast Asia experienced a four-fold increase in loans from Japan.[23] During the 1970s Japan transferred $27 billion in ODA to ASEAN, about twice as much as the United States or the EEC.[24] By 1976 Japan was providing just under half of total ODA to Southeast Asia.[25] In the 1980s ASEAN's share of Japan's ODA diminished as Japan's aid program broadened geographically, but ASEAN still receives about one-third of Japan's bilateral ODA. Prime ministers and other cabinet members who visit Southeast Asia continually reassure the nations of that region of Japan's continued commitment to strong relations with them. It also remains the favored site for new Japanese aid programs such as the Asian Industrial Development plan (AID), the ASEAN Japan Development Fund, and the Japan-ASEAN Industrial Development Organization (JAIDO). Here again we see the emphasis on aid as part of Japan's trade and investment strategy: AID is designed to coordinate aid, trade and investment flows from Japan to Asia, while AJDF and JAIDO are intended to augment the Japanese aid program with private sector activities. Southeast Asia has also been the site of Japan's new environmental aid initiatives.

Despite its geographic concentration in East Asia, Japan's ODA now has a global reach. As the volume of its aid increased in the 1980s, Japan came under pressure from the United States and the DAC to expand its program in new areas. Expansion of the aid program has benefitted some Southeast Asian recipients, namely strategic aid in the Thai case and the MAI in the Philippines, but it has also worked against them. The ASEAN countries complained loudly when Japan moved China to the top of its recipient list in the early 1980s, to no avail. More recently, Japan has taken an important role in providing debt relief to Latin America and in assisting the debt and economic restructuring efforts of the former Communist states in Eastern Europe. These efforts have shifted resources that might otherwise have gone to the ASEAN countries.

The shift is not entirely Japan's doing. On the one hand, the developed countries expect more from Japan's aid program. On the other, the ASEAN nations have had trouble absorbing the increasing amounts of Japanese assistance they have been getting. Singapore and Malaysia account for a decreasing share of ODA; Indonesia and the Philippines have trouble using the aid they get in a timely fashion. Orr suggests that the shift away from Southeast Asia after 1978 is due in part to ASEAN's signal failure to prepare appropriate projects to take advantage of Japan's offer of $1 billion to support cooperative regional development as part of the Fukuda Doctrine.[26]

The Japanese government prefers to give bilateral aid as an extension of bilateral diplomacy with key developing nations. Rix has characterized bilateral aid to Asia as a "preoccupation" of aid officials. The aid process has resulted almost exclusively in government-to-government aid requests. Cultivation of bilateral aid relationships has created interdependence between donor and recipient, in which "those countries to which Japan's aid was directed in greatest quantities often depended on Japan as the largest source of their foreign aid receipts."[27] Despite the increase in multilateral ODA from Japan, bilateral ODA accounts for about 70 percent of total ODA. The Ministry of Foreign Affairs sees aid as an efficient diplomatic tool, and as it acquired influence in the aid program in the 1980s, Japan continued to emphasize bilateral aid.[28] Japanese aid officials are concerned that aid be visible, and that it be part of an exchange, criteria which are best served by close bilateral relations.[29]

Organization of the Aid Bureaucracy

Japan's aid program is reactive. The aid bureaucracy relies upon aid requests from recipient governments, and it will not act in the absence of a formal request made through appropriate diplomatic channels. The normal pattern for aid policymaking is as follows: request by a recipient government, either through the Japanese embassy abroad or through the recipient's embassy in Tokyo; assessment by the relevant ministries and agencies in the Japanese government; decision and budget request; exchange of notes between governments; and implementation by the relevant agencies. The aid process differs among aid types, both as to decision makers and process.

Japan's aid disbursement lacks overall planning for several reasons. For one thing, aid policy makers react to applications from recipient governments rather than seeking out projects on their own. The aid bureaucracy has steadfastly avoided the "stigma" of being perceived as an active donor in order to avoid political repercussions from recipients, a viewpoint it has begun to shed only recently and with hesitation.[30] As a result, aid requests come from developing country governments, in whose abilities to find and develop suitable projects the Japanese have little faith. The Overseas Economic Cooperation Fund (OECF) invites members of recipient governments to Tokyo every year to learn how to formulate and prepare aid requests.[31] The results are bound to be disjointed, since individual recipient government requests are unlikely to be coordinated with those of other recipient governments.

At the same time, Japan prefers project loans for specific purposes, which reduces the amount of money it can give. Moreover, recipients' absorptive capacities for aid may limit the amount of aid they can effectively use. For example, this has been a continuing problem with aid to Indonesia and the Philippines since 1986. As Japan has tried to fulfill its international commitments to double its aid volume, money has ended up chasing projects.

The Japanese government cannot coordinate aid policy. It cannot coordinate because its bureaucratic structure prevents unity of purpose. The plethora of ministries and agencies involved helps explain this. There is no aid ministry, rather there are numerous ministries with jurisdiction over parts of the aid program. The Japan International Cooperation Agency (JICA), created in 1974 as an attempt to rationalize the aid process, does not have ministerial status (it is a quasi-independent agency under the MFA), and its jurisdiction encompasses only the implementation of grant aid, technical assistance, and loans not handled by the OECF.

Aid policy is generally set by the "big four": the Ministry of Foreign Affairs (MFA), the Ministry of Finance (MOF), the Ministry of International Trade and Industry (MITI), and the Economic Planning Agency (EPA). Because there is no ministry that sits above the four on aid policy, each enters aid consultations with its own bureaucratic perspective. A situation of equal partnership exists among the four on aid policy in general, although one or two might predominate in specific areas. OECF loans, which make up about half of Japan's ODA, are decided upon jointly by the big four. Grant aid is handled by MFA and MOF, which gives MFA greater influence in deciding its disbursement. Implementation of aid projects is handled by the relevant line agencies in the Japanese government, further decentralizing the program. The centrifugal tendencies of having up to sixteen aid participants is lessened by the fact that the big four occupy the central position in aid policymaking, a position they guard jealously.

Although all aid proposals must pass through the annual budgetary process, and thereby through MOF scrutiny, that process does not necessarily lead to coordinated aid policy. The budget process begins in September for the fiscal year starting April 1. When all proposals have been received, the MOF oversees interministerial negotiations. The draft budget is completed in December, at which point MOF submits it to the cabinet for approval. After senior cabinet approval and adjustment, the budget is sent to the Diet early in the calendar year. Aid items are listed by implementing agency, not by country: country allocation occurs in the ministries after Diet approval of the aid budget. As noted below, the Diet pays little attention to the aid budgetary process, with the result that "de facto authorizations" are made during budget preparation before Diet consideration.[32]

Budget requests come from each ministry for its part of the total aid program. As a result, fluctuations, especially in the 1960s and 1970s, occurred as individual programs were separately augmented or curtailed. Rix found, however, that a balance in aid allocations was preserved among MITI, MFA, and MOF. He also found that MOF influence over the aid budget weakened in the 1970s as more ministries became involved in the aid process, although MOF continually monitored the aid process throughout the year. MOF oversight of the budgetary cycle provides the only means of overall coordination of the aid program, but MOF resources are too limited and its scrutiny too fleeting to really coordinate aid flows.[33]

Annual budgeting is the rule in the MOF, and aid is no exception. Reparations and multilateral aid, however, have been managed on a multi-year basis. The inability of the government to separate the aid program from the single-year budget process prevents flexibility in aid programming, especially for multi-year projects. Annual budgets encourage incremental changes in aid planning and quantitative increases over qualitative improvements in aid policy. They also limit Japan's ability to coordinate aid program implementation with recipients because funds cannot be guaranteed beyond the current budget. In those cases in which recipient countries have initiated medium-term "rolling plans" to provide continuity in their aid programs, JICA and the OECF have had to rely on informal promises of future assistance.[34]

The diffusion of responsibility at the policymaking level continues at the implementation level. There are three agencies charged with implementing aid programs, each under a separate ministerial authority, with practically no coordination among them in the field. The Export-Import Bank occupies a middle ground between true ODA and commercial lending, extending loans to domestic corporations in the forms of export supplier's credit, technical service credit, import credit for goods vital to the Japanese economy, and overseas investment credit. It extends direct loans to foreign governments and their agencies, foreign local public institutions, foreign corporations, and foreign financial institutions. The Bank refinances loans to enable recipients to repay existing debts owed to Japan. It also extends loans in conjunction with private commercial banks for export supplier's credit, import credit, and technical service credit. The Export-Import Bank's role in Japan's aid program diminished in the course of the 1970s as Japan relied more and more on the OECF, but it has continued to play a role in debt rescheduling agreements and in such new programs as the MAI in the Philippines.

The OECF was founded in 1961 to promote overseas economic cooperation in Southeast Asia and other developing areas. It was designed to extend funds in cases where it was difficult to obtain loans from Exim Bank or private banks. In 1975 overlapping functions between OECF and Exim Bank were abolished, although their scope of activities still resemble one another. OECF extends loans to foreign governments and their agencies and to Japanese corporations. It also invests in Japanese corporations, and participates in international agreements such as those maintaining international commodity buffer stocks. OECF extends loans when the grant element of such loans is 25 percent or greater. Although the Export-Import Bank in principle provides loans to Japanese corporations, OECF may do so in some cases.[35] OECF is nominally under EPA supervision. Because it extends about half of total ODA loans, OECF occupies a major position in the aid process.

JICA, created in 1974, extends grant and technical assistance to developing countries. Although it is technically a nongovernmental entity (*tokushu hojin*), it is supervised directly by MFA.[36] JICA took over the functions of the Overseas Technical Cooperation Agency (OTCA) and the Japan Emigration Service (JEMIS). It also carries out international cooperation efforts for MAFF and MITI. JICA extends technical assistance, grant aid, and is responsible for the administration of the Japan Overseas Cooperation Volunteers (JOCV). It also trains Japanese experts for overseas technical cooperation, conducts training programs for foreign participants, and conducts development surveys for technical cooperation.[37]

The small size of the aid bureaucracy contributes to the inefficiency of its policy making. The aid bureaucracy is small compared to other donors, and staff growth has not kept pace with the increasing amounts of aid disbursed over the last two decades. Overall ODA grew five times from 1976 to 1986, while total staff increased barely one percent (from 1,308 to 1,476), with the result that ODA volume per staff was two to three times larger than in other major donor countries.[38] During that period, for example, JICA's budget increased fourfold while its staff decreased slightly to under 1,000 in 1987. The OECF had less than 270 staff members at OECF and fourteen offices overseas that same year.[39] In 1991, as Japan was poised to become the largest bilateral donor in the world, OECF staff had increased to only 291, and total ODA personnel totaled 1,625. In contrast, USAID had 4,512 people that same year, and Germany, with aid volume two-thirds the size of Japan's, had over 4,800.[40] The consequence of recent aid budget augmentations has been to overwork the aid staff severely.

The embassies occupy a position in the aid bureaucracy that is at once critical and limited. Most aid requests from recipients go through Japan's embassies, and in that capacity the embassies act at the forefront of bilateral aid relationships. Rix found that they handled much of the negotiation of aid agreements leading up to the exchange of notes between donor and recipient governments. More generally, embassies maintain the bilateral relationships of which aid relationships are a part. They serve a door-opening function to the recipient ministries. They also engage in intelligence gathering which Rix argues defines the options for policy makers in Tokyo.[41]

Yet, the ability of the embassies to influence aid policy is limited. Several factors explain this. First, the bureaucracy in Tokyo allows the embassies little initiative in aid policy. Second, there is no specialist staff in the embassies, which inhibits the embassies' ability to stake out alternative policy options. Career patterns generally prevent the appointment of economic cooperation personnel to embassy positions. Third, in the absence of specialists, the personnel posted from the various ministries respond to the needs and interests of their own ministries. Consequently, the divergent aid philosophies found in the bureaucracy at home are replicated in the embassies. Not surprisingly, given the relationship between Tokyo and the embassies, domestic interests predominate over advice from the field in the aid relationship. As a result, embassies cannot affect aid allocations, except in unusual circumstances, and thus reinforce the prevailing aid policy.[42]

The reporting functions of the embassies are inadequately fulfilled. The slack is taken up by OECF and JICA offices in a number of developing countries. These officials often conduct economic and aid reporting and act as unofficial aid liaisons. Their presence magnifies the bureaucratic inclination to favor those few recipient countries with such offices. This suggests that once a recipient has established an aid relationship with Japan, that relationship is likely to persist except under extraordinary circumstances, if for no other reason than bureaucratic inertia.

How well the JICA and OECF field offices fulfill the reporting function is questionable. Japan rarely has more than a few OECF and JICA officials posted in a recipient country at one time, and they are posted in the capital cities. Because the number of aid personnel is small, the aid bureaucracy cannot maintain an "extensive network of aid missions in developing countries" able to seek out and assess worthy projects,[43] a weakness that is reinforced by a staff organization that favors clerical and auditing skills over analytic skills.[44] In 1991, for example, the JICA office in Manila had 14 people, most of whom were clerical staff recruited locally.

The gap is filled on an ad hoc basis by numerous survey teams sent by the government. The short-term survey mission is the most common form of contact between Japan's aid staff and recipients. Rix argues that the flow of the later stages of projects consulting firms were funded by governme. ants or loans.[49] Other ministries have similar relationships with the con- ltant associations attached to them.

Consulting for most companies is a means to profit in related business, t an end in itself. Not everyone is happy with this arrangement. The tential for questionable practices exists. Moreover, the ability of this formal system to provide projects that truly benefit recipients while pro- ling efficient use of Japanese aid funds is at least debatable. One Japanese ficial noted that in this situation it is hard to discern the recipients' interests d needs from those of the consultants.[50]

Actors on the Outside Looking In

l policy as described here is dominated by the bureaucracy and certain ts of the private sector that support it. While public awareness of Japan's A has increased markedly in recent years, influences outside the bu- ucracy and business community remain limited. Thus, bureaucratic dom in the aid program has remained stable throughout the 1970s, 0s and early 1990s.

The Diet has the legal authority to participate in aid policy, but it rarely s. While the cabinet must approve all grant and loan aid, it usually omes actively involved when an aid issue has become too controversial eal with through routine channels. The Liberal Democratic Party (LDP) ntains a special committee on aid in the Policy Affairs Research Council. ies abound of influence exerted by LDP leaders on behalf of specific ects, but in general the Diet only becomes interested in aid at budget time hen an aid scandal emerges. From time to time the opposition parties raised issues surrounding aid projects in order to embarrass the prime ster and cabinet, but Diet investigations have little impact on aid policy: pposition parties' 1986 investigation of the aid scandal involving the ppines was limited by LDP and ministry obstruction. In sum, the Diet rmally part of Japan's aid organization, but its inactive posture puts it de the pale of active players.

The ability of the media to affect Japan's aid policy is also limited. to the mid-1980s, the popular media did not pay much attention to aid y. When it did, its coverage was fragmented and episodic, reporting r government statements or scandals involving contracts. Media cover- f aid increased in the mid-1980s in the wake of the Marcos scandals Japan's rise to prominence as the world's largest aid donor. Media

survey teams inhibits continuity in the Japanese aid progra
wanted by the recipient governments. One aid official descril
as "survey pollution."[45]

The lack of official personnel with the requisite tec
administer the aid program has forced Japan to rely heavil;
sector. Private sector personnel fill gaps in the technical
policy agencies as well as in JICA and the OECF.[46] Private
play a significant role in the engineering and construc
foreign aid projects, since they possess skills and knowledg
aid bureaucracy. Japanese firms operating overseas fill t
the understaffed aid bureaucracy and inadequate recipient
tions. Unlike embassy personnel, who are stationed in an
or two years, Japanese firms are staffed by experts far
languages, cultures, and political and economic situati
firms are involved in all aspects of the aid process, from
to project proposal. Consultants often help the recipient g
official proposals for submission to the Japanese embass
aid bureaucracy in support of the project. One MITI offi
almost all loan proposals originated in Japanese compani
officials comment that their success in getting propo
funding is much lower.[47]

In essence, the consultants act as the unofficial rep
government. Understandings about which projects are su
oped between the aid agencies and the companies, altho
companies themselves to convince recipient governmer
projects. In this position they occupy a critical role in th
act as intelligence gatherers who augment the efforts of
personnel. They serve as a link between earlier and late
and, as such, help coordinate aid policy. They also serve
the Japanese aid bureaucracy and new projects in recij
between the aid bureaucracy and new recipients.[48]

A relationship of interdependence exists between
aid bureaucracy. Rix states flatly that the overseas cons
the creature of Japanese foreign aid. Japanese consultin
tended to be internationally uncompetitive, garnering on
of multilateral bank contracts. Some depended on Ja
contracts for half of their work. The government suppor
contracts and direct assistance designated as technical
Consulting Firms Association (ECFA), the main consu
ation, relied on MITI's technical aid budget for one qu

survey teams inhibits continuity in the Japanese aid program, and is unwanted by the recipient governments. One aid official described the process as "survey pollution."[45]

The lack of official personnel with the requisite technical skills to administer the aid program has forced Japan to rely heavily on the private sector. Private sector personnel fill gaps in the technical staff in the aid policy agencies as well as in JICA and the OECF.[46] Private consulting firms play a significant role in the engineering and construction aspects of foreign aid projects, since they possess skills and knowledge lacking in the aid bureaucracy. Japanese firms operating overseas fill the gap between the understaffed aid bureaucracy and inadequate recipient project applications. Unlike embassy personnel, who are stationed in an embassy for one or two years, Japanese firms are staffed by experts familiar with local languages, cultures, and political and economic situations. Consulting firms are involved in all aspects of the aid process, from the initial search to project proposal. Consultants often help the recipient governments write official proposals for submission to the Japanese embassy, then lobby the aid bureaucracy in support of the project. One MITI official declared that almost all loan proposals originated in Japanese companies, although other officials comment that their success in getting proposals accepted for funding is much lower.[47]

In essence, the consultants act as the unofficial representatives of the government. Understandings about which projects are suitable have developed between the aid agencies and the companies, although it is up to the companies themselves to convince recipient governments to request their projects. In this position they occupy a critical role in the aid process. They act as intelligence gatherers who augment the efforts of embassy and field personnel. They serve as a link between earlier and later stages of projects and, as such, help coordinate aid policy. They also serve as the link between the Japanese aid bureaucracy and new projects in recipient countries, and between the aid bureaucracy and new recipients.[48]

A relationship of interdependence exists between consultants and the aid bureaucracy. Rix states flatly that the overseas consulting industry was the creature of Japanese foreign aid. Japanese consulting firms in the 1970s tended to be internationally uncompetitive, garnering only small percentages of multilateral bank contracts. Some depended on Japanese government contracts for half of their work. The government supported the industry with contracts and direct assistance designated as technical aid: the Engineering Consulting Firms Association (ECFA), the main consulting industry association, relied on MITI's technical aid budget for one quarter of its assistance.

In the later stages of projects consulting firms were funded by government grants or loans.[49] Other ministries have similar relationships with the consultant associations attached to them.

Consulting for most companies is a means to profit in related business, not an end in itself. Not everyone is happy with this arrangement. The potential for questionable practices exists. Moreover, the ability of this informal system to provide projects that truly benefit recipients while providing efficient use of Japanese aid funds is at least debatable. One Japanese official noted that in this situation it is hard to discern the recipients' interests and needs from those of the consultants.[50]

Actors on the Outside Looking In

Aid policy as described here is dominated by the bureaucracy and certain parts of the private sector that support it. While public awareness of Japan's ODA has increased markedly in recent years, influences outside the bureaucracy and business community remain limited. Thus, bureaucratic freedom in the aid program has remained stable throughout the 1970s, 1980s and early 1990s.

The Diet has the legal authority to participate in aid policy, but it rarely does. While the cabinet must approve all grant and loan aid, it usually becomes actively involved when an aid issue has become too controversial to deal with through routine channels. The Liberal Democratic Party (LDP) maintains a special committee on aid in the Policy Affairs Research Council. Stories abound of influence exerted by LDP leaders on behalf of specific projects, but in general the Diet only becomes interested in aid at budget time or when an aid scandal emerges. From time to time the opposition parties have raised issues surrounding aid projects in order to embarrass the prime minister and cabinet, but Diet investigations have little impact on aid policy: the opposition parties' 1986 investigation of the aid scandal involving the Philippines was limited by LDP and ministry obstruction. In sum, the Diet is formally part of Japan's aid organization, but its inactive posture puts it outside the pale of active players.

The ability of the media to affect Japan's aid policy is also limited. Prior to the mid-1980s, the popular media did not pay much attention to aid policy. When it did, its coverage was fragmented and episodic, reporting either government statements or scandals involving contracts. Media coverage of aid increased in the mid-1980s in the wake of the Marcos scandals and Japan's rise to prominence as the world's largest aid donor. Media attention still focuses on short-term phenomena such as illegal practices or the involvement of particular politicians.[51] Such reporting tends to be forgotten as new, hot topics emerge. Overall, the media's focus on the underside of the aid program limits its impact on aid policy, because the information it provides is short-term and fails to provide the public with a larger understanding of aid policy and its process.

Reasons for Giving Aid

Japan gives aid for a number of reasons. At different times the government has perceived the utility of aid-giving differently. Aid policy, moreover, is subject to the pressures of various ministries and agencies, each with its own agenda. Nevertheless, a few major reasons for aid-giving are clear. Brooks and Orr outline four phases of postwar Japanese aid policy. They are: 1) war reparations from the mid-1950s to 1965; 2) tied aid designed to promote Japanese exports, from the 1950s to the early 1970s; 3) aid in the 1970s designed to promote interdependence with resource-rich aid recipients, with the aim of fostering resource diplomacy; 4) emphasis on basic human needs, LDC aid, and "sensitivity to the humanitarian needs of countries of strategic importance."[52] Yasutomo emphasizes the change in aid policy in the late 1970s and 1980s toward aid giving for political and strategic reasons.[53] More recently, Japan has included debt alleviation measures in its aid program as the international debt crisis has emerged as an international economic problem. Finally, Japan has begun to wrestle with defining its leadership role in the international aid community.[54]

The common thread running throughout is the economic motive for aid giving. Japan has often been accused of extending aid as a mere extension of private overseas investment. In the 1950s and 1960s the government found it convenient to blur the distinction between aid per se and private flows by referring to both as economic cooperation, a term MITI still uses. This ambiguity enabled different ministries to define their own priorities within this policy area, and allowed the government to soften the image of an overt policy of postwar export promotion. Aid policy facilitated this export through aid and reparations loans and grants tied to procurement of Japanese goods, a policy that continued well into the 1970s.

As Japan's economic drive continued into the 1970s, its dependence upon imported natural resources became acute. The "soybean shock" of 1972 and the oil crisis of 1973-74 heightened the sense of vulnerability to external resource dependence. Given the trend toward continued industrialization, the government foresaw heavy resource dependence in the future, regardless of short-term measures to reduce consumption. The Japanese solution was to develop its "resource diplomacy." One aspect of this new policy was to expand the number of suppliers in order to avoid dependence on any one. Second, Japan began to develop processing industries in countries which have natural resources vital to the Japanese economy. The Asahan aluminum complex in Indonesia is an example of these development-aid package programs.[55] It also instituted a policy of cultivating friendly diplomatic relations with supplier countries. Foreign aid was part of this effort. The Export-Import Bank was already making efforts to channel funds to developing countries. At the beginning of the 1970s the bank increased its credit for natural resources development projects overseas. Following the Arab oil embargo, Japan offered aid packages to oil producers and their allies, which resulted in a reduction of oil cutbacks to Japan in late 1973.[56]

In the 1970s Japanese aid strategy changed from one based purely on economic considerations to one that considered international security and the integrity of the western alliance. In 1979, following events in Iran and the Soviet invasion of Afghanistan, Japan increased its economic assistance to Turkey and Pakistan: theretofore neither country had been a major recipient of Japanese aid. That same year Japan suspended its aid to Vietnam, in the wake of that country's invasion of Cambodia, and increased its aid to Thailand. These cases fell under the new rubric of aid to "countries bordering on areas of conflict," which were considered strategically or politically important to Japan and the western alliance. The shift occurred simultaneously with a debate about the political and strategic possibilities of aid giving. The Ohira cabinet (1978-1980) began a search for a comprehensive national security policy that transcended economic diplomacy.

What comprehensive national security and strategic aid are remains unclear. Yasutomo's research on this change suggests that the relevant ministries are not of one mind about how to formulate strategic aid policy: some see it as a substitute for military power; others see it as a supplement. Since the Ohira cabinet, aid has been accepted by all cabinets as a part of comprehensive security, but it has never been specifically defined nor have its consequences fully examined. Moreover, there is a great deal of ambiguity in the Japanese government's position on the reasons for giving aid. While the LDP and the ministries are clear that aid is given for strategic reasons, and also as a cover for defense budget increases, the relationship between comprehensive national security and aid is ambiguous.[57]

While cabinets have used aid for "strategic" purposes the government hesitates to say as much. This term has been used by outside observers and the media, but not within the government. Government officials are at pains to point out that it is not "strategic" in the American sense even though it is in line with American security interests. Officials worry about the public's understanding of security aid. Moreover, the opposition parties have rejected the idea. In the 1990s the dual discussion of ODA and the dispatch of Self Defense Force personnel for multilateral peacekeeping efforts as parts of Japan's contribution to maintaining international stability has served only to heighten the ambiguity.

If we do not know exactly what strategic aid is, it is clear what it is not. Although strategic aid is given to countries that are politically and militarily important to western interests, strategic aid is not military aid per se. It is given with the intention of indirectly maintaining the political and military status quo by stabilizing the recipient economically. Japanese aid to stabilize the Philippine economy in the aftermath of Marcos' departure in 1986 is an example of this kind of thinking. Moreover, not only does aid to the Philippines stabilize the Philippine economy, it contributes to regional political security. This last point suggests that there is no hard and fast distinction between recipients of strategic aid and recipients of purely economic aid. In either case, countries like Thailand and the Philippines are major recipients of Japanese aid. Finally, no matter what the political motivation of aid, the actual content is for economic projects. For example, in 1983 South Korea requested additional Japanese aid under the rubric of "security-related economic assistance," thereby emphasizing Japan's reliance on South Korea's security needs. The $4 billion finally agreed upon was for infrastructure that included the construction of waterworks and a dam. The government has refused specific proposals because of the possibility that the projects would be used for military purposes.[58]

Given Japan's renunciation of war, economic diplomacy occupies center stage in Japanese foreign policy. Japan became an aid donor in the 1960s as part of its OECD membership. In the ensuing three decades Japan has gradually come to terms with the expectation that it supports the international economic system in which it has succeeded so well. Aid is an effective way for Japan to fulfill its responsibility to the international economic order. It simultaneously works well as a tool of Japan's diplomacy. When Japan talks of being an "aid great power" it can claim it is assuming world leadership commensurate with its economic power while promoting its trade and investment policies and avoiding the potential backlash of military buildup.

The bureaucracy does not unquestioningly accept aid as Japan's contribution to the international economic order. While the MFA in the 1960s and 1970s championed aid as a priority in satisfying international and regional responsibilities, and was thus more sensitive to DAC and recipient criticisms of aid performance, the MOF and EPA are more concerned with aid's budgetary impact. MITI, in particular, remains concerned that aid serve Japan's economic policy goals.

Two obstacles remain. One is the nature of Japan's aid bureaucracy, discussed above. To answer its critics Japan has within the last few years announced various plans to improve its aid to keep up with its global responsibilities. Yet, while Japan continues to raise the volume of its aid budget, actual disbursements lag. The second is the current debate in Japan about its proper role in the world. The government is still reluctant to cut too large a swath in the international system, thereby limiting aid's utility as a tool of global foreign policy. In no small part the ambiguity of strategic aid policy reflects the unfinished nature of this debate. The most recent attempt to articulate an aid philosophy was found in the 1992 ODA Charter. Yet, with the exception of an explicit commitment to using aid to promote environmental protection and a pledge to work more closely with non-gov-ernmental organizations (NGOs), the Charter largely ratifies the existing policies of providing aid for humanitarian, economic and strategic reasons to those regions of the world to which Japan already provides assistance.[59]

The upshot of these two factors is that Japan is neither a world leader, except in the narrowly economic sense, nor is it an aid leader. Rix argues that although Japan provides more aid to Asia than anywhere else, Japan is not setting a development agenda for the region, not is it setting a develop-ment agenda anywhere else.[60] Despite recent attempts to articulate a Japan-ese model of development, Japan's policy impact on institutions like the World Bank remains limited.

Finally, Japan gives aid because it is a politically acceptable diplo-matic tool. It is not military, which soothes the fears of wary Asian neighbors and satisfies pacifist sentiments at home. Its obvious economic orientation is in line with Japan's postwar economic policy, foreign and domestic. In an era marked by "aid fatigue" in other donor countries, public approval of aid programs remains strong in Japan. With the exception of a few critics in intellectual circles, practically all parties and key interest groups support the idea of foreign aid. Finally, because aid giving is seen as desirable by donor and recipient alike, aid initiatives have become important Japanese agenda items at G-7 summits and Southeast Asian trips attended by Japanese prime ministers. The latter point is important. Given Japan's reluctance to use military force beyond its borders, aid is one of a few foreign policy tools it can use.

Conclusion

Several characteristics of Japanese aid have emerged in this chapter. One trend in the last four decades has been the expansion of the volume and scope of Japanese foreign aid. In terms of volume, Japan has changed from a minor aid donor to the world's largest. From the recipient's viewpoint, it has become a major source of external funding. Meanwhile, it has gradually, and reluctantly, softened the conditions of its aid to favor recipient and DAC expectations. Second, it has expanded the scope of its aid policy to encompass more than economic goals. Third, the administrative process has not kept pace with these changes. The diffusion of overall responsibility for the aid program, the multiplicity of decisionmaking and implementing actors, the small size of the aid bureaucracy, and the importance of nongovernmental actors to all stages of the aid process cast doubt on the ability of the Japanese government to ensure the effectiveness of its aid program. It is not clear that Japan is accomplishing either its developmental goals or its more broadly political goals with its foreign aid program. Finally, aid is a policy area largely insulated from outside pressures. Aid policymaking tends to be routine, with only occasional problems requiring or amenable to outside solution.

As noted at the beginning of this chapter, the structure of the a donor's aid administration and the nature of its aid program are givens with which a prospective recipient must contend. It is improbable that the recipient will be able to affect either of those aspects of its aid environment. Moreover, the routine nature of most aid decisions means that there are few channels of access outside the Japanese aid bureaucracy that can be used consistently to a recipient's advantage. Yet the fact remains that the recipient is included in the aid process. From that point, it is possible that the recipient can affect some outcomes in the aid process. Moreover, the existence of the aid regime reminds us that Japan's aid program, while retaining its own character, resembles other donors' programs in many ways. Active private sector consultants, reliance on project requests from recipients, rotation of officials in the field, agency competition for funds, and "survey pollution" are found in other countries.[61] Long-term beneficiaries of bilateral aid relationships will undoubtedly have learned to use the process to their own advantage. It is likely that recipients will try to press their claims at the request phase, since application for projects is up to them. Given the crucial position that private consultants play in the aid process, it is also likely that recipients rely on them to lobby the Japanese aid bureaucracy. The following chapters explore these access points and how they are used by recipients.

2

Overview of Japan's Foreign Aid to Thailand and the Philippines

Introduction

Chapter One outlined the general developments and characteristics of Japan's foreign aid program. Chapter Two explores the history and characteristics of its aid programs in Thailand and the Philippines. Broadly, it will examine what each recipient got, and when. It will describe the origins of Japan's aid program in each country, then examine the programs in terms of amounts of aid received and sectoral and regional distribution of that aid. Finally, it will examine the terms of Japan's aid to each recipient over time. This will enable us to more fully examine the bilateral relationships in subsequent chapters.

The Japanese Aid Program in Thailand

Through the end of 1993 Japan has given eighteen yen loan packages to Thailand. It has given grant aid almost annually since 1970. Since the mid-1980s, Japan has provided about two-thirds of Thailand's total bilateral ODA. How has the program changed? We would expect that over time Japan would give Thailand larger amounts of aid, both in terms of loans and grants, for more projects. We would also expect that the sectoral distribution of Japan's aid to the Thai economy would expand, and that Japan would progressively give aid to more regions within Thailand. Finally, we would expect that the terms of lending would soften across successive yen loans.

The aid program really began in April 1966 at the first World Bank-sponsored Consultative Group meeting in Tokyo. At that meeting, the Thai government made a formal request for long-term yen loans from Japan. Negotiations got underway when the Japanese foreign minister visited Thailand in October of that year, and an agreement was reached in 1968. Japan pledged 21.6 billion yen in loans to finance development projects under the Thai government's Second Economic and Social Development Plan. Half the amount would be funded by the Export-Import Bank of Japan, with terms of fifteen to eighteen years' repayment with five years' grace period and a 5.75 percent interest rate. The other half was to be funded by the OECF with a twenty-year repayment period, a five-year grace period, and a 4.5 percent interest rate. All parts of the loan package were tied. All projects were for infrastructure development. The unused portion of the loan package was cancelled in 1972.[1]

Volume of Japan's Aid to Thailand

Table 2.1 presents data on Japan's aid to Thailand from 1968 to 1989. As expected, the volume of both yen loans and grants increased over time. The Fifteenth Yen Loan, signed in February 1990, amounted to 81.154 billion yen, almost four times larger than the First Yen Loan. The increase in the volume of grant aid was even more spectacular, from 24 million yen in 1970 to 14.42 billion yen in 1983. Total aid for fiscal year 1991 was 90.64 billion yen, more than four times larger than total aid for 1968.

Beginning in 1977, annual commitments of both yen loans and grants became the norm. (The exception occurs in yen loans in 1986, when no commitment was made.) Since the Fukuda Doctrine was announced in 1977, it is natural to assume that Japan would show greater commitment to ASEAN countries thereafter. One way of achieving that would be to establish a continuous aid presence in the recipient countries. In 1977 Thailand and Japan began annual bilateral consultations on aid. The results of these trends are clear: aid commitments show much greater continuity from year to year from 1977 on, especially after 1979. In the case of grant aid the continuity can be seen as early as 1974, but there is clearly a major leap in funding levels after 1977.

Table 2.1 reveals that the lion's share of aid was in the form of loans. Because the World Bank classifies Thailand as a middle income country it does not qualify for much grant aid, a policy to which Japan adheres. In the early 1970s the share of grants in years in which both grants and loans

TABLE 2.1
Japan's ODA to Thailand, 1967–93
(Hundred Million Yen)

Year	Loans	%Total	Grants	%Total	Total	Total ODA
1967	216	100	0	0	216	na
1970	0	0	0.24	100	0.24	na
1971	0	0	0.13	100	0.13	na
1972	640	99.75	1.63	0.25	641.63	na
1973	0	0	0	0	0	na
1974	0	0	7.9	100	7.9	na
1975	168.4	94.3	10.13	5.7	178.53	na
1976	0	0	10.31	100	10.31	na
1977	574	96.75	19.3	3.25	593.3	3825
1978	103	73.4	37.4	26.6	140.3	4663
1979	390	84	73.68	16	463.68	5781
1980	500	82.4	107	17.6	607	7491
1981	550	95.9	123.25	21.5	573.25	6993
1982	700	83.5	138.46	16.5	838.46	7529
1983	637.6	82.4	144.2	17.6	817.2	8933
1984	696.4	83.4	138.8	16.6	853.2	10258
1985	720.7	84.4	131.8	15.6	853.49	9057
1986	0	0	127.18	100	127.18	9495
1987	817.3	87	123.7	13	941.05	10782
1988	758.18	88.4	99.8	11.6	858.01	11705
1989	811.54	89.5	95.41	10.5	906.95	12368
1990	0	0	66.66	100	66.66	13350
1991	846.87	93	59.53	7	906.4	14840
1992	1273.75	97.5	32.14	2.5	1305.89	14354
1993	1044.62	97	31.45	3	1076.07	

Source: *Waga Kuni no Seifu Kaihatsu Enjo*, selected years.

were given was low. From 1979 on the share of loans to grants stabilized at about 83 percent to 16 percent. In the late 1980s the proportion of grants to loans decreased as grant levels declined. By 1989 Japan's grant aid had fallen to two-thirds of the 1983 level. This trend will be discussed in Chapter Three.

As noted in the introduction to this book, the literature on Japan's foreign aid has focused almost exclusively on how Japanese aid policy is made. Discussions of aid to specific recipients have tended to explain certain aspects of that policy process. Looking at specific aid programs by

TABLE 2.2
Sectoral Distribution of Japan's Loan Aid to Thailand
(Number of Projects)

Sector	1967-75	1976-80	1981-85	1986-90	1991-93
Roads & Bridges	4	7	7	6	8
Transportation	2	4	8	5	4
Energy/Electricity	3	5	6	6	7
Communications	5	3	2	3	3
Waterworks	7	2	8	7	7
Agriculture/Forestry	1	6	16	5	3
Industry/Mining	1	0	5	6	0
Education/Manpower	0	0	1	0	0
Medicine & Health	0	0	0	0	0
Social Services	0	1	1	0	0
Food Aid	0	0	0	0	0
Disaster Relief	0	0	0	0	0
Other	0	0	0	0	4

Source: *Waga Kuni no Seifu Kaihatsu Enjo,* selected years.

themselves, however, reinforces the fact that Japan's aid program is based upon bilateral relationships with recipient countries. This clearly emerges when we compare Japan's total ODA for any given year with the ODA received by a specific recipient. The far right column of Table 2.1 shows total amounts of Japanese ODA by year. Column Three shows the total amounts of Japanese ODA Thailand received per year. Until 1978 the amounts vary widely. In some years Thailand received no aid at all; in others, it received either grant aid or loan aid or both. Despite the greater continuity in aid to Thailand after 1977, there has never been a one-to-one correspondence between Thai aid and the overall Japanese aid program. Increases in overall Japanese ODA does not necessarily reflect corresponding increases in total Japanese ODA to Thailand. Conversely, there are years in which ODA to Thailand increases despite decreases in overall ODA. In 1985, for example, total Japanese aid to Thailand increased marginally from 1984 despite a drop of almost 12 percent in overall ODA from the previous year. The increase in Thai aid from 1981 to 1982 is more dramatic: overall Japanese aid in 1982 increased 7 percent from 1981 while ODA to Thailand increased 46 percent from 1981 to 1982. Although the trend in this period is toward increases

TABLE 2.3

Sectoral Distribution of Japan's Grant Aid to Thailand

(Number of projects)

Sector	1970-75	1976-80	1981-85	1986-90	1991-93
Roads & Bridges	0	0	0	3	1
Transportation	0	0	0	0	0
Energy/Electricity	0	0	1	0	0
Communications	3	0	0	1	0
Waterworks	0	1	4	3	1
Agriculture/Forestry	0	3	9	6	3
Industry/Mining	1	1	3	6	0
Education/Manpower	3	9	24	18	13
Medicine & Health	0	2	5	2	2
Social Services	0	6	9	6	0
Food Aid	0	5	5	3	0
Disaster Relief	0	4	5	7	0
Other	0	0	1	2	0

Source: *Waga Kuni no Seifu Kaihatsu Enjo*, selected years.

in aid amounts over time, there appears to be no relationship between the amount of aid in one year and the amount in the subsequent year.

Sectoral Distribution of Japan's ODA to Thailand

As expected, the number of loan commitments increases over time. Table 2.2 presents data on the sectoral distribution of Japan's yen loans to Thailand. The data have been aggregated into five-year periods to filter out changes in specific years. The nearly exclusive concentration of loans in the areas of infrastructure development, agriculture (fisheries and aquaculture have been included in this category) and industry is striking. Only three project commitments during the entire period fall into other categories. 70 percent of all loan projects committed between the 1968 and 1993 fall into the infrastructure category. Furthermore, while the number of loan projects generally increase over time, the sectors to which they are directed show little variation.

Table 2.3 presents data on the sectoral distribution of grant aid to Thailand from 1970 to 1993. In the first three periods the number of grant projects increases. In the last two periods it declines compared to the third period: this can be attributed to the general decline in grant aid funding seen in the previous section.

Grant aid sectors and loan aid sectors are almost mutually exclusive. Non-infrastructure sector projects account for just over 90 percent of all grant aid projects. Education and manpower alone accounts for 37 percent of the total.[2] Agriculture and forestry are well represented in grants as well as loans, comprising 12 percent of total grant projects. Infrastructure projects account for just 7 percent of all grant aid. In the case of roads and bridges, aid was designated for repair of small-scale rural sites and thus differs in scale and purpose from its loan aid counterparts.

In contrast to loan aid, grant aid has become more diversified over time. Projects were funded in only three sectors in the first five-year period; by the fourth period grant aid was being committed to twelve sectors. Moreover, although the grant aid program has favored the "soft" sectors, like social services and rural development, some grant aid was committed to infrastructure development in all periods. In terms of sectoral distribution, we may conclude that the grant aid program is more diversified and flexible than the loan program.

Regional Distribution of Japan's ODA to Thailand

Japan has been accused of giving aid largely to capital regions in recipient countries. The data here, however, do not appear to bear out that contention. Table 2.4 presents data on the regional distribution of yen loans to Thailand. Across the first three periods the number of projects allocated to the metropolitan Bangkok region remains flat, then drops off markedly in the fourth period before returning to its former importance in the early 1990s. It would be difficult, given the sharpness of the decline, to attribute it merely to the lack of a yen loan package in 1986. Furthermore, projects are allocated to all regions in all periods, although the North and Northeast receive less than the Central and Bangkok regions in the first two periods. The exception is the South, which lags in project allocation behind other regions in all periods. The number of interregional and national projects is remarkably large, reflecting Japan's manner of reporting projects.[3]

All governments face the problem of allocating limited resources. Table 2.4 suggests how the Thai government has made such decisions in the case of Japanese aid. Note that yen loan allocations for the Central region, the area surrounding metropolitan Bangkok, fall off markedly in the third period. Note also that the Eastern Seaboard Development Project

TABLE 2.4
Regional Distribution of Japan's Loan Aid to Thailand
(Number of projects)

Region	1967-75	1976-80	1981-85	1986-90	1991-93
North	2	1	5	2	3
Northeast	2	1	5	2	0
Central	5	4	1	0	1
South	1	0	0	0	1
Bangkok	8	7	10	3	7
ESDP	na	na	13	9	5
National	6	14	22	21	19

Sources: JICA, *Kunibetsu Enjo Kenkyukai Hokokusho*, 1989; *Waga Kuni no Seifu Kaihatsu Enjo*, 1994.

(ESDP) receives the largest number of projects of any region in that period and the fourth period. At the same time, allocations to the Bangkok region level, then fall off. The evidence suggests that the Thai government made the decision to allocate aid resources away from the capital region to the ESDP. In so doing, it also drew resources away from the rest of the Central region, of which the ESDP is part. This decision will be discussed more fully in Chapter Three.

Grant aid was distributed differently. Table 2.5 presents data on the regional distribution of Japan's grant aid to Thailand. The North received the least grant aid in all periods. The South fared better with grant aid allocations than with yen loans, although it received fewer grants than the Northeast, the Central region, or Bangkok. The latter received many more grants than any other region in all periods. Finally, note that the ESDP received only one grant, an environmental protection study carried out in 1984. Overall, the spatial pattern of grant aid distribution supports the criticism that Japanese grant projects are overwhelmingly clustered in the capital region and the immediately surrounding areas. The farther away a region lies from the capital, the less likely it is to get Japanese grant aid.

The Northeast is an anomaly in that its distance from Bangkok is not in inverse proportion to the number of grant projects it was allocated. This can be explained by the fact that the Northeast received a great deal of relief and other grant aid following the influx of Cambodian refugees into the region following

TABLE 2.5

Regional Distribution of Japan's Grant Aid to Thailand, 1970–93

(Number of projects)

Region	1970-75	1976-80	1981-85	1986-90	1991-93
North	1	1	3	2	1
Northeast	3	7	7	10	2
Central	3	6	10	6	0
South	1	2	3	7	3
Bangkok	10	12	31	29	5
ESDP	na	na	1	0	0
National	1	10	19	16	7

Sources: *Tai Kunibetsu Enjo Kenkyukai Hokokusho*, 1989; *Waga Kuni no Seifu Kaihatsu Enjo*, 1994.

the outbreak of the Third Indochina War in 1979. The politically motivated intent of Japan's aid to the Northeast is reflected in the large number of projects allocated to that region. With the diminution of the Vietnamese threat to Thailand in the early 1990s, that region has received less aid.

Terms of Japan's Yen Loans to Thailand

As expected, loan terms become more concessional in all categories across time. Table 2.6 shows the terms of Japan's yen loans to Thailand. Loans are arranged by date of exchange of notes rather than by loan package, allowing us to see different loan terms within annual aid commitments. The repayment column shows the actual repayment period followed by the grace period indicated in parentheses. Repayment terms soften in a fairly orderly fashion. For example, the terms of the Thirteenth Yen Loan (1987) included a repayment period five to ten years longer, a grace period two to five years longer, a slightly lower interest rate, and the ability to more freely award project contracts than the First Yen Loan (1968). The trend is not even, however; the repayment terms of the Twelfth (1985) and Thirteenth (1987) Yen Loans and the interest rates in the Eleventh (1984) and Twelfth Yen Loans (1985) are harder than the trend would otherwise suggest. In all years, special yen loans received in addition to the usual loan packages carry harder terms in at least one category.

TABLE 2.6

Terms of Japan's Loan Aid to Thailand, 1968–93

Year	Amount	Agency	Repayment	Interest	Tying
1968	10800	Exim	15-18 (5)	5.75	Tied
1968	10800	OECF	20 (5)	4.5	Tied
1972	1821	Exim	20 (7)	5.0	Tied
1972	4179	Exim	20 (7)	5.0	Tied
1972	6000	Exim	20 (7)	4.0	Untied
1972	17000	OECF	25 (7)	3.25	Untied
1972	17000	OECF	25 (7)	2.75	Untied
1972	10000	Exim	20 (7)	3.75	Tied
1972	8000	OECF	20 (7)	3.75	Tied
1975	9550	OECF	20 (7)	4.0	LDC
1975	7290	OECF	25 (7)	2.75	LDC
1977	24900	OECF	25 (7)	3.25	Untied
1978	32500	OECF	25 (7)	3.25	LDC
1979	10300	OECF	25 (7)	3.75	Tied
1979	26536	OECF	30 (10)	3.25	Untied
1980	15536	OECF	30 (10)	3.0	Untied
1981	10536	OECF	30 (10)	3.0	Untied
1982	15000	OECF	30 (10)	4.25	Untied
1982	10536	OECF	30 (10)	3.0	Untied
1983	67360	OECF	30 (10)	3.0	Untied
1984	69638	OECF	30 (10)	3.5	Untied
1985	68018	OECF	30 (10)	3.5	Untied
1985	4059	OECF	25 (7)	3.5	Untied
1987	4915	OECF	25 (7)	3.0	Untied
1988	75818	OECF	30 (10)	2.9	Untied
1990	81154	OECF	30 (10)	2.7	Untied
1991	84687	OECF	25 (7)	3.0	Untied
1992	34375	OECF	30(10)	2.5	Untied
1992	93000	OECF	25(7)	3.0	Untied
1993	104462	OECF	25(7)	3.0	Untied

Source: MITI, *Keizai Kyoryoku no Genjo to Mondaiten*, selected years.

Although the status of aid tying becomes more liberal over time, a pattern is harder to distinguish. As early as 1972 Thailand negotiated a completely untied aid package. This concession, however, should be seen in light of the strong anti-Japanese sentiment in Thailand at the time. The terms of subsequent yen loan packages are harder, and more in line with the overall trend. Untying did not reappear until 1977, and not continuously until after 1979. LDC untied loan portions are relatively scarce.

Japan's Aid Program in the Philippines

Concurrent with the reparations program, Japan's technical cooperation program began in the 1950s. The Philippines was among the first countries to receive Japan Overseas Cooperation Volunteer (JOVC) assistance.[4] Japan also participated in United Nations programs in the Philippines and extended relief aid for natural disasters during this period. In the late 1960s, Japan committed technical assistance resources for projects in polio prevention, rice research, and a center for the development of cottage industries. Japan's contribution through the mid-1960s in this area, however, was quite small. Given the nature of bilateral relations during most of this period, it is not surprising that the Japanese presence would be so.

In 1966, the Philippine government approached Japan for OECF loans. The First Yen Loan was agreed upon in February 1969. The loan, to pay for the foreign exchange portion of construction of the Pan-Philippine Highway, was funded by private loans and the Export-Import Bank of Japan. The loan, tied to procurement of Japanese products, amounted to 10.8 billion yen, with a repayment period of nineteen years with five years' grace, and an interest rate of 5.125 percent.[5] Japan gave its first grant of food aid, valued at 360 million yen, in 1970.

Through February 1993 Japan extended eighteen yen loan packages to the Philippines. By 1987, Japan accounted for two-thirds of total bilateral aid to the Philippines. Table 2.7 presents data on loan and grant aid amounts from 1968 to 1993. As expected, the overall trend is toward increases in each category. Unlike aid to Thailand, the increases are more consistent: one year's yen loan or grant package is somewhat higher than the previous year's. The same holds true for decreases. This pattern generally persists for yen loans through the early 1980s. Fluctuations in yen loan commitments occur from 1984 through 1986, a period of Philippine economic crisis. In 1987, the Fourteenth Yen Loan amount increases dramatically to more than twice the 1986 level. Thereafter it returns to a pattern of incremental change at that higher level, with a drop again after 1990. The factors behind the wide changes in yen loans after 1983 will be taken up in Chapter Four.

The pattern of change in grant aid amounts appears to conform even more closely to an incremental model of aid giving. The Philippines received grant aid every year after 1971. Although there is a notable increase in

TABLE 2.7

Japan's ODA to the Philippines, 1968–93

(Hundred million yen)

Year	Loans	%	Grants	%	Total	Total ODA
1968	108	100	0	0	108	na
1970	0	0	3.6	100	3.6	na
1971	234	100	0	0	234	na
1972	123.2	98.14	2.34	1.86	125.53	na
1973	153.29	98	3.08	2	156.37	na
1974	147.52	97	4.62	3	152.14	na
1975	147.88	99.95	0.07	0.05	147.95	na
1976	233	95.75	10.33	4.25	243.33	na
1977	275	93.5	19	6.5	294	3825
1978	395	92	34.7	8	429.7	4663
1979	0	0	44	100	44	5781
1980	360	88	48.2	12	408.2	7491
1981	420	87.45	60.25	12.55	480.25	6993
1982	500	88	68.4	12	568.4	7529
1983	650.5	88.6	83.56	11.4	734.06	8933
1984	425	83.7	82.94	16.3	507.94	10258
1985	232.18	74	81.84	26	314.02	9057
1986	495	83	100.05	17	595.05	9495
1987	1206.67	91.6	110.57	8.4	1316.65	10782
1988	1260.67	91	127.54	9	1388.21	11705
1989	1149.63	89	141.78	11	1291.41	12368
1990	1985.48	93	143.32	7	2128.9	13350
1991	367.7	72.4	140.17	27.6	507.87	14840
1992	815.8	84.7	146.57	15.3	962.37	14354
1993	470.36	73	166.42	27	636.78	

Source: *Waga Kuni no Seifu Kaihatsu Enjo,* selected years.

amounts from 1974 to 1979 it is not as great as the increase in grant aid to Thailand during the same period. Moreover, grant aid levels do not swing nearly as widely after 1983 as do yen loan amounts, reinforcing the conclusion in Chapter One that the two aid types are determined independently of one another.

The ratio of grants to loans steadily improved through the early 1980s. By 1984, grants comprised 16 percent of total Japanese aid to the Philippines. In the Aquino period, however, the trend reversed; grant aid as a proportion of total aid approximates the situation in the early 1980s. This is attributable

TABLE 2.8

Sectoral Distribution of Japan's Loan Aid to the Philippines, 1968–93

(Number of projects)

Sector	1968-75	1976-80	1981-85	1986-90	1991-93
Roads & Bridges	4	7	4	14	2
Transportation	1	7	5	12	2
Energy/Electricity	1	4	6	4	2
Communications	0	1	2	7	1
Waterworks	3	4	4	11	0
Agriculture/Forestry	3	5	3	4	2
Industry/Mining	1	1	3	3	1
Education/Manpower	0	1	0	1	1
Medicine & Health	0	0	0	0	0
Social Services	0	1	1	0	0
Food Aid	0	0	0	0	0
Disaster Relief	0	0	0	0	0
Debt Rescheduling	0	0	2	2	2
Commodity Loans	4	3	1	3	1
Program Loans	0	0	0	6	0

Source: *Waga Kuni no Seifu Kaihatsu Enjo*, selected years.

to the fact that, while grant aid has increased at a fairly constant rate, the volume of yen loans from 1987 increased greatly. In the early 1990s, the grant portion of the aid program improved as the loan program suffered.

Sectoral Distribution of Japan's ODA to the Philippines

As in the Thai case the concentration of yen loans in infrastructure development is clear. Table 2.8 presents data on the sectoral distribution of yen loans to the Philippines. Infrastructure comprises about 60 percent of the total number of projects. As is the case with Thailand the agriculture and forestry category accounts for the largest number of non-infrastructure projects, numbering fourteen over the entire period. It is also remarkable that yen loans show little expansion across categories in successive periods.

Unlike the case of Thailand, a notable feature of Japan's lending to the Philippines is the inclusion of nonproject lending. This category,

TABLE 2.9

Sectoral Distribution of Japan's Grant Aid to the Philippines, 1968–93

(Number of projects)

Sector	1968-75	1976-80	1981-85	1986-90	1991-93
Roads & Bridges	0	1	0	3	3
Transportation	0	0	0	1	0
Energy/Electricity	0	0	0	0	0
Communications	0	0	0	0	1
Waterworks	1	2	1	1	6
Agriculture/Forestry	0	4	4	8	7
Industry/Mining	0	0	7	3	0
Education/Manpower	1	6	15	17	13
Medicine & Health	0	1	3	5	2
Social Services	0	1	3	5	2
Food Aid	4	5	5	5	3
Disaster Relief	0	0	2	7	8
Other	0	0	0	5	1

Source: *Waga Kuni no Seifu Kaihatsu Enjo*, selected years.

including debt rescheduling, commodity loans and program loans accounts for 13 percent of all commitments to 1993. Commodity loans constitute the largest component of this category with thirteen committed. As can be seen in Table 2.7, the most commodity loans were given in the early 1970s. Thereafter they taper off, with a small increase during the Aquino administration in the late 1980s. Debt rescheduling occurs only after 1983, as do program loans. The latter, committed in conjunction with World Bank lending, have been important elements of Japan's aid during the Aquino and Ramos administrations.

As expected, grant aid was given largely for noninfrastructure projects. Table 2.9 presents data on the sectoral distribution of Japan's grant aid to the Philippines. 70 percent of total grant projects were given for sectors other than infrastructure development. Again, overlap between yen loans and grants appears in agriculture and forestry, which accounts for 13 percent (23 projects) of total grant commitments. Moreover, education and manpower account for the largest number of grant projects, partly due to inflation of this category by cultural grant aid.

TABLE 2.10

Regional Distribution of Japan's Yen Loan to the Philippines, 1969–93

(Number of projects)

Region	1969-75	1976-80	1981-85	1986-90	1991-93
North Luzon	1	8	3	3	0
Central Luzon	2	3	4	11	3
South Luzon	0	1	0	1	0
Visayas	0	5	6	6	2
Mindanao	0	0	2	2	0
Manila	5	4	5	7	2
National	7	17	10	32	7

Source: JICA, *Fuiripin Enjo Kenkyukai Hokokusho*, 1987; *Waga Kuni no Seifu Kaihatsu Enjo*, 1994.

Regional Distribution of Japan's ODA to the Philippines

Japanese aid was allocated to more regions of the Philippines over time. Table 2.10 presents data on the regional distribution of yen loans to the Philippines. Regional dispersion across time is visible in the table. The most dramatic change occurs between the first two periods, although classification of the Pan-Philippine Highway as a national project understates regional dispersion in the first period. Concentration of projects is heaviest in central Luzon and Metro Manila. Excluding the Pan-Philippine Highway, 66 projects were allocated to Regions 3, 4 and Metro Manila (29 percent of the total.) The concentration is heavier than the numbers suggest; although Region 4 includes Palawan Island, Mindoro Island and the Calamian Islands in the west, no projects were allocated outside Luzon. Northeastern Luzon and the Visayas also received substantial numbers of projects. Southern Luzon was almost completely neglected, as was Mindanao, although projects in the national category were carried out there.

Grant aid was concentrated in fewer regions than loan aid. Table 2.11 presents data on the regional distribution of grant aid to the Philippines. Regional concentration in Central Luzon and Metro Manila in the last three periods is evident. These three regions account for almost half of all grant projects to specific regions: Metro Manila alone accounts for just over one-quarter of the total. If we include portions of national projects, the

TABLE 2.11

Regional Distribution of Japan's Grant Aid to the Philippines, 1969–93

(Number of projects)

Region	1969-75	1976-80	1981-85	1986-90	1991-93
North Luzon	0	3	3	3	0
Central Luzon	1	3	10	3	12
South Luzon	0	0	1	3	0
Visayas	1	0	8	4	6
Mindanao	0	0	2	0	1
Manila	4	10	12	22	2
National	5	9	10	27	26

Sources: JICA, *Fuiripin Enjo Kenkyukai Hokokusho*, 1987; *Waga Kuni no Seifu Kaihatsu Enjo*, selected years.

concentration would no doubt be higher. Even so, a process of regional dispersion is clear across the first three time periods. Between the first two periods, the wider distribution of grants can be attributed in part to the larger number of projects available for allocation. In the early 1980s, grant projects were allocated to all but two regions. Interestingly, despite the Aquino administration's avowed objective of encouraging regional development, the distribution of grant projects within the Philippines in the late 1980s and early 1990s narrowed somewhat. At the same time, the number of grant projects to Metro Manila almost doubled over the early 1980s figure. On the other hand, the number of projects allocated to the national category rose dramatically during the Aquino administration and the first two years of the Ramos administration, suggesting a correlation between Japanese grants and the Philippine government's policy of promoting regional development.

Terms of Japan's Yen Loans to the Philippines

As expected, the terms of yen loans soften across time. Tables 2.12 and 2.13 show data on the terms of Japan's yen loans to the Philippines. Notice that Export-Import Bank funding terms are higher than OECF terms in all years. The Export-Import Bank has cofunded debt rescheduling agreements with the OECF since 1986; under the agreements, OECF lending has also had

TABLE 2.12

Terms of Japan's Project Loans to the Philippines, 1969–92

Year	Amount	Agency	Repayment	Interest	Tying
1969	10800	Exim	19(5)	5.13	Tied
1971	9000	OECF	20(7)	3.5	Tied
1973	4729	OECF	25(7)	3.25	LDC
1974	7252	OECF	25(7)	3.25	Tied
1975	14788	OECF	25(7)	3.25	LDC
1977	11120	OECF	25(7)	4.25	LDC
1977	27680	OECF	25(7)	3.25	LDC
1978	30000	OECF	30(10)	3.25	Untied
1978	7000	OECF	30(10)	3.25	Tied
1980	36000	OECF	30(10)	3.0	Untied
1981	42000	OECF	30(10)	3.0	Untied
1982	50000	OECF	30(10)	3.0	Untied
1983	9600	OECF	30(10)	4.0	Tied
1984	7298	OECF	30(10)	3.5	Untied
1985	16605	OECF	30(10)	3.5	Untied
1987	40400	OECF	30(10)	4.0	Untied
1987	50208	OECF	30(10)	3.0	Untied
1988	14003	OECF	30(10)	3.0	Untied
1988	36061	OECF	30(10)	2.7	Untied
1989	74963	OECF	30(10)	2.7	Untied
1991	83395	OECF	30(10)	2.7	Untied
1991	30084	OECF	30(10)	2.5	Untied
1992	35145	OECF	30(10)	3.0	Untied

Source: MITI, *Keizai Kyoryoku no Genjo to Mondaiten*, selected years.

terms harder than usual. In the early period, food aid lending was consistently softer than normal yen loans. As with lending to Thailand, all special yen loans to the Philippines carry harder terms than normal yen loans. The pattern of untying exhibits more continuity than the Thai case. Loan commitments that carry LDC untied terms occur exclusively between 1973 and 1977. Thereafter, all but two commitments were untied, the two exceptions being special yen loans.

The data also suggest that the terms of special types of lending have carried harder terms since the mid-1980s. Note first that commodity loans in the 1970s carry softer terms than the commodity loan in 1984. Interestingly, the commodity loans to the Aquino government in 1987 carry terms that are softer than the 1984 and 1985 commodity loans. This suggests that

TABLE 2.13
Terms of Japan's Non-Project Loans to the Philippines

Year	Amount	Type	Agency	Repayment	Interest	Tying
1971	14400	C*	OECF	20(7)	3.5	Tied
1972	12320	C	OECF	20(7)	3.5	Tied
1973	10600	C	OECF	25(7)	3.25	Tied
1975	7500	C	OECF	25(7)	3.25	LDC
1976	5000	C	OECF	25(7)	3.25	LDC
1977	5000	C	OECF	25(7)	3.25	LDC
1978	2500	C	OECF	30(10)	3.25	Untied
1984	35202	C	OECF	20(5)	3.5	Untied
1985	32895	C	OECF	20(5)	3.5	Untied
1986	23218	R**	OECF/Exim	NA	3.5/5.125	NA
1987	30000	C	OECF	25(7)	3.5	Untied
1988	26473	R	OECF/Exim	NA	3.2/5.125	NA
1988	52500	C	OECF	25(7)	2.7	Untied
1989	40000	C	OECF	25(7)	2.7	Untied
1990	49940	R	OECF/Exim	NA	3.2/5.125	NA
1990	28200	C	OECF	30(10)	2.7	Untied
1991	37013	C	OECF	30(10)	2.7	Untied
1992	39373	R	OECF/Exim	NA	3.2/5.125	NA
1993	7062	R	OECF/Exim	NA	3.2/5.125	NA

*commodity loan **debt rescheduling

Source: MITI, *Keizai Kyoryoku no Genjo to Mondaiten*, selected years.

the 1984 commodity loan was as an exception given to a country in economic crisis. This impression is reinforced when we examine the terms of the two debt rescheduling agreements concluded in 1986 and 1988. In both cases, repayment terms are shorter and interest rates higher than normal lending.

Second, note also that even OECF lending to the Philippines in the late 1980s has been somewhat harder than it might be otherwise. In the Fourteenth through Eighteenth Yen Loans (1987 to 1993) the regular yen loan packages were split, with some parts of the packages carrying the maximum thirty-year repayment period with ten years' grace while others carry shorter repayment periods of twenty-five years with seven years' grace. This is explained by the presence of a commodity loan in 1987 and program loans cofinance with the World Bank in 1988 and 1989. The impression one gets is that while Japan has been willing to lend more to the Aquino government, it has also been more careful to insure that its loans will be well managed.

Conclusion

This chapter has outlined the main contours of Japan's aid to Thailand and the Philippines. It has described the beginnings of the aid programs and their origins in postwar reparations and semi-reparations agreements. As expected, Japan's aid to Thailand and the Philippines has increased in quantity. It has become more complex in terms of regional and sectoral distribution, but there are also fairly well defined limits to this complexity. Finally, the terms of aid to Thailand and the Philippines have become more concessional although, as will be discussed in later chapters, not as much as these governments would like.

There are several differences between Japan's aid to Thailand and its aid to the Philippines. The increase in aid volume to the Philippines from year to year is much smoother than that for Thailand, as is the progressive softening of yen loan terms. The Philippines also exhibits more complexity in its aid program because it has availed itself of more kinds of Japanese aid. The Philippines has received project loans, commodity loans, food aid loans, program loans, debt rescheduling loans, and cofinanced loans from Japan. Thailand has received only project loans and two-step loans.

This chapter described some of the surface differences between Japan's aid to Thailand and its aid to the Philippines. It is possible that the differences between the two aid programs are the result of happenstance. It is more likely, however, that the differences have occurred in no small part because the governments of Thailand and the Philippines want different things from the Japanese aid program. Those priorities, and the degree to which they are reflected in Japan's aid, are the subject of the next four chapters.

3

Japan's Aid and Thai Development

Introduction

Chapter Two discussed the overall trends of Japan's aid to Thailand. Japanese aid has tended to become more complex as it has been allocated to more sectors of the Thai economy and to more regions of Thailand. The terms of aid have become more concessional over time. How well have these trends conformed to Thai development priorities? Have Japanese aid projects been carried out in those regions and economic sectors that the Thai government has identified for development efforts? Has the Thai government found aid terms satisfactory? This chapter will discuss Japanese aid in light of the sectoral and regional priorities set forth by the Thai government in its five-year development plans. It will also deal with the terms of that aid. Due to the paucity of information on this topic, especially in the Japanese literature, its treatment will be episodic.

Overview of Thai Sectoral and Regional Priorities

The Thai economy is generally of the free market type. A limited number of state enterprises participate in production of public goods such as power and telecommunications or support private commercial enterprises. In line with World Bank development strategies, the government has seen its role as allowing private sector economic development while providing supportive infrastructure for that development.[1] To this end the Thai government has undertaken five-year economic plans since 1961 to forecast the future directions of the economy, and to allocate government resources accordingly. In 1992 Thailand began its Seventh National Economic and Social Development Plan. Because the Japanese aid program in Thailand began in the Second Plan period (1967-71), this chapter will focus on the plans since then.

Foreign aid comprised a significant portion of the development budgets in all plans. Foreign loans made up between one-quarter and one-third of the early plans' development budgets.[2] Sectoral allocations of public development expenditures were programmed in all Plans. The development of public infrastructure such as roads, seaports, and urban facilities always occupied an important place in the development budgets and carried over into the foreign aid arena. In fact, some sectoral budgets were dependent on external assistance; foreign loan and grant aid was expected to equal or surpass funding from domestic sources.

Regional development policy in Thailand has followed two main trends. First, the government has continually expressed the desire to develop the regions outside Bangkok and the Central Plain. Since the first plan, Thailand has pursued a growth pole strategy to carry out economic decentralization. In this strategy, urban centers in each region were designated as focal points for the development of the surrounding provinces. In 1960 the Thai government designated the following as growth poles: Chiang Mai—Lamphun in the North; Khon Kaen, Udon Thani, Ubon Ratchasima and Nakhon Ratchasima in the Northeast; Krung Thep and Maha Nakhon in the Central Plain; and Phuket and Songkhla in the South.[3] Despite elaboration in subsequent development plans, these centers have remained the core of the growth pole strategy.

Second, the Thai government has been interested in developing metropolitan Bangkok as the country's economic, political, cultural and administrative center. Despite the formulation of a regional growth pole strategy, policymaking in Thailand is highly centralized in the national bureaucracy in Bangkok. Through the 1970s, Thai government allocations of public resources such as transportation, irrigation systems, and schools were based on a policy of "building on the best," which reinforced the dominance of Bangkok and, secondarily, other urban centers that already had basic infrastructure and services in place.[4] The result was that "Bangkok policy-makers (sic) defined a series of resource investment priorities that allocated scarce resources most often to elites rather than the masses, Bangkok rather than the provinces, Bangkok elites rather than Bangkok masses, and provincial elites rather than provincial masses."[5]

Regional development has largely been defined in terms of its utility to the central government. All regions outside the Central Plain contain ethnically non-Thai populations. The difficulty of political and cultural integration, a policy favored by the central government, has resulted in delayed economic development. The government has tended to look at the development of the regions, or the lack thereof, in terms of political threat to the capital and the government.

The Northeast is an excellent example. Containing one-third of the Thai population, that region has had the highest levels of poverty in the nation throughout the period under study. Until the 1960s the government largely ignored the region. The external threat from war in Indochina changed the policy of neglect to one of counterinsurgency, in which regional underdevelopment was linked to political instability. With aid from the United States the government in the 1960s began to implement "social overhead" programs based largely on road building, communications, and counterinsurgency measures such as the accelerated rural development plan.[6]

Japanese aid has followed the general priorities outlined above. First, Japanese aid has been given predominantly to capital projects like highways, bridges, and dams. Second, Bangkok has benefitted from more aid than any other region; assistance not flowing to the capital has gone to regional growth centers. Third, Japan has allocated more aid to the Northeast than to other regions outside of the Bangkok and Central Plain areas because development of that region is politically important to the Thai government. Finally, rural development aid commenced later than other types of infrastructure aid as the Thai government began to deal seriously with the problems of rural poverty.

The Second Plan (1967–1971)

The public development budget presented in the Second National Social and Economic Development Plan allows us to see the sectoral priorities of the Thai government during the Plan period. Figure 3.1 shows a breakdown of sectoral allocations in the plan.

The emphasis on heavy infrastructure development in the Second Plan is unmistakable. Of a total development budget of 57.52 billion baht, transportation and communications was allocated the largest share, followed by agriculture, public utilities, education, power, health, and industry and mining and commerce (designated "other"). As expected, the emphasis carries over into the plan's calculations of foreign aid funding. Transportation and communications, public utilities, and agriculture were programmed for the largest amounts of foreign aid. The power sector stands out in this regard: projected

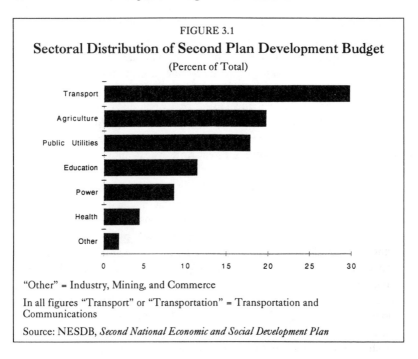

FIGURE 3.1

Sectoral Distribution of Second Plan Development Budget

(Percent of Total)

"Other" = Industry, Mining, and Commerce

In all figures "Transport" or "Transportation" = Transportation and Communications

Source: NESDB, *Second National Economic and Social Development Plan*

foreign aid expenditures were slightly greater than the projected expenditures from the national budget and the state enterprise budgets combined. Unlike later plans, the distinction between sectors to be funded by loans and those to be funded by grants was not clear. Transportation and communications, for example, was allocated the largest amounts of both types of aid.[7]

The Second Plan committed the government to alleviate regional income disparities, a concern prompted by economic and security considerations.[8] The inclusion in the development budget of counterinsurgency programs carried out with American assistance points to the Thai government's concern for stability in the Northeast. External threat from war in neighboring Indochina was coupled with increasingly vocal complaints by northeastern members of the National Assembly about the growing economic imbalance between the poor, agricultural Northeast and the industrializing Central region. During the plan period the Northeast absorbed just over one-quarter of the total development budget, with stress on transport and irrigation and, to a lesser extent, social services in the region.[9]

Japan became the largest bilateral aid donor to Thailand in the course of the Second Plan period. It surpassed the World Bank and the ADB as a donor of loan aid, as well as becoming the largest grant aid donor of the Colombo Plan countries. The beginnings of Japan's true aid program in that country corresponded to the peak and subsequent decline of American aid. After 1967, security assistance from the United States to Thailand and the rest of Southeast Asia declined, as did its aid presence.[10] While Japanese aid did not necessarily fill the gaps left by the American withdrawal—Muscat notes that the reduction was most prominent in fields related to security, areas for which Japan does not provided assistance—it provided an alternative source of external funding.

During the Second Plan period Thailand and Japan negotiated the First Yen Loan. Although the exchange of notes took place in 1968, agreement on the details of specific projects continued until April 1972. In general, the sectoral distribution of projects follows the priorities expressed in the plan. Four projects in the first two phases of the loan package, funded by the Export-Import Bank of Japan and private banks, were committed for telephone expansion in metropolitan Bangkok, improvement of ports and coastal navigation routes, and expansion of the state railway. Two grants were made in 1970 and 1971 for the Thailand-Laos Microwave project, adding to Japan's contribution to transportation and communications development. Parts of the power loans also benefitted agricultural development. Loans for two hydroelectric power projects in the Northeast, both for construction of dams, were designed not only to provide electricity but irrigation and flood control as well.[11]

Japan's aid for the power sector was especially significant. As noted above, the power sector relied most heavily on foreign financing during the Second Plan period. The OECF provided nine loans, almost its entire allocation, for power development. Moreover, the projects funded by the OECF were high priority. All of the projects in the First Yen Loan were listed as ongoing Priority 1 projects (of three levels of priority) in the Third Plan. They formed the basis, moreover, of a number of new Priority 1 projects programmed in the latter plan.[12]

Two explanations for the sectoral concentration of Japan's aid under the Second Plan can be given. First, the transport and communications projects funded in the First Yen Loan are quite similar to those funded under the Special Yen Account, the economic cooperation agreement concluded after World War II. Given the newness of a large Japanese aid presence in Thailand, we can assume that the aid policy makers in both countries would want to expand in areas with which Japan already had experience. The same seems to be the case in the power sector: Japanese companies and the Overseas Technical Cooperation Agency (OTCA), through Mekong

Committee cooperation, had experience in the survey and construction of dams in the region.[13]

Second, the concentration was fostered by institutional capacities within the Thai government. While the expenditures programmed for the agricultural sector in the Second Plan, for example, represented a significant increase over those of the First, actual implementation fell short of stated policy. Project proposals for agricultural development were insufficient in number, and project priorities were not made explicit. Resources for pre-investment studies in the Second Plan period were inadequate, resulting in a lack of satisfactory agriculture and rural development projects in the Third Plan as well. Loan lists concentrated foreign resources in the heavy infra-structure sectors at the expense of rural development. In 1973 the National Economic and Social Development Board admitted that Thailand had yet to come up a successful loan program to promote rural development.[14] At the end of the Second Plan Period, 2.2 billion yen from the First Yen Loan remained unused because of poor assessment and implementation by the Thai government.

The First Yen Loan shows a regional concentration in Bangkok and the Northeast. All but four projects were located in or intended to provide support for the Bangkok metropolitan region. Two power projects were located in the Northeast, as were a portion of a power transmission and substation project and the Thailand-Laos Microwave project. One power project was carried out in the North.[15] The projects were carried out in growth pole areas.

The Third Plan (1972–1976)

The Third Plan's development budget emphasized infrastructure and public services development. The sectoral breakdown is presented in Figure 3.2. Education was allotted the largest portion, a change from the Second Plan. Transportation and communication was allocated the second largest share, followed by urban and rural development, agriculture, power, health, and social welfare development, industry and mining, and commerce.

Foreign aid was again expected to play a greater role in the infrastruc-ture sectors. Beginning in 1973, the government decided to expand external borrowing to promote economic development. Projected foreign aid ac-counted for about one-quarter of the infrastructure budget; it accounted for just over one-tenth of the social services budget. The allocation of loan aid and grant aid followed this distinction. Transportation and communication and power were allocated the largest shares of loan aid and significantly cerning foreign financing in those sectors: foreign loans were projected amount to one-third of total power development expenditures in the :ond Plan. A similar situation existed in the transportation and communiions sector, with foreign loans accounting for one quarter of total develnent expenditures in that sector. Japan's loan aid to these sectors generally iformed to Thai objectives as well. The plan emphasized improvement of ver supply and distribution, and to rural electrification. The power develnent projects funded by Japanese loans either provided additions to sting facilities or constructed new facilities in anticipation of future nand increases. Two projects for reinforcement of power distribution tems targeted provincial cities.[18]

The Third Plan placed priority on completion of transportation and nmunications networks largely accomplished in the Second Plan. Highy construction remained a high priority, especially in the provinces. Three ns were given for transportation. Two were for engineering services and istruction of Sathorn Bridge in Bangkok. The third was for construction a highway in the South, part of an ongoing Thai project to link that region h Bangkok. Three Export-Import Bank loans in the Second Yen Loan for les for the telephone network in metropolitan Bangkok followed similar rk carried out under the First Yen Loan in the preceding period. A fourth, nmitted by OECF in the Third Yen Loan, was intended to develop the g-distance network between Bangkok and the provinces.[19]

The industry and mining sector was allocated a small portion of the ird Plan development budget and was not programmed to receive foreign ns. Nevertheless, the Plan noted that Industrial Finance Corporation of ailand (IFCT) and OECF had entered into negotiations for loans during Plan period for relending to private investors in agroindustrial projects.[20] e Second Yen Loan included five commitments to IFCT, together worth billion yen, funded by the Export-Import Bank.[21] The element of windfall nmistakable; Japan had helped finance the establishment of the IFCT in 59, and it is one of only two DAC donors willing to support industrial jects with concessional loans.[22]

Japan's agricultural aid accounted for one-quarter of total aid to that tor in the Third Plan period.[23] That aid was largely allocated to the velopment of agricultural exports, an important component of Thailand's icultural development policy. In the Third Plan, special projects were lertaken to accelerate production of maize, soybeans, mulberry and silk, onuts, shrimp, and cattle. Japan indicated its willingness to help Thailand rect its balance of trade by emphasizing agricultural export promotion of se potentially marketable commodities. Thailand, in turn, prepared pro-

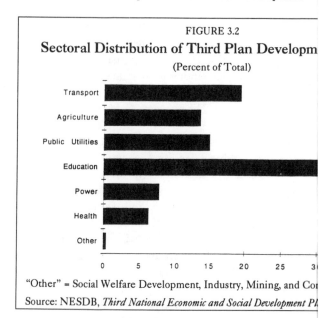

FIGURE 3.2
Sectoral Distribution of Third Plan Developm

(Percent of Total)

"Other" = Social Welfare Development, Industry, Mining, and Co₁

Source: NESDB, *Third National Economic and Social Development Pl*

smaller shares of grant aid. Agriculture was to receive bot
as the largest grant aid allocation in the infrastructure secto
were to receive mostly grants.[16]

The Third Plan continued to focus regional developn
and Northeast. While the Plan mentioned development
regions, the North and Northeast received the most exte
Allocations were to be distributed according to the growth p
Chiang Mai—Lamphun in the North and Khon Kaen in th
developed. Foreign aid was expected to be a major source
funding. In the case of the Northeast, the plan again empha
tion, agriculture and social services, although American aio
play the most significant role.[17]

The Third Plan period corresponds with the Secon(
Loans. Projects were agreed upon between April 1973 a
Again, loan aid largely corresponded to Thai sectoral priori
in budgetary allocations. Almost two-thirds of the 74 billio
in the Second Yen Loan package was allocated to power (
transportation and communications. Power sector loans ao
largest sectoral allocation in the loan package, followed b
and communications. The size of the allocations is in line

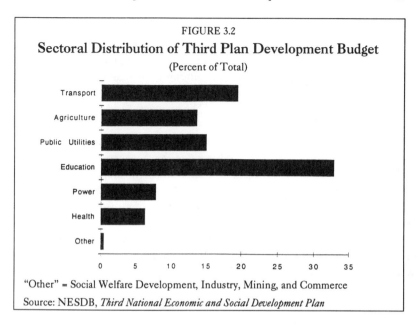

FIGURE 3.2

Sectoral Distribution of Third Plan Development Budget

(Percent of Total)

"Other" = Social Welfare Development, Industry, Mining, and Commerce

Source: NESDB, *Third National Economic and Social Development Plan*

smaller shares of grant aid. Agriculture was to receive both loan aid as well as the largest grant aid allocation in the infrastructure sector. Social services were to receive mostly grants.[16]

The Third Plan continued to focus regional development on the North and Northeast. While the Plan mentioned development strategies for all regions, the North and Northeast received the most extensive treatment. Allocations were to be distributed according to the growth pole strategy, with Chiang Mai—Lamphun in the North and Khon Kaen in the Northeast to be developed. Foreign aid was expected to be a major source of development funding. In the case of the Northeast, the plan again emphasized transportation, agriculture and social services, although American aid was expected to play the most significant role.[17]

The Third Plan period corresponds with the Second and Third Yen Loans. Projects were agreed upon between April 1973 and March 1977. Again, loan aid largely corresponded to Thai sectoral priorities as expressed in budgetary allocations. Almost two-thirds of the 74 billion yen committed in the Second Yen Loan package was allocated to power development and transportation and communications. Power sector loans accounted for the largest sectoral allocation in the loan package, followed by transportation and communications. The size of the allocations is in line with Thai policy concerning foreign financing in those sectors: foreign loans were projected to amount to one-third of total power development expenditures in the Second Plan. A similar situation existed in the transportation and communications sector, with foreign loans accounting for one quarter of total development expenditures in that sector. Japan's loan aid to these sectors generally conformed to Thai objectives as well. The plan emphasized improvement of power supply and distribution, and to rural electrification. The power development projects funded by Japanese loans either provided additions to existing facilities or constructed new facilities in anticipation of future demand increases. Two projects for reinforcement of power distribution systems targeted provincial cities.[18]

The Third Plan placed priority on completion of transportation and communications networks largely accomplished in the Second Plan. Highway construction remained a high priority, especially in the provinces. Three loans were given for transportation. Two were for engineering services and construction of Sathorn Bridge in Bangkok. The third was for construction of a highway in the South, part of an ongoing Thai project to link that region with Bangkok. Three Export-Import Bank loans in the Second Yen Loan for cables for the telephone network in metropolitan Bangkok followed similar work carried out under the First Yen Loan in the preceding period. A fourth, committed by OECF in the Third Yen Loan, was intended to develop the long-distance network between Bangkok and the provinces.[19]

The industry and mining sector was allocated a small portion of the Third Plan development budget and was not programmed to receive foreign loans. Nevertheless, the Plan noted that Industrial Finance Corporation of Thailand (IFCT) and OECF had entered into negotiations for loans during the Plan period for relending to private investors in agroindustrial projects.[20] The Second Yen Loan included five commitments to IFCT, together worth 10 billion yen, funded by the Export-Import Bank.[21] The element of windfall is unmistakable; Japan had helped finance the establishment of the IFCT in 1959, and it is one of only two DAC donors willing to support industrial projects with concessional loans.[22]

Japan's agricultural aid accounted for one-quarter of total aid to that sector in the Third Plan period.[23] That aid was largely allocated to the development of agricultural exports, an important component of Thailand's agricultural development policy. In the Third Plan, special projects were undertaken to accelerate production of maize, soybeans, mulberry and silk, coconuts, shrimp, and cattle. Japan indicated its willingness to help Thailand correct its balance of trade by emphasizing agricultural export promotion of these potentially marketable commodities. Thailand, in turn, prepared projects and submitted requests in the form of technical assistance and grant aid. In the course of the plan period Japan initiated technical assistance for development of maize and shrimp, and continued to provide it for a soybean, silk, cattle, and rice improvement projects.[24] The Second Yen Loan included two loans to the Bank for Agriculture and Agricultural Cooperatives (BAAC) for relending to farmers and agricultural cooperatives for diversification of agricultural products for export.[25]

The emphasis on capital aid in the Japanese program during the Second and Third Plans can be explained by two factors. First, Japanese aid was concentrated in the capital-intensive sectors anyway. Second, Japan was one of a few donors willing or able to fund large projects the Thai government wanted to undertake. During the Second Plan period the Thai government had foreseen a large increase in development expenditures. In order to meet that requirement, it tried to diversify its sources of capital assistance to include as many donors as possible. This approach was successful at the beginning of the Second Plan period, and terms and conditions of aid were generally consistent with Thai expectations. By 1970, however, it became clear that the "sources of funds" approach had become less effective because of a lack of competition: only a few donors—Japan, Germany, Australia, the World Bank and the ADB—provided loan aid on a large scale. Thai planners had therefore programmed the infrastructure budget with the expectation that funds would be forthcoming from Japan.[26]

Japanese loan aid was concentrated in Bangkok. Only two of nine loan projects in the Second Yen Loan were implemented outside of Bangkok and the Central Region. Those two, a loan for construction of the Southern Thailand Highway and a loan for reinforcement of power distribution systems, clearly support the growth pole strategy since they were designed to connect urban centers. The concentration in Bangkok is also striking: of the remaining seven projects, five were for development of Bangkok infrastructure. The Third Yen Loan shows a similar distribution: a loan for construction of a bridge in the capital, one for construction of water works in Chiang Mai, and another for reinforcement of the power distribution systems of provincial cities. The grant and technical assistance program exhibits a great degree of geographical concentration. Only two projects were located outside of the Central Plain region, while the rest were located in metropolitan Bangkok.[27]

The Thai government had mixed success in obtaining the terms it wanted in the Second and Third Yen Loans. The terms of the Second Yen Loan were better than the First. The interest rate on the OECF portion of the Second Loan was 1.25 percent lower than its predecessor, and the Export-Import Bank portion was 0.5 percent lower.[28] The repayment periods were extended to twenty-five years and twenty years, respectively, and the grace period for both types of loans were lengthened to seven years from five. Moreover, in certain cases, part of the loan could be used to finance the local cost portion of the project.

The Thai government was dissatisfied because the loan package was tied. It strongly requested that Japan untie the loans. Following a year of negotiations, the Japanese Minister of International Trade and Industry in January 1973 promised to untie the project loan portion of the package, but not the loans to IFCT and BAAC. In late 1973 a general untying clause was added to the original Exchange of Notes on the loan package. During Prime Minister Tanaka's goodwill visit to Thailand in January 1974 he promised to speed the utilization of loans and reduce the interest rates on half the amount of the project loans. Accordingly, the interest rate on 17 billion yen of OECF funding was reduced to 2.75 percent, and the rate on six billion yen of Export-Import Bank funding was reduced to 4 percent.[29]

Japanese concessions on aid terms were influenced by the exigencies of bilateral relations during this period. The large influx of Japanese goods into Thailand and the perceived cultural insensitivity of Japanese business-men were sore points in the two countries' relations in the early 1970s. Resentment about the commercial motives of Japanese economic coopera-tion and its concern with profits boiled over in 1972 in the form of a ten-day university student boycott of Japanese goods at department stores in Bang-kok. Tanaka's 1974 trip to Southeast Asia was greeted with riots and demonstrations, including in Thailand.[30]

Although the aid program was not an object of criticism in Thailand, the Japanese government used aid concessions to assuage Thai anger in other areas. The timing of Japanese concessions matches the major political events of the time. The Japanese foreign ministry announced it would ease its yen loan terms six days after the outbreak of the Thai student boycott in November 1972.[31] MITI's announcement on untying of project loans followed within two months. Similarly, Tanaka announced the last round of Japanese concessions during his "goodwill" tour in 1974. Examination of subsequent loan packages in Table 2.6 reinforces the impression of political expediency in this case, since their interest rates returned to a normal, higher, level after 1974.

The Fourth Plan (1977–1981)

The period of the Fourth Plan marks an important turning point in the aid relationship between Thailand and Japan. In 1977 Japan and Thailand began annual bilateral discussions aimed at setting each year's aid package. Japanese aid not only increased in volume thereafter, but became more uniform in terms of the timing of package commitment. The regularity of aid commitments is especially visible in the grant program; grant aid packages have been committed annually since then. Although it retained its characteristic emphasis on capital projects, Japan's aid to Thailand became more complex. Project allocations were made in new areas and for purposes not seen in the aid program theretofore.

The changes in the relationship occurred for reasons internal to both countries. Japan formally acknowledged that Southeast Asia was an important region in Japan's foreign policy. The Fukuda Doctrine was an outcome of that thinking. Although most observers agree that the doctrine marked no major change in Japan's foreign policy toward Southeast Asia, it indicated a new level of seriousness on the part of the Japanese government in dealing with its counterparts in the region.[32] The political significance of the Fukuda Doctrine can be seen in the timing of yen loan packages to Thailand. The Fourth and Fifth Yen Loans were agreed upon in 1977, an unusual circumstance. Negotiations for the Fifth took place during and immediately after Fukuda's visit to Southeast Asia in August of that year. In both cases, aid procurement was untied, a concession afforded no other ASEAN member at that time.

Changes in Thailand also affected the aid relationship. The second oil shock of 1979 forced a reassessment of Thailand's economic development. At the same time, however, it accelerated its medium and long-term public borrowing.[33] Instability in Indochina, coupled with American military withdrawal from Thailand, was also a cause for concern. The Vietnamese invasion of Cambodia in early 1979 threw the problem of political and economic instability in the Northeast into high relief, forcing the Thai government to deal with a huge influx of Indochinese refugees while simultaneously reexamining its rural development strategies.

Sectoral allocation in the Fourth Plan budget generally followed that of the Third Plan, but on a larger scale. Figure 3.3 presents data on the distribution of the development budget. Education was allotted just under 40 percent of the development budget, almost as much as the entire infrastructure budget. Agriculture was allocated the second largest share, followed by transportation and communications, public utilities, public health, power, and social development, industry and mining, and commerce.

As with the Third Plan, foreign aid was to play an important role in the development of infrastructure, comprising one quarter of that portion of the development budget. Conversely, foreign aid amounted to only 5 percent of

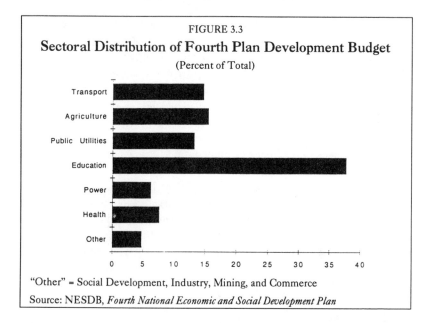

FIGURE 3.3
Sectoral Distribution of Fourth Plan Development Budget
(Percent of Total)

"Other" = Social Development, Industry, Mining, and Commerce

Source: NESDB, *Fourth National Economic and Social Development Plan*

the social services budget. As in the previous plan, loan aid was concentrated in infrastructure and grant aid in social development; no loan aid was programmed for education and health. The largest portion of loan aid was allocated to the power sector, which accounted for just over two-thirds of that sector's budget. Foreign loans were programmed for public utilities, transportation and communications, agriculture, industry, mining and commerce, and social development. Agriculture was also to receive the highest single allocation of grant aid in the development budget.[34]

The Fourth Plan continued the stated policy of developing urban centers outside of Bangkok in order to relieve migration into the capital region and to develop the regions. The government also formulated a master plan for Bangkok to rationalize development of public utilities. It also tried to slow the growth of Bangkok by moving major public facilities, such as international seaports, outside of the metropolitan region. Development programs to improve Bangkok included development of the urban transport system, increased coordination of public utilities, incorporation of new areas, and administrative reform.[35]

As for regional development, the Fourth Plan recognized that, with most of its large infrastructural development goals complete, its new task was to concentrate on completion of existing projects to increase the benefits from them. As such, the government gave less emphasis to new large infrastructural development and more to extending facilities to rural inhabitants.[36]

By the end of the Fourth Plan, Japan had become Thailand's single largest aid donor. Between 1978 and 1981 Thailand received $688 million in aid from Japan, making it the second largest recipient after Indonesia, accounting for 9 percent of total Japanese ODA. Between 1979 and 1981 Japan accounted for just over half of total loan aid to Thailand, more than twice multilateral loan aid and four times larger than the next biggest bilateral donor, West Germany.[37]

Despite the increase, Japan's aid largely followed Fourth Plan guidelines. This is especially true in terms of project goals, although loan amounts to the infrastructure sectors differ from the plan budgets. The power sector is a good example. Its share of the development budget declined compared to the Third Plan as power development began to receive lower priority. Yen loans declined accordingly: Japan funded construction of only one dam, a holdover project given priority in the Fourth Plan.[38] Thereafter, power sector loans were given for projects designed to improve distribution of existing power systems. Two loans in particular were directed at provincial electrification. Japan also provided a special loan in 1978 for the purchase of a power generating barge for the South, and another in June, 1979 for oil tankers.[39]

A significant portion of Japanese aid went to projects in the Bangkok region. This distribution is especially noticeable in the transportation and communications sector: 11 of 17 yen loan commitments went to projects in metropolitan Bangkok. The projects funded were largely for bridge and road construction and telephone network expansion, activities that would strengthen Bangkok's transportation and communications system. Two of the 11 loans were given for construction of facilities at Bangkok International Airport. Japan also committed loans for feeder road and provincial highway construction and expansion of the communications network throughout the country, the former given high priority in the Thai transportation budget in order to link agricultural areas to markets.[40]

The commitment to assisting Thailand's development outside of the capital can be seen in the emergence of aid for rural development. In addition to the feeder road and rural power development projects mentioned above, Japan committed three loans specifically to this area: one to the New Village Development Program in 1979, one for *tambon* (district) electrification in 1979, and one for a village electrification project in 1981. The latter two were for construction and installation of equipment to unelectrified local areas throughout the country and in the North, Northeast and Central Plain respectively.[41]

The commitment can also be seen in the expansion of aid for agriculture. During the plan period Japan supplied just over 35 billion yen in loans for the agriculture sector. It committed five loans to BAAC. In contrast to earlier yen loans, agricultural projects funded, especially in irrigation, were not byproducts of power sector projects. Japan thus committed two loans to small-scale irrigation involving the construction of over two thousand small irrigation projects in rural areas. It also gave loans for the construction of electric irrigation pumps and engineering services for an irrigated agricultural development project near Bangkok. Moreover, it made loans for fisheries promotion in the Gulf of Thailand and inland swamps, and for seed multiplication centers.[42]

Grant aid for agriculture continued. Two projects were funded through Kasetsart University, and grants were made to the Songkhla Coastal Cultivation Center and the Rice Species Storage Center. Beginning in 1977 Japan supplied grant aid for food production increases in the form of fertilizers and agricultural machinery. Technical assistance projects included aid for natural rubber products improvement, irrigated agricultural development and technical assistance in tandem with the grant aid for the Songkhla Coastal Cultivation Center.[43]

The incorporation of a strategic component in Japan's aid program, as part of the formulation of comprehensive national security, coincided with the latter part of the Fourth Plan. Thailand was one of the first countries to be designated by the Ohira cabinet as a "country bordering areas of conflict" after the Third Indochina War broke out in 1979, and therefore worthy of greater attention and increased aid. Yasutomo argues that for Thailand, assistance under the new formula did not constitute a change in aid policy direction. In announcing its intention to grant 57 billion yen in aid to Thailand in April 1979, for example, the Japanese government stated that the increase over the previous year's package was due to Thailand's membership in ASEAN as well as the large influx of refugees fleeing the Indochina war. For Yasutomo, the only real difference in aid to Thailand under the countries bordering areas of conflict formula was the amount of new aid committed.[44]

The emphasis on the change in aid volume hides the change in content of Japan's aid during this period. Beginning in 1979 Japan's grant program included several commitments to refugee aid each year. Of particular note was the establishment of a Japanese medical aid presence in the refugee camps in the Northeast under JICA supervision, an ongoing effort that lasted until 1982. Japanese teams also engaged in construction of wells for the camps and for Thais displaced by them.[45]

There was also a reorientation of part of the loan program toward addressing the problems caused by the dislocation of the war in Indochina. The rural development projects noted above are good examples. The New Village Development Program is remarkable because of Japan's assistance despite its avowedly political purpose. The project's objectives were to provide facilities to the rural poor to increase productivity and income, to improve the physical environment of specified villages, and to mobilize and support community selfhelp efforts. Villages selected for the program, all in the North and Northeast, were to be poor, remote, lacking government infrastructure services, and "sensitive to political and security management."[46] The timing of Thailand's request, in late 1978, indicates the program's importance in stabilizing the North and Northeast as instability in the rest of Indochina increased. In its announcement of the exchange of notes in January 1981 for a loan to continue the project, the Thai government noted that the project was aimed especially at Thais displaced by refugees, a growing concern at the time.[47] It also marks one of Japan's earlier attempts to assist projects directly at the rural village level.

Strategic aid added another feature to Japan's aid program in Thailand: during the Fourth Plan period Japan's aid to projects in the Northeast became noticeably larger, particularly after 1978. The geographic concentration, which continued until the early 1990s, is the result of refugee relief and other aid designed to mitigate the effects of the Indochinese influx into Thailand's poorest region.

Fifth Plan (1982–1986)

The Fifth Plan has been called a "milestone document" in the government's development effort. In particular, the plan sought information from a wider range of sources than had previously been the case, and attempted to link overall goals with operational plans in the line agencies.[48] The Plan did not include an explicit development budget: Figure 3.4 presents the sectoral distribution of the annual budgets for the years 1984 to 1986.

The continuity with the previous Plans is clear. In all three years education accounted for the highest expenditures, about 20 percent per year. Agriculture ranked second, followed by transportation, public health, and social services. Mining and industry, tourism and commerce, and "other"

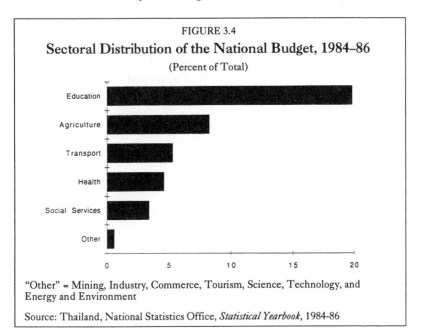

FIGURE 3.4

Sectoral Distribution of the National Budget, 1984–86

(Percent of Total)

"Other" = Mining, Industry, Commerce, Tourism, Science, Technology, and Energy and Environment

Source: Thailand, National Statistics Office, *Statistical Yearbook*, 1984-86

(science, technology, energy, and environment) accounted for less than 1 percent respectively during the period.

Foreign borrowing was programmed to follow the trend of the Fourth Plan as well. The power sector, however, was programmed to absorb about 30 percent of total foreign borrowing in order to fund projects to create substitute energy sources. Agriculture's share was also programmed to increase from just under 10 percent in the Fourth Plan to 15 percent of total foreign borrowing in the Fifth Plan.[49]

The Fifth Plan recognized the primacy of Bangkok in the urban development of Thailand in terms of population and economic concentration. It therefore stressed the need to develop the surrounding towns, provinces, and the Eastern Seaboard to absorb a greater share of economic activity. At the same time, it also called for development of public utilities and infrastructure in the capital itself. In particular, the plan noted the need for planning and improvement of the transportation system.

The Fifth Plan continued the policy of promoting efforts to decentralize economic activity outside of Bangkok. It observed that the existing regional growth centers lacked sufficiently strong economic bases to absorb a growing labor force, and that the infrastructure necessary for industrial and other development was still inadequate. The traditional regional growth centers were to be further developed and six provinces were to be planned for future development. The plan emphasized social services and public utilities development in the centers. In keeping with a greater sensitivity to the problems of regional development, the Fifth Plan noted the economic problems in each region and measures to counteract them. Specific plans for the economic development of each of the targeted growth centers were formulated as well.[50]

Japanese prime minister Suzuki visited the ASEAN countries in January 1981. His trip ended in Thailand, which his cabinet considered a top priority. In his final address, he outlined four areas Japan would emphasize in its aid program: development of the rural and agricultural sectors, development of new energy sources, technical assistance for human resources development, and support for small and medium size industries.[51]

The task for the energy sector was to develop alternative power sources following the second oil shock in 1979. Japanese aid to the sector reflects the shift: it provided three loans for energy development, all of which were for non-traditional power sources available domestically, such as natural gas and lignite. Japanese loans continued to fund rural power distribution and electrification projects.[52]

The agricultural sector continued to receive sizeable amounts of Japanese aid during the Fifth Plan. Japan committed thirteen loans to that sector. Loan aid generally went to irrigation projects, although several were committed to inland swamp fisheries development. The grant aid program also funded a number of agriculture projects. Grants ran heavily to the construction or expansion of research and training facilities. Fertilizer and equipment were provided under the rubric of aid for agricultural productivity expansion.[53]

Until the Fourth Plan period Thai government policy was to "develop basic agricultural infrastructure in areas where natural conditions yield high returns to investment programmes." Once dams and irrigation canals were in place, the government would shift to supplying more modern inputs such as fertilizer, extension services, credit, and market systems.[54] Japanese aid followed this pattern. The early aid program, especially loan aid, was directed toward basic irrigation infrastructure. In the Fourth and Fifth Plan periods, the program became more diversified as aid for agricultural productivity, begun in the Third Plan period, increased. BAAC loans also increased during the Fourth and Fifth Plan periods. The change occurred earliest in the regions outside the Northeast because those regions were better suited for earlier agricultural development. Japan's fisheries aid program, for example, began in the South, an area recognized in the Third Plan as suitable for such development.[55] The lag in the Northeast is apparent from the distribution of Japan's aid: until the Fourth Plan period agricultural aid to the Northeast was almost exclusively for irrigation. Beginning in the Fourth Plan period, but really taking off in the Fifth, Japanese aid to the region began to be allocated for projects designed to enhance agricultural productivity.

Aid for transportation and communications also demonstrated sensitivity to Thai priorities. As noted above, transportation and communication's share of the development budget declined throughout the Plan period. In particular, highway development was cut back, and new construction after 1983 was focused on feeder roads.[56] Of six loans for transportation (excluding harbor construction in the Eastern Seaboard), three were for road construction, one of which was for feeder roads. All transportation projects were committed by 1983. One telecommunications project loan, for cables for regional public telephone expansion, was committed during the Plan period.[57]

Bangkok was the major recipient of transportation aid from Japan. The bias toward the capital region reflects Thai policy to improve its transportation and other infrastructure. Two highway project loans were allocated there, as well as one for bridge construction. One of two loans to the State Railway of Thailand was for railway cars to help relieve railroad commuter traffic in the metropolitan region. Two loans were also committed for improvement of Bangkok's sewage system; Khon Kaen was the only other city to receive such a loan.[58] In sum, almost all of Japan's transportation and public utilities aid went to Bangkok.

The aid program shows an expansion into the social sectors. Japan's second commitment for the New Village Development Program constituted a significant portion of the Thai government's poverty alleviation efforts in the first two years of the Plan.[59] The trend is marked in the grant program. As with agriculture, grant aid for construction of manpower and education training facilities increased. The increase is particularly noticeable for industrial training facilities.[60]

Development of the Eastern Seaboard was the centerpiece of the Fifth Plan. Centered in the Rayong growth center southeast of Bangkok and bordering the Gulf of Thailand, it was the most developed area outside of the capital region. By the Fifth Plan period it possessed better infrastructure facilities than other regions, with an airport, good communications and transport networks, and a deep-sea port. Natural gas extracted from the Gulf of Thailand was brought ashore in the area. It also bordered the Northeast, whence it was supplied with labor and raw materials. Based on these factors, the government designed a policy to develop the provinces of Chonburi, Rayong, and Chachoengsao. The region was to act as a growth center and the location of future basic industries, in line with the policy of decentralizing economic and industrial activity outside of Bangkok.[61]

Following discussions between Japan and Thailand about the Fifth Plan, the Japanese government announced in June 1981 its preliminary intention to aid development of water resources for industrial use in the Eastern Seaboard Development Project (ESDP).[62] Throughout the Fifth and Sixth Plan periods, aid for development of the Eastern Seaboard constituted a major portion of Japan's loan program. Between 1982 and 1986, it committed 13 of 48 loans to the Eastern Seaboard Development Project, which accounted for approximately one-third of the total amount of yen-loan funding in the Plan period. Japan provided loans for work on all three deep-sea ports to be constructed, as well as for infrastructure support projects such as rail cars, a reservoir, and a water pipeline. It committed loans for the natural gas separation plant project, the fertilizer plant complex, and was prepared to assist the ASEAN-sponsored soda ash plant, the former two of which constituted the centerpieces of the Laem Chabang and Mab ta Phut seaport development plans. It also provided loans for construction of industrial estates at Mab ta Phut and Laem Chabang.[63]

Japan's concentration on the Eastern Seaboard Development Project limited the regional distribution of its overall aid. All but one loan project in the Central Plain region were carried out in the ESDP. Loan aid was directed to the growth centers, particularly in the North and Northeast. Grant aid was allocated largely to the Northeast, reflecting continued Thai interest in stabilizing that region. No loan aid was allocated to the South, and only two grant aid projects were carried out there, again both in growth poles.

Despite the government's stated policy of developing the South, actual budgetary allocations to the region during the Fifth Plan suggest its neglect: between 1982 and 1988 the South received less of the national rural job creation budget than any other region.[64] In 1983 the National Economic and Social Development Board (NESDB) chose the upper South for development of a future industrial zone along the lines of the ESDP. JICA carried out the feasibility study in 1983-84. NESDB accepted the results of the survey, but no further Japanese activity was apparent during the Fifth Plan period.[65]

We saw above that the ESDP absorbed most of Japan's infrastructure aid. For example, we find fewer communications or bridge construction loans during the Fifth Plan period than in previous plans or in the Sixth Plan. The following incident suggests the implications of ESDP aid for other projects. In 1985 a survey team was dispatched to investigate a Thai request for a loan to improve its rail system. The head of the survey mission reported that during his initial meeting with Japanese embassy officials in Bangkok he was told that because the Thai government wanted a large loan from Japan to construct one of the ESDP's ports it would not be possible for Japan to make another for railway improvement. Moreover, he was informed, the Thai government had recently decided to limit its foreign borrowing because of its concern over its external debt. The survey team was therefore encouraged to limit the scale of its loan recommendation.[66] Such conversations must have occurred frequently.

In 1985, the Thai government initiated two policies that attempted to change the basis of the aid relationship with Japan. The first was its decision to limit its external borrowing in order to reduce its external debt. The second was to present the "White Paper for Improving Thailand-Japanese Economic Structure," the first Thai government attempt to coordinate aid, trade, and investment policies toward Japan. The course of negotiations on those two issues illustrates the extent to which Thailand can achieve its objectives in the aid relationship with Japan.

In October 1985, concerned about what it saw as a deteriorating external debt situation, the Thai government set a limit on foreign borrowing for the Sixth Plan period. The ceiling was set at $1 billion per year for the beginning of the plan, although it could be adjusted upward depending on the country's capacity to earn foreign exchange.[67] This policy's enactment coincided with the sharp appreciation of the yen beginning in 1985. The Thai government in 1986 curtailed its loan requests, with the result that no yen-loan package was agreed upon that year.[68]

Thailand's policy of refusing Japanese loan aid could not endure. The Department of Technical and Economic Cooperation (DTEC) made an effort in the Fifth Plan to seek grants and technical assistance in lieu of foreign loans in order to reduce the foreign debt burden.[69] This effort made little headway. Grant aid from Japan peaked in 1983, then declined somewhat thereafter. As a proportion of total ODA, moreover, Japanese grant aid remained flat throughout the plan period at about 16 percent. In subsequent bilateral negotiations, the Japanese government argued that Thailand would have to continue borrowing from Japan if it wished to continue its development program, particularly in the Eastern Seaboard.[70] In 1986, Japan suggested that the Thai government concentrate its efforts on infrastructure and human resources development in order not to spread limited resources too thinly. The Thai government ultimately agreed with the Japanese recommendation, in no small part because it realized the need for such development itself.[71] In any case, yen loan borrowing remained flat at about 80 billion yen through 1991.

Thailand accepted the argument that it continue to borrow from Japan, because its options were limited. By the mid-1980s, Japan accounted for over half of Thailand's external concessional lending. Following two structural adjustment loan (SAL) agreements with the World Bank in 1982 and 1983, the Thai government decided to diversify its aid program away from multi-lateral, especially Bank, funding. In the face of recession the government dropped plans for a third SAL in 1986, in effect forgoing the World Bank's guarantee to fund one third of the Fifth Plan, including the ESDP, in exchange for economic adjustments.[72] In interministerial fights over contin-uation of the project in 1985, the World Bank sided with project opponents in the Thai government. When the NESDB and its allies carried the day, supported in part by Japanese official and corporate lobbying, the Bank's opposition foreclosed its further financial support.[73] To the extent that the government wished to continue developing the Eastern Seaboard, it would have to rely on Japan. The United States and West Germany, the second and third largest bilateral donors, could not provide the level of loan funding Thailand required for such large-scale priority projects.

Borrowing from the multilateral banks was unattractive for other reasons. The multilaterals lend funds drawn from their members with strong currencies. As a result, Thailand would simply be substituting yen from the World Bank and ADB for yen from the OECF. Worse, it would be accepting appreciated yen on less concessional terms because the multilaterals' interest rates are higher and their repayment terms are shorter than Japan's. Thailand has had no other donor to turn to for concessional lending for its priority programs, and has therefore had to content itself since then with limiting its borrowing from the OECF to the level of the mid-1980s.

The "White Paper on Improving Thailand-Japanese Economic Struc-ture" represented the Thai government's attempt to reform its economic relationship with Japan on a broad scale. The White Paper presented Thai concerns about its chronic trade deficit with Japan and its recommendations for reducing the imbalance. They included guidelines for bilateral trade, investment and economic cooperation, and marked the first time the Thai government had ever attempted to coordinate its economic policies toward Japan.[74] The discussion here will include only economic cooperation, as it is most relevant to this study.

Thai aims for economic cooperation expressed in the White Paper were straightforward. Thailand wished to adjust its economy to promote export of manufactured goods based both in agriculture and industrial production, and it wanted Japanese assistance for research and development on quality standards and design for exported goods. On a broader level, it wanted Japan to revise its loan conditions to allow greater participation of Thai contractors in construction projects. It also called for Thai agencies to draw up indicative plans of required Japanese aid.

The initial Japanese reaction was cautious. The Japanese government was taken aback by the idea of the White Paper, but gradually it agreed to some of the Thai demands. By 1989, elements of the White Paper were incorporated into JICA's country study for Thailand, although it did not fully endorse the Thai position that aid, trade, and investment should be linked.[75] Japan found Thai demands for assistance with export promotion development easiest to accept, and grant and technical assistance for an industrial standards research center and other projects related to export promotion were included in subsequent grant aid packages. In terms of aid planning, Japan agreed in principle to provide grant aid within the framework of a three-year indicative plan for 1987-89 drawn up by DTEC.[76] Participation in the rolling plan, however, was conditioned by the fact that Japan continued to budget aid annually.

Sixth Plan (1987–1991)

Allocation guidelines for foreign aid in the Sixth Plan followed the pattern of its predecessors. Loan aid was to emphasize infrastructure and development of urban and regional areas. The Plan specifically mentioned telecommunications, air transport, reinforcement of private investment, and promotion of projects that could generate foreign exchange. Emphasis was to be placed on repair, maintenance, and improvement of highways and rural roads, and on construction of new roads to complete farm-to-market systems for export promotion. Grant aid was to emphasize social and human resources, rural development, mineral resources, science and technology, and research and administration development.[77]

National budget expenditures for 1987 to 1990 repeated the general trend of the Fifth Plan. Figure 3.5 shows the sectoral breakdown of expenditures from those years. Education accounted for about 18 percent during the period. Agriculture accounted for the second largest share, followed by transportation and communications, public health, and social services. Tourism and commerce, industry and mining, and science, technology, energy, and environment continued to receive a small fraction of the annual budgets. While mining and industry remained almost constant in 1990, tourism and

FIGURE 3.5

Sectoral Distribution of the National Budget, 1987–90

(Percent of Total)

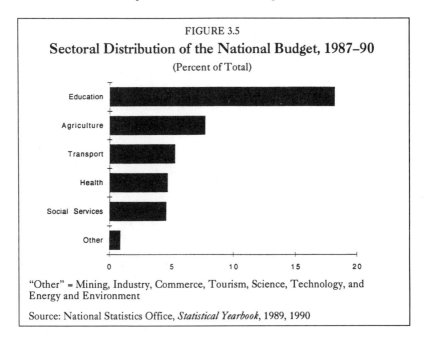

"Other" = Mining, Industry, Commerce, Tourism, Science, Technology, and Energy and Environment

Source: National Statistics Office, *Statistical Yearbook*, 1989, 1990

commerce and science, technology, energy, and environment rose to 0.8 percent and 1.3 percent, respectively.[78]

During the Sixth Plan period the Thai government again sought to develop the capital and the regional growth centers. The concentration of development resources in Bangkok was justified on the grounds that "premature attempts to slow the growth of the metropolitan areas may be economically inefficient," and that managed growth of those areas would be preferable. The government, moreover, could not deny that Bangkok would continue to grow and retain its primacy, putting off to the mid-1990s the prospect that the regional growth poles and the ESDP would begin to significantly reduce migration into the capital region. It also continued the development of the Eastern Seaboard, and to prepare to develop other regions, especially in the South, to further its decentralization policy.[79]

By the Sixth Plan, the Thai government realized that with world economic conditions improving slowly, technical assistance during the plan period could not be expected to increase rapidly. DTEC expected technical assistance during the Plan period to be about the same level as during the Fifth Plan, with any nominal increase deriving from the devaluation of the baht.[80]

During the Sixth Plan the Thai government expected Japan to remain an important source of foreign aid. In 1987, the first year of the new plan,

Japan's bilateral ODA accounted for 70 percent of total bilateral ODA. The total volume of Japan's annual aid, however, peaked that year at 102.3 billion yen, the highest level ever, then declined through 1990 as loan borrowing dipped. Beginning in 1991, loan amounts rose again, pushing up the volume of aid.[81] The grant aid program registered a decline, a trend in line with Japanese government expectations that Thailand should increasingly rely on concessional and nonconcessional loan aid as it prepared to graduate economically into the ranks of the newly industrializing economies.[82]

As expected, Japan committed substantial loan aid for infrastructure development. In its 1989 *Country Study for Development Assistance to the Kingdom of Thailand,* Japan voiced its assessment that further development of port and harbor facilities, transportation, and communications was urgently needed. The study noted that aid would be extended to promote decentralization of industries and population, and to promote comprehensive regional development in the growth centers and the ESDP. In particular, Japanese aid would be extended to transport and communications as well as industrial complexes in the regions. It also observed that to enhance linkages between the regions as well as between the cities and the rural areas, transport and communications networks would have to be developed.[83] The loan program continued to favor the ESDP. As with the Fifth Plan period, the ESDP represented the largest group of loans, twelve by the end of 1991.

The loan program showed a remarkable degree of continuity with previous plans because much of its loans were continuations of earlier projects. The ESDP is the most visible example. In addition, several loans were for reconstruction or rehabilitation of existing facilities in the power and transportation sectors. Although those sectors were previously supported by Japanese aid, the focus on upgrading and repairing existing infrastructure was new.

Tourism development provides a good example of the role the Japanese government considered desirable for its aid program. Tourism promotion had figured in previous plans, but had never been programmed to receive foreign aid. In the Sixth Plan, tourism promotion received high priority as a foreign exchange earner. Japanese government support came in the form of infrastructure to support the industry since tourism projects are largely carried out in the private sector.[84] In 1987 Japan committed a loan for a tourism program designed to develop roads, communications, water supply, and other facilities in eight designated areas.[85] In 1990 it funded a series of road projects for tourist areas in the South.[86] In essence, Japan applied its preference for infrastructure development to a Thai priority area.

The loan program clearly supported private sector development. Loans for ESDP development were the most visible part of that effort, but were not the only types of support. Japan also made loans to the IFCT for relending to small and medium size enterprises, with several of them specifically aimed at businesses producing for export.[87] A great deal of infrastructure aid was also directed at supporting private sector development. Loans for transportation and public utilities in Bangkok and in provincial cities supported the plan's long-term goal of preparing the provincial centers for industrial development.

Japan's expressed intention to help promote regional development was carried out in its aid program. The linkage function in particular is noticeable. Communications loans to the Telephone Organization of Thailand included projects to extend telephone networks between Bangkok and the provinces. In 1988 it committed a loan to upgrade roads in the Northeast and Central regions. A number of projects were allocated to improvement of public utilities in provincial cities as well. In line with previous plans and its own policy, Japanese aid to specific areas tended to benefit growth centers directly.[88]

In accordance with its policy to assist development in the Northeast, Japan committed a sizeable portion of its loan and grant programs to that region. Relief aid for refugee camps and for Thais displaced by them continued, comprising about half of the grant aid projects to the region. A number of projects in the Northeast were for agricultural development, including commodity production in the form of road improvement and rehabilitation.[89]

The aid program branched out in new directions during the Plan period. The publication of *The Country Study for Development Assistance to the Kingdom of Thailand* in January 1989 was the most important aspect of this diversification. Reflecting the importance of its aid relationship with Thailand, JICA in 1987 commissioned a country study group to review its aid performance there and to analyze the performance of the Thai economy and the Thai government's development policies. The result was the most comprehensive analysis of Thai economic development policy and appropriate areas of Japanese assistance to date.

Japan also extended grant aid and technical assistance for environmental protection in response to new Thai efforts to deal with the problems of pollution and natural resource destruction. In 1989 it extended a grant for construction of an environmental research institute in Bangkok, and in 1990 and 1991 it agreed to dispatch experts to staff it. JICA also agreed to accept Thai trainees for pollution assessment training in Tokyo.[90] These efforts reflected new thinking on the part of the Thai government. Previous conceptions of environmental assistance had been much more broadly conceived, and consequently assessments of "environmental assistance" had included some public utilities projects, human settlements improvement, and even cultural projects.

The Thai government found Japan's aid terms generally satisfactory during the plan period. Commitments included local cost financing of projects and the introduction of sector loans cofinanced with the World Bank and the ADB. The Thai Ministry of Finance acknowledged in 1988 that the OECF's interest rates of 3 percent were favorable compared to international capital markets or loans from the ADB and World Bank. Nevertheless, Thailand requested a drop in the OECF's interest rate on the Fourteenth Yen Loan to 2.5 percent.[91] The interest rate was settled at 2.9 percent.[92]

The role of Thai and Japanese companies in the implementation of aid projects presented a thornier problem. The boom in Japanese investment in Thailand beginning in 1986 provided a catalyst for Thai perceptions of domination by Japanese companies, a perception that spilled over into the aid program. Although the contracting portion of Japanese loans was untied, the continued success of Japanese companies in project bidding received a great deal of public criticism.[93] At bilateral consultations in early 1988, the Thai government requested opening to Thai businesses of specifications for loan and grant conditions, and priority of Thai products in materials supply. The Japanese government replied that the requests would be difficult problem from the "systemic viewpoint," meaning that such decisions would have to be worked out at the policy level in Japan and were therefore not easily agreed to.[94] Nevertheless, Japan agreed to untie consultancy services in its loan aid that year, thus completely untying that program. By 1990, Japan had agreed to Thai demands for more participation for Thai firms and greater usage of Thai goods and services in grant aid projects.[95] At the same time, the government of Thailand began to approach the ADB as an alternate source of project design studies.[96]

Conclusion

In general, Japan's aid has conformed to the priorities established by the Thai government in its five-year plans. Japanese aid has been allocated to those sectors for which Thailand programmed aid receipts. Moreover, areas that received a lot of attention in the plans, as measured by proportion of funding in the development budgets, also received Japanese aid, although the relationship was never one-to-one. As expected, the Japanese aid program favored capital assistance, and branched out into the "soft" sectors in later plans. Changes in Japanese aid policy, such as the inclusion of strategic aid and policy statements by the Suzuki cabinet in the early 1980s, largely meant that Japan expanded its aid funding to sectors for which the Thai government had already planned external funding; Japan's aid simply augmented expected aid levels.

Japan's bias toward capital projects in its aid program is well known. Its aid program in Thailand is no different; infrastructure projects have tended to dominate the loan aid program. Even in the grant program, aid has tended to be in the form of provision of equipment or construction of facilities. The benefits to the Japanese companies that are awarded contracts for these projects are real. The capital project emphasis, however, does not exist solely on the Japanese side. The agencies of the Thai government share this orientation. As seen above, infrastructure development has constituted a major portion of all seven plan budgets.

The Thai case is also interesting because it cautions us against simplistic assumptions about the relationship between aid and other aspects of the economic relationships between the two countries. In particular, it suggests that the link between trade and aid is not one-way. We saw in the negotiations that followed the anti-Tanaka riots and the formulation of the White Paper an attempt to link the two. It is significant that the linkage came from the Thai negotiators. Given Japan's economic presence in Asia, the issue for them was not simply the link between Japan's aid and trade success, but how to use Japanese aid to promote Thai producers' ability to export to the region's largest market. Thai negotiators during the White Paper negotiations went so far as to request technical assistance intended specifically to teach Thai exporters how to meet Japanese import standards for processed agricultural products. While this may smack of dependent development in microcosm, it is useful to consider the direction of negotiations.

The bias exists even in sectors such as rural development. The Thai Foreign Ministry noted at the beginning of the Fourth Plan that "the Central Government agencies have limited absorptive capacity to plan and carry out rural development programmes and are generally oriented towards basic physical infrastructure or big projects."[97]

The emphasis in the Japanese aid program on capital aid has resulted in the overwhelming emphasis on projects. The technical assistance program has grown over the years, but remains a small portion of Japan's annual aid. With the exception of loans to IFCT and BAAC, the loan program has been exclusively oriented to individual projects. The result has been that Thailand's largest aid donor has not been actively involved in assisting the planning of the Thai economy. As one observer noted, the World Bank has played the leadership role in Thai development, while Japan has been the largest aid donor.[98] While this situation keeps Japan from being criticized for "interference in domestic affairs," it has limited its scope to help shape Thai development in ways it considers appropriate.

Japan's capital aid allowed Thailand to substitute for the changes in other donors' programs. In the 1950s USAID carried out a sizeable infrastructure aid program emphasizing transportation development. Most of the projects had been completed by the early 1960s, just as American interest shifted to counterinsurgency and other security aid. In the mid-1970s, just as Japan's aid program was shaping up, USAID turned its focus to poverty alleviation and basic human needs development.[99] Similarly, while the World Bank allocated three-quarters of its loans to Thailand between 1954 and 1972 for infrastructure, it shifted its emphasis to agriculture and rural development in the mid-1970s, as did the ADB.[100] Throughout most of its aid history, then, Japan has been Thailand's major supplier of loans for infrastructure development.

Japanese aid has generally followed the sectoral and regional priorities of the Thai government. The terms of aid, however, are another matter. Discussion of interest rates, repayment periods, the ratio of loans to grants, and the status of untying have been problematic throughout the period under investigation. Japan has made concessions in these areas, but because decisions on terms of aid are made at the policy level in the four-ministry system, and because these decisions affect all recipients, Thailand has little power to consistently affect such decisions. Aid terms, moreover, are based on DAC norms. As a middle-income economy, Thailand can expect a certain level of concessionality in the aid it receives, but not beyond a certain level.

Two recent Japanese decisions illustrate Thailand's vulnerability to changes in donor policies. In February 1990 Japan closed ranks with international donors in suspending aid to Thailand in the wake of the February coup d'état. While Japan was careful to argue that the suspension covered only discussions of "new aid,"[101] the result was to postpone the signing of an aid package until late 1990. The most dramatic change in terms for Thailand occurred during the Seventh Plan period. In April 1993 Japan announced its decision to suspend new grant aid beginning that year. The decision resulted from Japan's adherence to an earlier World Bank judgment that Thailand had "graduated" to NIC status and therefore no longer qualified for grants.[102] While Japan has room to adjust its aid terms for specific recipients, those adjustments will be made within a framework set outside the bilateral aid relationship.

4

Japan's Foreign Aid and Philippine Development

Overview of Philippine Sectoral and Regional Priorities

The Philippine government, like its Thai counterpart, has seen its role primarily as a supporter of private sector initiative. To that end, it has allocated its public expenditures in part to the development of infrastructure necessary for economic growth and projects beyond the reach of private firms. In all periods, heavy infrastructure has occupied a large place in Philippine government expenditures. Between 1975 and 1985, for example, infrastructure expenditures accounted for 42 percent of government capital outlays, with utilities, power and energy, water, and transportation and communications taking the largest shares.[1]

Until the 1970s economic policy makers in the Philippine government did not recognize the need to develop the areas of the country outside of Manila and its immediately surrounding regions. This attitude changed in the early 1970s, resulting in decisions to develop the economic foundations of the regions.[2] Immediately following the declaration of martial law in September 1972, the government undertook a series of reforms to strengthen local governments and coordinate central government programs at the local level.[3] The government also promulgated the Integrated Reorganization Plan. As part of the plan, regional urban centers were designated in each region. Since, historically, the islands of Luzon, the Visayas, and Mindanao had developed largely autonomous regional urban centers, government resources tended to flow to them before radiating out to the rural areas around them.[4]

Despite the government's recognition of the need to promote regional development, obstacles hindered its policies. Development planning was centralized, with little room for local and regional input. Development planning, moreover, focussed on export-led growth in both the agricultural and industrial sectors, and development of domestic agriculture and markets was largely ignored. Historically, government expenditure on rural areas has been low, and the areas outside major regional cities still have high incidences of poverty.[5]

Foreign aid was expected to play an important role in Philippine development. In the mid-1970s the World Bank suggested that at least one-third of all medium- and long-term lending come from concessional lending.[6] Unlike Thailand, however, the Philippine government viewed foreign aid in terms of its short-term utility. Aid could not only be used to fund capital projects, but could cover balance of payments shortfalls, too. For most of the 1970s and 1980s the Philippine government held this double view of the possible uses of aid; at times, the latter took precedence over the former, forcing postponement of development projects.

The creation of the World Bank Consultative Group for the Philippines was an important event in the history of aid to the Philippines; its inauguration in 1971 marked the beginning of a massive increase in aid to that country. Total ODA commitments to the Philippines from 1971 to 1974 were greater than those of the previous two decades; ODA accounted for just over one half of total foreign financing from 1972 to 1976.[7] The Consultative Group, composed of the World Bank, the ADB, the United States, Japan, West Germany, and others, provided a forum for the Philippine government to present its development objectives in order to familiarize an expanded number of donors with them. The Group's formation allowed for better coordination of external assistance, although donors were careful to insulate their bilateral aid machinery from undue Group influence.[8]

Japan's aid program in the Philippines began simultaneously with its participation in the Consultative Group. Japan participated in the first Consultative Group meeting in April 1971, and its first two yen-loan packages to the Philippines coincided with Group meetings.[9] While the Consultative Group provided Japan's entrance into the aid relationship with the Philippines in the first place, it also placed constraints on that aid. As will be discussed below, the division of labor among Consultative Group donors affected the composition of Japan's aid there.

Japan's aid has tended to conform to the sectoral and regional priorities of the Philippine government. Aid has been distributed to infrastructure projects in population centers, although a significant component has been diverted to debt and balance of payments relief. Manila and the

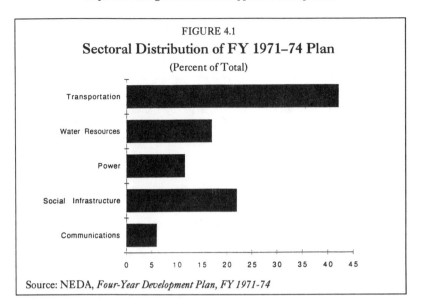

FIGURE 4.1

Sectoral Distribution of FY 1971–74 Plan

(Percent of Total)

Source: NEDA, *Four-Year Development Plan, FY 1971-74*

regions around it in central Luzon have been prime candidates for assistance, followed by other regional centers in the provinces.

Four-Year Development Plan, 1971–1974

The Philippine government undertook greater levels of public sector capital formation in the 1971-74 four-year plan than it had previously. Figure 4.1 shows the sectoral distributions of the public investment budget for the plan period. Public investment expenditures were targeted at 4.63 billion pesos during the period. Transportation development received the lion's share of resources from the public investment program between 1971 and 1974, accounting for 42 percent of total programmed expenditures. Social infrastructure, including school and hospital buildings and local government investments, was allocated the second highest amount. Water resources development was third, followed by power, and telecommunications.

Foreign aid was expected to play an important role in the development of these sectors. In fact, the Philippine government's expectation that it could avail itself of concessional lending spurred the increase in public investment. Foreign exchange requirements were programmed for all of the sectors listed above. As expected, transportation accounted for the largest portion, 46.5

percent of total foreign financing programmed in the four-year infrastructure budget. The power, water resources, and communications sectors were also allocated foreign aid funding. In contrast to its overall allocation in the public investment budget, social infrastructure expenditures accounted for only 3 percent of total foreign financing.[10]

Expanded foreign aid, made possible by the creation of the Consultative Group, served an additional Philippine foreign policy goal. In the 1970s the Philippines desired to reorient its relationship with the United States. It viewed bilateral security and economic relations as asymmetrical, with the advantages accruing overwhelmingly to the United States. One task of Philippine foreign policy, then, was to diversify its relations with other countries and blocs. To that end, the Marcos administration attempted to foster closer relations with the Philippines' regional neighbors as well as undertaking high-profile attempts to promote relations with socialist nations. A new policy toward Japan was at the top of the list of the Philippines' diversification attempts, and the aid relationship began in a climate of warming economic and political relations between the two countries.[11]

The 1971-1974 plan was created in the midst of a balance of payments crisis. Following decontrol of foreign exchange in 1962, imports rose dramatically; the value of imports in 1969 was almost double that of 1962. The resulting trade deficit was financed by external borrowing. "Massive" spending by the Marcos administration during the 1969 election campaign, also financed by external borrowing, provided the catalyst for the balance of payments crisis in February 1970.[12] The crisis affected Philippine government decisions about its foreign capital requirements for the early 1970s, with almost all of the external funding requirements for 1971-1973 to be used for debt service. To that end, the government made efforts to secure new aid commitments in the form of commodity loans. Japan was at the head of the list of possible donors.[13]

Japan's aid during the period amounted to 58.29 billion yen, a significant increase over its commitments of the 1960s. It was composed overwhelmingly of loans and a small proportion of grants, a pattern that would be repeated throughout the period under study. Yen loans accounted for 20.7 percent of total ODA loans to the Philippines, while Japan's grant aid was less than 5 percent of total grants. Commodity loans made up the majority of yen loans during the period. A commodity loan was included in each of the first three yen loan packages, committed in 1971, 1972, and 1973, respectively. $155 million of $227 million in yen loans were of this type. Japan's aid accounted for over two-thirds of all commodity loans received by the Philippines during the period.[14] The large amount of Japanese commodity loans reflected a lending policy in marked contrast to that toward Thailand, and contradicts the conventional wisdom about Japan's preference for project lending.

Commodity loans offered Japan and the Philippines a device for avoiding the implementation difficulties attendant on the new aid relationship. As noted in Chapter Two, implementation of Japanese loan aid to Thailand during the early 1970s lagged significantly behind project commitments. A like situation existed in the Philippines, where project loan disbursement was slow, and fundable projects were lacking. Many of those that were ready were being funded by other donors. The Japanese screening process also added to the problem. In another respect, commodity loan disbursement procedures were simple. The loan agreements provided general strictures on the management of imports, but not on specific commodities, and use of a given portion of total Japanese imports was credited to the commodity loans.[15]

The provision of commodity loans satisfied the Philippine government. Commodity loans provided substantial balance of payments support, allowing an increase of imports without straining the Philippines' short-term debt repayment position, and "provided peso-finance for development projects mutually agreed upon on a bilateral basis."[16] Commodity loans benefitted Japan as well. Japanese private exporters certainly benefitted from them, and they eased the disbursement and implementation responsibilities for an aid bureaucracy new to the Philippines.

Japan's loan aid followed the sectoral priorities set forth in the plan, although variation in allocations existed. Japan committed nine project loans in the First and Third Yen Loans, of which four loans were for water resources projects, three were for transportation projects, and one each was for power and agriculture.[17] In addition, a $30 million Japanese commodity loan for construction of the Pan-Philippine Highway had been committed in 1970, and was implemented during the Plan period. The difference in the proportion of transportation and water resources projects funded by Japanese aid and that of Philippine allocations of public investment and foreign exchange to those sectors can be explained by the small number of projects, which would tend to exaggerate the impact of Japan's aid on the water resources sector, and the fact that the Philippine government had planned to seek financing for transportation projects from the World Bank and the ADB.[18]

The objectives of Japanese-funded projects tended to follow Philippine priorities, again with some variance. Transportation projects showed the most consistency with stated Philippine goals. The Four-Year Plan's infrastructure program allocated just over 75 percent of planned foreign exchange to highway construction and 10 percent to railroads. Including the 1970 commodity loan for the Pan-Philippine Highway, three Japanese loans went to highway development, and one went to the Philippine National Railway.

Water resources and power present a different picture. While the infrastructure program allocated foreign exchange almost evenly between irrigation and water supply, with no foreign exchange allocated to flood control, Japanese-funded projects were divided between irrigation and flood control. Similarly, the infrastructure program allocated almost 80 percent of foreign exchange for power development to power plants and transmission lines, and 16 percent to rural electrification; the lone Japanese aid project for power was committed for electrification of the Cagayan Valley in northeastern Luzon. The flood control projects appear to be adjuncts to other priority projects. The plan emphasized waterworks and sewerage expansion in Metro Manila. One project loan committed in 1971 was for flood control and drainage work in that area, suggesting that the project was in support of larger sectoral work. The second project loan, committed in 1973, was for flood control dredging in the Bicol (southern Luzon), Cotabato (Mindanao), and Pampanga (central Luzon) river basins.

This work anticipated the Philippine government's efforts to develop these river basins in the subsequent four-year plan. Similarly, electrification of the Cagayan Valley was not a priority project. Preliminary surveys of the electrical system in the Cagayan Valley were undertaken in 1971, but the loan agreement for transmission lines was not completed until October 1974, suggesting that Japan had offered the Philippine government equipment before the project was "mature" enough to be suitable for foreign funding. In sum, Japanese loan aid for these sectors was supportive, but did not occupy a central place in the first four-year plan.

It is difficult to assess Japanese aid in terms of Philippine regional priorities during the plan period. The plan tended to stress projects, especially in its discussion of sectoral plans, suggesting that planning was more concerned with projects than regions. Some sectors, such as highway development, had a national and interregional character; others, such as the power sector, emphasized construction in Luzon. Japanese aid tended to focus on Luzon and Metro Manila. The Pan-Philippine Highway clearly had national scope, and the project loans associated with it were carried out accordingly. The two other transportation loans were for projects in Manila, as was a transportation master plan study for the capital.[19] The two flood control projects focussed on Metro Manila and Luzon. The irrigation and seed production projects were carried out nationwide.

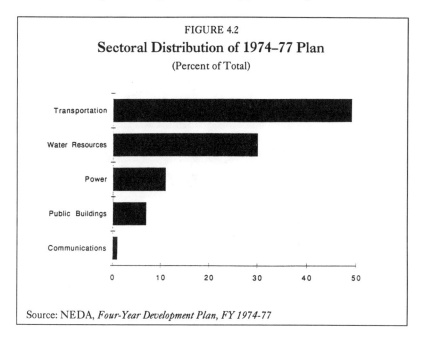

FIGURE 4.2
Sectoral Distribution of 1974–77 Plan
(Percent of Total)

Source: NEDA, *Four-Year Development Plan, FY 1974-77*

Four-Year Development Plan 1974–1977

The Philippine government continued to favor transportation development in the new four-year plan. Figure 4.2 provides a sectoral breakdown of the infrastructure budget for the Plan period. Transportation accounted for just under half of that budget, followed by water resources, power, public building, and telecommunications. Subsectoral breakdowns were also similar. Highway construction accounted for most of total peso funding in the transportation budget, with almost all of the rest going to railway construction. Irrigation accounted for almost one-half of the water resources peso requirement, and power plant construction continued to dominate power sector investment.

Sectoral foreign exchange requirements were allocated somewhat differently. Figure 4.2A shows the sectoral breakdown of planned for exchange during the plan period. Transportation and power were given almost equal shares of projected foreign exchange, accounting for about one-third each. The water resources sector was allocated one-quarter. The shares of estimated foreign exchange for power and telecommunications were higher than their shares of domestic finance in the public investment

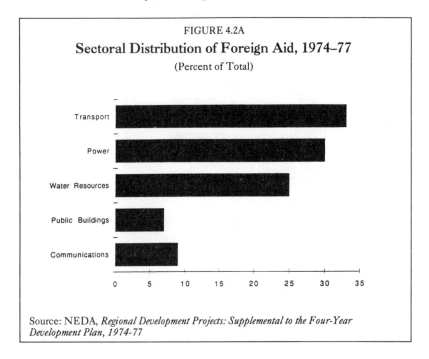

FIGURE 4.2A

Sectoral Distribution of Foreign Aid, 1974–77

(Percent of Total)

Source: NEDA, *Regional Development Projects: Supplemental to the Four-Year Development Plan, 1974-77*

budget, suggesting that they were more reliant on foreign financing than other sectors. Subsectoral breakdowns of foreign exchange requirements tended to follow those of domestic finance. Highway construction was to account for 58 percent of total foreign exchange for transportation. Irrigation was to take almost half of the foreign exchange estimated for water resources, with water supply and sewerage taking 39 percent, and flood control and drainage 17 percent. 78 percent of the foreign exchange planned for the power sector was allocated to power plant construction, while rural electrification was allocated 22 percent.[20]

Despite its recognition of the need to develop the regions outside Metro Manila, the Philippine government continued to concentrate its infrastructure resources in Central Luzon. On the eve of the 1974-77 plan period, it recognized that if national economic development were to continue, resources would have to be concentrated in those centers where they could be most efficiently utilized: the most notable case was Metro Manila. The National Capital Region and central Luzon accounted for almost 40 percent of the development projects planned for specific regions. Mindanao accounted for just under 30 percent, of which Southern Mindanao accounted for over half. The Visayan Islands and northern Mindanao fared the worst, receiving between one and three projects apiece.[21] This list formed the basis of the government's requests for external funding for its development program, so we would expect Japanese aid to conform to its regional priorities.

As in the previous plan period, Japanese project loan aid favored transportation development. More than half of the project loan commitments made between 1974 and 1977 were for that sector. Project loans for the water resources and power sectors followed, with two loans apiece, while agriculture received one. Loans show greater diversity than their counterparts in the previous plan period. In the transportation sector, port works projects are especially noticeable. Three loans were given to port works, second in number to highway construction loans, which accounted for four. Power sector loans were evenly split between power plants and rural electrification, the latter a continuation of the Cagayan Valley rural electrification project.[22]

The Pan-Philippine Highway was the focal point of Japan's transportation loan aid in the first two plan periods. It accounted for three of four highway loans during the second period. For the Philippines, it provided necessary linkage for all of the regions of the country except Western Mindanao. According to the Four-Year-Plan, the Highway was to constitute "the main artery of the national highway network of the country, serving various lateral secondary and feeder roads."[23] It opened opportunities for the economic development of previously remote regions. Successive loans provided funding for portions of the Highway progressively farther from central Luzon. For example, the last two loans of the period, parts of the Sixth Yen-Loan agreed upon in 1977, were to link the northern parts of Luzon, as well as to link the Visayan Islands and northern Mindanao by ferry. In 1977, the Philippine government noted that the near-completion of the northern portion of the highway, along with other infrastructure development, had enhanced the advantages of the Cagayan Valley as a supplier of farm products to Metro Manila and Northern Luzon. It also observed that the highway had finally made southern Luzon more accessible.[24]

Japan's assistance for the highway supported the development of other sectors. The Five-Year Plan for 1978-1982 emphasized streamlining the interregional transportation network to be built off the highway, based on the needs of other productive sectors. The highway supported the Philippine government's policy of promoting the development of export processing by linking agricultural export operations and tourist sites to the nationwide transportation system.[25]

While commodity loans were similar in purpose to project loans, differences did exist. Hospital construction was funded with commodity loans, a departure from the pattern of yen loans. Commodity loans were also to be used for other miscellaneous public works. Thus, while commodity loan allocations were similar to project loan allocations, the distribution of commodity loans points to greater Philippine freedom in the choice of sectoral targets than was the case with project loans.

The composition of Japanese loan aid to the Philippines in the period from 1970 to 1977 suggests that Japan established a niche for its aid. One of the results of the coordination of aid by the Consultative Group during that period was the sectoral concentration of aid by different donors. The World Bank and the ADB took the lead in financing power development projects, especially in Luzon and Mindanao. Similarly, the multilaterals were active in highway development; all major highway construction except the Pan-Philippine Highway was funded by the two multilateral donors. The effect of this concentration was to place Japan in competition with the multilaterals and not other bilateral donors. Japan also established a niche in road construction in Metro Manila. As noted above, an OTCA survey of transportation requirements in the capital region during the 1971-74 Plan period became the basis for the development of the transportation network in Manila in the 1974-77 plan period, which in turn prepared the way for road construction loans in the following period.[26]

By the end of the mid-1970s, then, Japan's loan aid in these sectors had the following profile. Power sector aid went to areas outside Central Luzon. Through 1977, aid in this sector went mostly to rural electrification; aid in subsequent plan periods went to power development in the Visayas or to support existing power plants in Luzon. Transportation aid went to financing the Pan-Philippine Highway, road projects in Metro Manila, or to projects for port works and railroads not dominated by the multilateral lenders.

The niche analogy is reinforced when we examine overall loan assistance during the 1970s. While total ODA loans to the Philippines from 1970 to 1979 favored agriculture (29 percent), followed by transport (18 percent), power (17 percent), industry (15 percent), and water supply (eight percent), Japanese ODA favored transport, with limited funding for agriculture. Flood control, a major part of Japanese ODA, accounted for 1 percent of total ODA loans. Similarly, projects funded by commodity loans amounted to just over 6 percent of total funding, most of which came from Japan.[27]

The composition of Japan's loan aid affected its regional distribution. Three areas are noteworthy for their concentrations of Japanese aid during this period: central Luzon, the Cagayan Valley, and the Visayan Islands.

Luzon accounted for the highest number of loans and grants; four loan projects were carried out in the Cagayan Valley. Three were power and electrification projects, which suggests that Japan had established a niche in that sector in that region. Two projects, one loan and one grant, went to the Visayan Islands.[28]

The 1974-1977 plan predicted that debt incurred from bilateral ODA sources would carry more concessional terms than private and multilateral debt. It expected bilateral ODA to carry average terms of twenty years' repayment after a four-year grace period and a 4 percent interest rate.[29] In all but one case, Japan's loan aid was more concessional than the anticipated average. All yen-loan packages during the period carried repayment terms of twenty-five years with a seven-year grace period. All but the second phase of the Fifth Yen Loan (1977) carried interest rates of 3.25 percent; that part of the Fifth Yen Loan had a 4.25 percent interest rate.[30] While the plan does not mention the Philippine government's expectations about the terms of Japanese aid within this period, those terms are within the limits of the plan's general outline. Japan's yen loans to the Philippines during this period were LDC untied, in conformity with most of its loans to other recipients.

Five-Year Plan, 1978–1982

The 1978-1982 Five-Year Development Plan reflected the Philippine government's reevaluation of investment priorities. While the infrastructure sectors continued to receive funding, their order of priority changed. Figure 4.3 provides a sectoral breakdown of the infrastructure budget. The power sector's share of the infrastructure budget increased to just under one-half of the total budget. Transportation allocations decreased markedly from the previous period. Water resources accounted for just under 28 percent and telecommunications for 1.5 percent.

Sectoral goals also differed from previous plans. On paper, the sub-sectoral distribution of resources was about the same as before. In the transportation sector, for example, highway development continued to take the lion's share of public investment expenditures. Irrigation development continued to dominate the water resources sector, as did power generation and transmission in the energy sector. The goals for the transportation and energy sectors, however, differed from prior development policies. Highway development was to focus on road construction and rehabilitation in remote areas, especially feeder roads to areas with potential for agricultural, mining, and industrial development. The plan specifically mentioned development

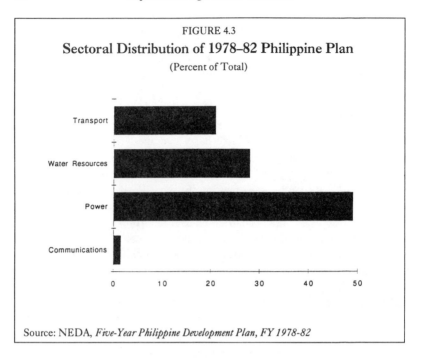

FIGURE 4.3

Sectoral Distribution of 1978–82 Philippine Plan

(Percent of Total)

Source: NEDA, *Five-Year Philippine Development Plan, FY 1978-82*

of road networks in Mindanao and the Visayas. Energy sector goals included diversification and development of indigenous energy resources. Although imported oil would continue to be the major source of energy, exploitation of local energy supplies was expected to decrease the Philippines' reliance on overseas oil.[31]

All sectors in the infrastructure budget were expected to receive substantial foreign funding. Foreign exchange projections for the ten-year period from 1978 to 1987 for all sectors averaged 40-45 percent of total funding. Foreign financing in the power sector was expected to account for more than one-half of total expenditures.[32] ODA in particular was expected to play a major role in financing capital expenditures in infrastructure and industrial project development. Most of that assistance was to be long-term loans with maturities of fifteen years or more. Most of that ODA was to come from the World Bank and the ADB, with the bilateral donors accounting for a comparatively small portion.[33] As with previous plans, however, Japan was to be an exception.

Japan was a major donor to the Philippines from 1978 to 1982, but it was not the largest. The World Bank, the ADB, Japan, the United States and the Federal Republic of Germany were the Philippines' main sources of ODA loans during the period. As planned, ODA from the multilateral donors comprised most of the total; World Bank lending constituted just over half of total ODA loans, while the ADB and Japan accounted for just under 20 percent each. In contrast, the United States and Germany accounted for 4 percent and 1.6 percent of total lending, respectively. The United States, Japan, and the United Nations were the principal grant aid donors to the Philippines. The United States accounted for 43 percent of the total, while Japan and the United Nations accounted for just under 20 percent each.[34]

Japan's loan aid during this period exhibits both sensitivity to new Philippine priorities and continuity from previous distribution patterns. Transportation loans constituted the largest number of loans to any sector, 14 of 37, in line with prior loan aid and reinforcing the image of a Japanese niche. Power and water resources loans were roughly equal in number, six and seven respectively. The industry sector was given two loans, similar to the 1974-1977 period. Japan provided three agriculture loans, an increase from previous plan periods. It also provided three loans to the communications sector, a new development. Japan provided one commodity loan in 1978, but did not commit such aid during the rest of the plan period.[35]

Power sector loans demonstrate the greatest sensitivity to new Philippine priorities. Unlike earlier loans, they were clustered in the power and transmission sector and not in rural electrification; the former sector accounted for five of six loans during the period. The geographic distribution of the projects conformed to Philippine priorities. The plan gave priority to power development in the Visayas, reflecting that region's low current capacity. Three of the five Japanese loans were for projects in that region, and a fourth included rural power development in the Western Visayas. Two of the three projects were carried out at the Tongonan and Palimpinon geothermal sites, slated for development in the plan period.[36]

The third loan reflected immediate power needs. In 1979 the Japanese government provided a special yen loan for power-generating barges, to be docked in the Visayas, to alleviate power shortages in the area. From the Philippine government's perspective, the project had two advantages. First, the barges were mobile, allowing the government to move them to power-deficient areas on short notice. (The government planned to move one barge later to provide power to the country's copper smelting facility, proposed for construction in Leyte.) Second, the loan could be implemented in a timely fashion. Unlike other power projects that would take years to complete, the barges could be in place within one year from the date of loan agreement.[37]

The composition of transportation loans shows a combination of ongoing distribution patterns as well as new priorities. As in previous plan periods, transportation development in Metro Manila and Luzon constituted a significant portion of total loans: of fourteen loans, five were for projects in Metro Manila and another four for projects in Luzon. Of the latter, one was for completion of the northern section of the Pan-Philippine. Highway, a continuation of an ongoing concentration in a Japanese niche. Two of the loans for Metro Manila were for general transport and traffic improvement.

New priorities were also evident in transport loans. With the exception of the Pan-Philippine Highway loan, all highway sector loans to Luzon were for construction of secondary and feeder roads; another loan was made for development of roads in Western Leyte. For the first time, in 1978, Japan committed a loan for airport modernization, an activity set forth in the plan. Similarly, the three port works projects funded during the period were for improvement and expansion of ports defined as primary in the plan.[38]

Japanese grant aid shows a greater degree of elaboration than in previous plan periods. First, the amount of funding increased from 1978 to 1982 due to larger numbers of projects funded as well as higher funding levels for some projects. Second, its composition changed. Grants prior to 1978 were made for the provision of rice aid, university education, water resources, and agriculture. From 1978 to 1982 the scope of grants broadened to include construction of technical training facilities and government educational programs, forestry conservation, fisheries, irrigation, and provision of fertilizer and machinery to increase food production.

Japan's loan aid was fairly evenly spread between northern Luzon, Manila and the Visayan Islands. The evidence suggests that Japan's aid in this period was an elaboration of previous distribution patterns. The Cagayan Valley and Ilocos Norte accounted for eleven of thirty projects in which specific regions were identifiable, a clear indication that it was building on its niche in the north. The Visayan Islands show a similar pattern, accounting for eight projects. Metro Manila continued to receive attention, being allocated five loan projects and all but three grants. Unlike earlier periods, Mindanao received three projects. As expected, loan aid was allocated largely to regional urban centers in those regions aided.

Japan's aid supported the Philippine government's integrated rural development program. The Philippine government established clear geographic priorities for the program, identifying the provinces of Cagayan, Isabela, Mindoro, Palawan, Samar, Leyte, the Bicol River Basin, the Agusan-Cotabato River Basin, and the Pampanga Delta as the initial priority areas of the program.[39] All but Samar and Palawan received funding for rural development-related projects during the period.

As expected, Japanese yen loans became more concessional during the plan period. While the Seventh Yen Loan, committed in 1978, carried the same terms as those of the previous plan period, subsequent loan packages carried a lower interest rate of 3 percent. Procurement for regular loan packages was also generally untied. The special yen loan for power plant barges in 1978 was an exception, as it was tied to procurement of Japanese goods. It is doubtful that the concessionality of terms had to do with Philippine initiative; loan terms for Thailand and the Philippines were similar, a pattern discernable throughout the period discussed in this chapter. Likewise, in announcing the untying of yen loans to the Philippines in 1978, Prime Minister Fukuda stated that the move was in accordance with OECD procedures.[40]

Despite a great deal of attention to issues of tying and aid terms in the literature on foreign aid, little attention is paid specifically to the costs of loan aid use. This is important in the Philippine case because its ability to actually use committed loans became a problem in the late 1970s. Among bilateral donors, OECF loans had the highest rate of disbursement, 78 percent. In contrast, disbursement rates for West Germany and USAID were 56 percent and 35 percent respectively. Reyes attributed the high availment rate of OECF loans to the fact that a Presidential Cabinet Committee and a corresponding Implementing Officer coordinated programming and disbursement of its loans, a mechanism that existed for no other donor.[41]

Given the difficulties the Philippine government experienced with aid use, the willingness of donors to cancel unused loans should be considered part of their terms of aid. Cancelled loans increased the costs of aid because they had to be foregone by the recipient. By this measure, the OECF compared favorably with other donors. Between 1973 and 1983 USAID and ADB canceled the largest amount of loan aid, $13.95 million and $13.57 million, respectively, just under 70 percent of total cancellations during the period. The World Bank followed with $7.35 million, or 18.4 percent of total cancellations. OECF canceled $4.856 million, or 12 percent of total cancelled loans. OECF also had the second lowest ratio of canceled loans to committed loans, 1.5 percent.[42] Overall, OECF loans cost the Philippine government less to use than those of the other major donors.

Japanese aid was also more concessional than other donors' because the Japanese government does not impose commitment fees for failure to utilize yen loans. The World Bank, ADB and West Germany charge commitment fees on the undrawn balance of committed loans: essentially this

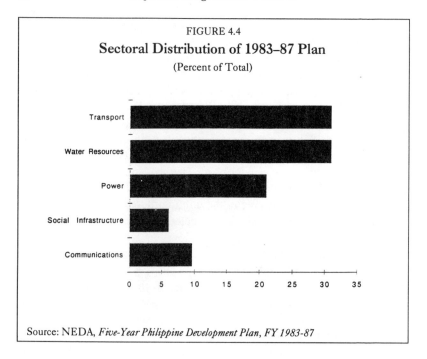

FIGURE 4.4

Sectoral Distribution of 1983–87 Plan

(Percent of Total)

Source: NEDA, *Five-Year Philippine Development Plan, FY 1983-87*

acts as an insurance payment by the recipient to keep the loan available past its original commitment period. OECF and USAID, on the other hand, do not.[43] In effect, their terms of aid were softer because the cost of delays in loan availment were lowered by the value of potential commitment fees. During the financial crisis of 1983 to 1986 this must have made OECF and USAID loans more attractive to the Philippine government.

Five-Year Plan, 1983–1987

The sectoral shares of the public investment budget for 1983-1987 were more even than in the previous plan. Figure 4.4 shows the sectoral distribution of public investment funds during the Plan period. An evening out of expenditures among the sectors is visible. Transport and water resources were to account for just under one-third of total investment. Power and electrification was to account for about 21 percent, about half its share from the previous period. Telecommunications' share rose to 9.6 percent, a marked increase over all prior plans. Social infrastructure was to account for just over 6 percent of the public investment budget. Subsectoral distributions were similar to previous plans.

As in the previous plan period, the Philippine government undertook the diversification of economic development outside of Metro Manila. The new plan specifically mentioned that the government would make sizable infrastructure and other public service investments in regional cities. Yet, it backed away from complete support for regional development. Metro Manila was still recognized as the trendsetter for the nation requiring further infrastructure development. In particular, further investment in water and flood control would be required, as well as housing, pollution control, transport, and other services.[44]

The plan also called for more concessional terms of foreign financing. Specifically, it called for diversification of funding sources, generation of funds with longer maturity periods, and more favorable interest rates. It also asserted that the maturity of project loans would be aligned with the gestation periods of the projects being funded;[45] presumably, the government would ask for longer grace and repayment periods for long-term projects such as energy plants.

Japan's ODA as a proportion of total ODA to the Philippines during this period rose dramatically. In 1983 Japan's ODA accounted for 42 percent of all bilateral ODA, and 36 percent of total ODA from all sources. In 1987, it had increased to 54 percent of all bilateral ODA, and 49 percent of total ODA. The rising share of Japan's aid to the Philippines was matched by declining proportions of multilateral aid. The United States' share diminished as well, from about 38 to 33 percent.[46] Thereafter, it dropped precipitously. Since this watershed period, Japan has continued to be the Philippines' largest aid donor.

As with previous aid, Japan's yen loans were largely directed toward the major infrastructure sectors.[47] Distribution of projects among sectors generally followed the Plan's objectives: the transportation and water resources sectors received the most loans, eight and six, followed by the power sector with four, and communications with one. Subsectoral distributions followed the familiar pattern. Transportation loans went to construction of roads, railways and port works. Water resources loans were concentrated on flood control, with one loan each being given to rural water supply and irrigation projects. Three of the power sector loans were given for power plant construction in the Visayas, transmission line construction, and provision of power plant barges.[48] Essentially, these projects represented continuations of development efforts already taking place.

Loan aid followed the usual geographic pattern. Metro Manila received a plurality of projects, most for road construction. The Visayas received three loans, second only to the capital. Projects were spread throughout the rest of Luzon, with Regions 2 and 4 receiving more than the others. Inadequate information prevents a breakdown of aid by cities outside of Metro Manila, but the extant evidence shows that loans for regional cities supported water resources and transportation development.

In October, 1983 the Philippines entered the worst balance of payments crisis in its postwar history. Economist James Boyce blames the policy of debt-financed development for the crisis, and argues that the Marcos administration's reliance on new debt to repay old obligations made the crisis inevitable. He also considers the assassination of Benigno Aquino in August, the growth of short-term debt, the deterioration of the Philippines' terms of trade following the two oil shocks, the sharp rise in international interest rates in the early 1980s, and the mismanagement of investment from external borrowing as contributing factors. The declaration of a 90-day moratorium on external debt amortization in October 1983 hastened the closure of commercial lines of credit already begun following the Aquino assassination. The government was forced to negotiate standby credit from the International Monetary Fund (IMF) and rescheduling of its commercial debt in the following two years.[49]

Japan responded to the crisis in two ways. First, it reintroduced commodity loans into its loan packages. Commodity loans committed in 1983 and 1984 were significantly larger than the project portion of the loan packages in which they were included. Unlike earlier commodity loans, however, their terms were harder than the project portions: while project loans carried thirty year repayment terms with ten-year grace periods, commodity loans had twenty-year repayment terms with five-year grace periods. This apparently reflected a tougher Japanese attitude toward "soft" financing as well as concern over the stability of the Philippine economy. Second, it agreed to two debt reschedulings, both of which were signed in January 1986, for a total of 23 billion yen. This was the first time Japan had ever agreed to reschedule Philippine debt.[50] As we would expect, the terms of rescheduling were stricter than for regular loans: the rescheduled portions had a repayment period of ten years with five years' grace. The reschedulings were cofinanced by the OECF and Export-Import Bank: the OECF portions carried interest rates of 3.5 percent and 3.25 percent, while the Export-Import Bank portions carried interest rates of 5.125 percent.

Clearly, Japan tightened its lending terms to the Philippines in response to the financial crisis. Japanese loan terms from 1983 to 1987 were harder than in the previous period. Interest rates rose, and loan repayment and grace periods for commodity loans and debt reschedulings shortened. Terms for the regular portions of the Eleventh Yen Loan package, in 1983, were the same as for the previous three years. The Twelfth and Thirteenth packages, however, carried interest rates of 3.5 percent, 0.5 percent higher than in the previous plan period. Shorter repayment periods for commodity loans made the terms even stricter. In comparison, the interest rates charged for the debt rescheduling agreements were lenient.

Medium-Term Plan, 1987–1992

The Aquino administration came to power following the so-called "February Revolution" in early 1986. The new government adopted a rhetoric of "People Power" and promised to end and correct the abuses of the previous administration. Among other reform efforts, the new administration launched an investigation of Marcos administration financial misuse, including corruption in the Japanese aid program. The Philippine and Japanese press also produced stories on other weaknesses in the aid program. The Japanese Diet, particularly the opposition parties, used the opportunity to launch investigations of Japan's aid practices, efforts that ultimately produced few results.

Given the new government's mandate for reform and the revelations about the defects and corruption in the Japanese aid program, we would expect changes in the aid program after the 1986 transition. We would expect the new plan to address new developmental problems in the Philippines, and that Japan's aid would reflect those new priorities. Finally, we would expect that Japan and the Philippines would take measures to rectify those conditions that had contributed to corruption and misuse of Japan's aid in the Philippines.

While the Japanese government initially supported the Aquino administration, its response to requests for aid in 1986 was guarded. In February, signing of the exchange of notes for the Thirteenth Yen Loan was postponed. The investigation into Marcos-era irregularities and the renegotiation—at the Aquino administration's insistence—of four projects in the loan package delayed final agreement through the spring.[51] Conclusion of the agreement in November and the promulgation of a new Medium-Term Philippine Development Plan appeared to restore Japanese confidence. During President Aquino's state visit to Japan in November 1986, Prime Minister Nakasone pledged support for Philippine recovery.[52]

The Aquino administration undertook several reforms of its aid program. First, it reorganized the aid bureaucracy. It reassigned some of the programming functions of the National Economic and Development Authority (NEDA). It created the Committee on Official Development Assistance (CODA), to which it gave the tasks of coordinating the ODA activities within the executive branch and monitoring agency and project performance. In order to administer the Multilateral Assistance Initiative it established the Coordinating Council for the Philippine Assistance Program (CCPAP), charged with deliberating ODA policy, giving policy advice to NEDA, and acting as the contact for top-level donor missions. NEDA was to continue to program project funds and to negotiate projects with donors. In addition, the president created the Project Facilitation Committee (PFC) to improve the government's aid absorptive capacity. Finally, it appointed project implementing officers to all agencies undertaking projects assisted by foreign aid.[53]

Second, it instituted a Medium-Term Public Investment Program (MTPIP). The MTPIP was designed to translate the policy goals of the Medium-Term Philippine Development Plan into specific projects and programs designated as top priority. The MTPIP was to serve as the basis for sectoral and regional allocations of public resources and to act as the pipeline for ODA projects. The MTPIP includes all capital projects of the central and local government agencies requiring national or ODA funding. In accordance with the MTPIP's role as priority setter, individual projects requested for inclusion therein were to be rigorously screened, and subsequently monitored during implementation.[54]

The reform most directly relevant to Japan's aid program involved the implementing officer for OECF loans. As noted above, the Philippine government's aid procedures for OECF loans included an implementing officer directly responsible to the president and responsible for coordinating the implementation of Japanese loan projects. After the fall of the Marcos government in February 1986, it became clear that the implementing officer's informal mission had been to divert kickbacks from Japanese contractors to President Marcos and, in some cases, to Japanese politicians. The implementing officer was replaced when the Aquino government took over, and eventually the position was abolished at NEDA's insistence.[55]

The Philippine government's sectoral priorities in the development budget were similar to those of previous plans. The new plan continued to support the heavy infrastructure sectors. Figure 4.5 provides a sectoral breakdown of public investment during the plan period. The public investment budget for the period was set at 257.6 billion pesos. Again, a balanced distribution of public investment among the largest sectors is evident, with

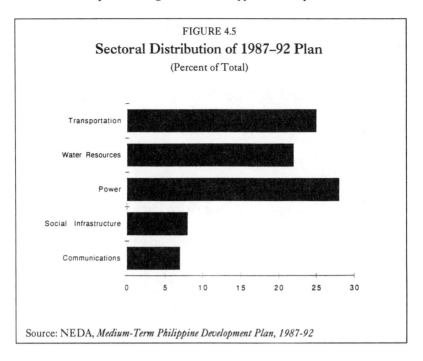

FIGURE 4.5
Sectoral Distribution of 1987–92 Plan
(Percent of Total)

Source: NEDA, *Medium-Term Philippine Development Plan, 1987-92*

just under 28 percent to be allocated to energy development, 25 percent to transportation, and 22 percent to water resources. Social infrastructure and communications accounted for less than 10 percent.

Subsectoral priorities were similar to previous plans: power development was to receive the majority of energy sector funding, highway development was allocated most of the transport sector budget, water supply and irrigation comprised most of the water resources budget, and telecommunications dominated the communications budget. The new plan differed from its predecessors by placing emphasis on the rehabilitation and maintenance of existing facilities. Similarly, ongoing projects were to receive funding priority in order to ensure their completion.[56]

The new administration committed itself to greater regional development efforts. The new government's regional development strategy attempted to correct regional economic and social imbalances caused by previous development policies. The plan undertook such measures as the development of rural transport and communications and the inauguration of its Countryside Agro-Industrial Development (CAID) program. More broadly, the government also attempted to rectify the regional biases in public investment by spreading the responsibility of project formulation to local and regional governmental authorities.[57]

While the plan called for regional development, not all of its statements were consistent with that goal. The public investment budget continued to favor Luzon. That island and its neighbors were allocated almost 40 percent of the total public investment budget. Metro Manila and the surrounding areas were allocated over half of that. The Visayas, in contrast, were allocated just over 10 percent, and Mindanao was to receive just under 18 percent. Thus, the emphasis on funding ongoing projects would reinforce interregional imbalances.

The Aquino administration responded to a debilitating debt burden from the previous administration in three ways. First, it decided to honor the outstanding debt incurred by the previous government. In so doing, it ruled out debt repudiation. While this decision angered critics of the administration, it allowed the Philippines the option of continuing to borrow from international lending institutions. Second, it undertook renegotiation of outstanding debt. Finally, it placed priority on concessional lending, in the form of grants and official loans, for new lending during the plan period.[58]

The transition from the Marcos to the Aquino government, and the allegations it produced regarding misuse of Japanese aid funds, prompted the Japanese government to reassess its program in the Philippines. The most visible result of that reassessment was the production of the *Country Study for Development Assistance to the Republic of the Philippines,* published in early 1987. The study marked a watershed in the aid relationship: it was the first comprehensive country study in the history of Japan's aid program. Contrary to previous aid evaluation efforts, this study embodied the results of discussions between the aid bureaucracies of both countries, at the working and policy levels, about the new administration's aid priorities and Japan's role in it. The study surveyed past Japanese aid practice in the Philippines and the current state of the Philippine economy, and made recommendations for future Japanese aid.

The Country Study's recommendations are particularly important to this analysis. The study began by noting the policy priorities to be addressed by Japan's aid. They included targeting the poor; support for land reform under the condition that the Philippine government produce feasible policies and projects; improvement of productivity in agriculture and industry through the provision of appropriate goods and training; support of employment generation through technical cooperation projects for medium and small-sized industries; and support for basic human needs and educational development. The study recommended continuation of commodity loans to help solve the country's balance of payments problems. It also argued that Japan should support revitalization of economic activities in the medium-sized provincial cities.

The report also called for changes in types of aid, such as the diversification of yen loans to include sector-specific loans, expansion of local cost financing, introduction of structural adjustment loans, and cofinancing with international agencies. It argued for increasing the ratio of grant aid to loan aid, for introducing regional programs, and for dispatching advisory experts to Philippine government agencies to assist with the formulation and implementation of Japanese aid and the joint evaluation of aid programs. It also called for establishment of "rolling plans" in which aid requests and implementation would be planned in the medium term rather than yearly. Finally, it urged the introduction of aid for nongovernmental organizations operating in the Philippines.[59]

Japan's ODA to the Philippines increased markedly following the inauguration of the Aquino administration, as did that of the United States and other donors. As shown in Table 2.7, total yen loan aid for 1987 under the Fourteenth Yen Loan package and the special yen loan for the Calaca II power plant was more than twice that of the Thirteenth Yen Loan package, the last package negotiated by the Marcos administration. Grant aid also increased slightly. Loan aid increased further through 1990 with the Multilateral Assistance Initiative (MAI), then declined precipitously in the early 1990s as the aid pipeline clogged up. Throughout the period, Japan remained the Philippines' largest donor. In 1987, Japan's ODA represented just over 50 percent of total bilateral ODA to the Philippines; in 1988 it rose to 68 percent. In contrast, ODA from the United States showed an initial increase in 1986, then fell through the early 1990s. The result has been to entrench Japan as the Philippines' largest source of ODA. While this position carries the potential for Japan to exercise leadership in overall aid to the Philippines, it has been reluctant to do so. As will be seen below in the case of the MAI, Japan's position allowed the United States to continue to exercise aid leadership despite its declining share of aid to the Philippines.

As noted in Chapter Two, Japanese loan and grant aid generally support different sectors of recipient economies. The new plan period was no different. The disparity illustrates the limitations of the Country Study in prescribing aid policy to the Philippines. Carried out under JICA auspices, the study's sectoral recommendations were reflected most clearly in the grant program. Grant aid from 1987 to 1992 emphasized manpower training and education, rural and agricultural support, and health care, areas specified in the study. Land reform support, however, proved difficult (an issue explored in Chapter Six). Loan aid continued to be concentrated in the infrastructure sectors and does not exhibit the sectoral priorities written in the study. Moreover, the ratio of grants to loans has not changed; the proportion of grants to loans from 1987 to 1989 was about 10 percent, a figure that prevailed in the early 1980s. Somewhat higher grant ratios from 1990 to 1993 can be attributed to difficulties in negotiating yen loans rather than a reorientation of Japan's basic stance toward aid terms. The Country Study, then, did not bridge the gap between loan and grant aid found throughout Japan's aid program.

Despite the Country Study's limited impact, Japan's loan aid generally met Philippine priorities. In line with the new administration's policy, virtually all project loans committed from 1987 to 1991 were committed for projects included in the MTPIP. The major infrastructure sectors in the plan received loan support, with transportation receiving the largest number of commitments (24). Power development received fewer projects than expected, only three, probably due to the concentration of funding in the 1987 special yen loan for the Calaca II coal-fired power plant; that loan amounted to just over 40 billion yen, almost as large as the entire loan package in 1984. Loan aid for agriculture was limited to irrigation projects, a continuation of past practice. If we include forestry and fisheries loans, Japan's aid for the primary sector becomes more significant. Japan has also required that certain portions of some program loans be used for agricultural support.

In general, grant and loan aid demonstrate continuity with past practice as well as funding for new projects. The continuity is especially noticeable in 1987, when several grant projects clearly carried the imprimatur of the Marcos administration. Likewise, loans such as that for repair of the Pan-Philippine Highway were in line with the Aquino administration's policy of supporting and maintaining extant projects.

Japan's aid shows some variation from previous regional distribution patterns. Grant aid continued to be concentrated in central Luzon, and Manila continued to receive the lion's share. Northern Luzon, a Marcos stronghold, lost ground under the Aquino administration, accounting for only three projects between 1987 and 1993. Southern Luzon, largely neglected during the Marcos years, received aid for projects linking it to central Luzon and the capital. The Visayas continued to receive loan funding but no grants: Cebu in particular benefitted, accounting for four of eight project loans to the region. Mindanao continued to be neglected, although it received somewhat higher funding than it had previously.

To a certain extent, Japan supported the CAID program. It has committed some aid to the development of General Santos City, a regional growth center in southern Mindanao, and provided grant aid to help develop Samar. The bulk of Japanese aid for CAIDs, however, has been located in the so-called CALABARZON (the government's acronym for the provinces of Cavite, Laguna, Batangas, Rizal, and Quezon) area in Central Luzon. Japanese aid assisted the construction of the Cavite Export Processing Zone and the Batangas Fishing Port, both south of Manila.[60]

The regional distribution of Japan's aid in the Aquino period suggests that it was sensitive to changing political priorities. The shift away from northern Luzon and the eastern Visayas can be explained by the fact that those areas had been the Marcos' political strongholds. It is not surprising that Ilocos Norte would suffer, as it was President Marcos' birthplace and continued to support him politically even in exile. The shift of aid to Cebu away from Isabela suggests that the Aquino administration was distributing resources, in this case Japanese loan aid, to new allies and away from Imelda Marcos' home area of Tacloban in Leyte. To be sure, some interregional projects, such as the repair of the Pan-Philippine Highway, contained portions allocated to those areas. Yet the shift of projects is unmistakable.

Japan's lending terms softened during the period. It included commodity loans, at Philippine request, in 1987 and again in 1990 and 1992. It also committed three program loans in the Seventeenth Yen Loan in 1991 as relief for the Philippine economy in the wake of the Persian Gulf War. It lowered its interest rates from 3.0 percent in the Fourteenth Yen Loan in 1987 to 2.7 percent beginning with the Fifteenth Yen Loan in 1988, the most concessional rate the OECF offers. According to the Japanese embassy in Manila, the rate was given to help the Philippines manage its external debt problem.[61] The two commodity loans and the 1987 special yen loan carried the same terms as project loans, a departure from previous lending patterns, and more lenient for the Philippines.

Japan expanded the types of aid it gave the Philippines. In line with the Country Study, Japan's loan aid broadened to include program loans and cofinancing with multilateral agencies. Through 1993, Japan provided seven program loans, six of which were cofinanced with the World Bank or the ADB. Program lending significantly altered the profile of Japan's lending to the Philippines. First, the proportion of the value of program lending to project lending was high: 60 percent of the Fifteenth Yen Loan in 1988, 35 percent of the Sixteenth Yen Loan in 1989, and 31 percent of the Seventeenth Yen Loan in 1991. Second, the profile of Japanese lending has changed correspondingly. While project loans continue to be important, program lending has allowed Japan to finance short-term support for the Philippines.[62]

Cofinancing is a two-edged sword for the Philippines. On the one hand, it has helped augment donor inflows at a time when funding for balance of payments and structural adjustment have been sorely needed. It also gives the Philippine government greater leeway to allocate foreign loans within the sectors for which the funds are drawn. On the other hand, cofinancing has made overall ODA lending stricter. Japan does not apply conditionality to its aid, such as requiring that certain economic policies be carried out before funds are disbursed. In this respect, its project lending has been more lenient than that of the World Bank, ADB and USAID. Under the cofinancing schemes to which it has been party Japan has followed the multilateral lender's lead on conditionality. While the portions Japan finances do not contain conditions, those portions are disbursed or withheld depending on the multilateral's evaluation of the Philippine government's economic policy performance. As one Philippine government official put it, "Japan doesn't have conditions. It just tells you to do what the World Bank says."[63]

Cofinancing also strengthens donor leverage by limiting the number of donors to which the Philippines can turn if it wishes to avoid unpopular economic reforms. It thus helps donors create a united front in persuading the Philippines to undertake structural adjustment. A number of Japanese aid officials indicated their approval of cofinancing because they view the IMF and the World Bank as "strict teachers."

The cofinanced portions of Japanese yen loans carry harder terms than project loans. While project loans carry repayment terms of thirty years with ten-year grace periods, the cofinanced portions of yen loan packages have twenty-five year repayment periods with seven-year grace periods. The stricter terms are in line with multilateral lending policy. On the other hand, cofinanced program loans, including consultancy services, are untied. The result was to untie all parts of those portions of Japan's yen loans as early as 1988, two years before Japan untied consultancy services for Philippine loans.

Japan has also continued to provide debt relief to the Philippines. Debt reschedulings have been stock components of yen loan packages in the Aquino and Ramos administrations. While it has expressed repeated interest in helping the Philippines solve its debt problems, Japan's efforts have been limited by both external and internal factors. A major constraint on the Japanese government's debt relief policies has been the nature of Philippine debt itself. Most debt accumulated by that country was commercial rather than official. Public debt owed to Japan, which includes lending by the Export-Import Bank as well as ODA loans, hovered around 6 to 7 percent of total external debt, and did not exceed 8 percent in any year between 1975 and 1983.[64] Although Philippine official debt continued to mount under the Aquino administration, the government of Japan remained only one of a number of external creditors. Its ability and willingness to rectify the Philippines' debt problem through the use of ODA, then, has been limited. Institutional limitations have also hampered Japan's ability to respond creatively to the Philippine debt problem. It has not financed debt-for-nature swaps undertaken by the United States, and has also balked at debt-equity swaps, arguing that such schemes require further funding to make them work.[65] Ironically, the Japanese approach has been to offer reschedulings and new loans to cover old debts, at somewhat more concessional terms that are more or less in line with Paris Club negotiations involving private creditors.

Closer Japanese coordination with other aid donors was also evident in its participation in the MAI. The history of MAI is a good example of the limits of Japanese leadership in the international arena. The MAI was first broached in the United States Congress in late 1987. The original proponents envisioned an increase in multilateral assistance to the Philippines by $1 billion per year beginning in 1988. Over the next eighteen months the United States was active in promoting the MAI, holding talks with the Philippine government and its aid donors.

While the initial impetus for MAI came from the United States, Japan's participation was crucial to its progress. First, Japan has been the program's major financial mainstay. For the United States, MAI would "leverage scarce U.S. assistance into much larger benefits for a country of central importance to the U.S. policy interests—an innovative policy initiative in an environment of shrinking assistance resources."[66] Japan was clearly the donor most likely to provide enough funding to make the MAI work. Its financial importance to the program increased as some other donors, including the United States and Italy, cut their assistance.

That position has given Japan leverage in determining how the MAI works. Japan early on insisted on World Bank and IMF participation in the program, an extension of the practice of cofinancing. The Japanese government felt strongly that if international aid was to assist the Philippine government in its economic reforms, such assistance should be coordinated and strict. Thus, the release of MAI donors' committed funds have been conditioned upon the ability of the Philippine government to reach agreements with the IMF on economic reform packages. The donors enforced this decision in 1990, delaying the convention of the second MAI pledging session until the Philippines worked out a reform package with the IMF.[67] The long-awaited pledging session did not occur until February 1991.

While the framework for MAI is multilateral, implementation of member programs has remained bilateral. Consequently, Japanese aid under the program has continued to follow the rhythms of the traditional aid relationship. Japan resisted the notion that MAI funding should be determined by an external standard, instead making its commitments dependent upon the availability of fundable projects. Likewise, it resisted Philippine attempts to obtain a multiple-year commitment for the proposed duration of the MAI program, 1989-1992, preferring to make commitments annually. Bilateral commitments also allowed Japan to deny that its aid was linked to the maintenance of United States military bases in the Philippines or that it gave aid for security reasons.

MAI has had mixed benefits for the Philippines. While it has received more new money than it might have gotten otherwise, it has not gotten the levels of funding originally envisioned. Second, it finds itself faced with donors willing to act in concert to see that it undertakes prescribed reforms in exchange for new assistance. For example, attempts to break Japan away from the MAI framework in the autumn of 1990 by requesting Japanese ODA commitments ahead of the second pledging session proved unsuccessful. Japan has been careful to tie its annual aid packages to IMF agreements in order to ensure that aid supports economic reforms. Thus, it finds itself more constrained to make unpopular policy decisions. Moreover, the official donors' willingness to provide aid has limited its borrowing options with commercial lenders: in 1989, following the World Bank's announcement that donors had pledged $3.5 billion at the first pledging session in July, commercial creditors balked at Philippine requests for further private funding, arguing that to unclog the aid pipeline would make sufficient funding available from official sources alone.[68]

The Ramos administration has inherited the dual nature of the MAI framework. On the one hand, the potential volume of Japanese aid has remained at levels similar to the Aquino years. The withdrawal of the United States from its bases at Clark and Subic Bay in 1991 and 1992, and a corresponding loss of American aid, has not resulted in a diminution of Japanese assistance: the latter pledged $1.5 billion in loans at the 1994 donors' meeting in Paris.[69] On the other hand, fiscal stringency and de facto conditionality have limited the new administration's aid options. Ramos' inauguration found the government saddled with debt service amounting to almost 40 percent of the annual budget and a warning from Japan not to expect new aid until it had developed an economic program acceptable to the IMF.[70] The Eighteenth Yen Loan's project commitments were spread over 1992 and 1993 as availment rates continued to lag and the administration struggled to win an IMF seal of approval.

Conclusion

In general, Japan's foreign aid has corresponded to the sectoral and regional priorities set out by the Philippine government. At the broadest level, we may say that Japanese aid has made a meaningful contribution to Philippine development simply because it has been there. As noted above, Philippine economic development, especially in the 1970s, was predicated upon large foreign borrowings to finance key sectors. Japan has aided that process by making loans and grants available. In the 1970s in particular, Japan was seen as a major donor of concessional aid, an expectation it met.

Japan's loan aid has been allocated consistently to those sectors programmed for large public investment in the medium-term development plans. Although the evidence for determining priority projects during the Marcos era had gaps, we have seen that projects included in the medium-term development plan annexes in the 1970s tended to be funded with OECF loans. The creation of the MTPIP during the Aquino administration has established clear priorities for project funding, and Japan's loan aid followed suit.

Grant aid has also tended to follow Philippine priorities, but with some exceptions. Political considerations appear to have limited the developmental contribution of the grant program. First, a number of grant projects were funded by Japan after interference by the Marcoses in the normal grant request process. These projects will be discussed in Chapter Six. Second, as in the Thai case, there exists a whole class of grant aid projects administered by the Japanese Ministry of Foreign Affairs under the rubric of cultural grants. These grants are small, generally less that 40 million yen, and tend to be given when high-level Japanese officials visit the recipient countries. Many have been used to provide equipment or materials to educational facilities in the Philippines; a few, however, show much more political purpose. While their monetary value is small, they are nevertheless credited to the Japanese grant aid program and thus inflate its contribution.

Japan has tended to concentrate its aid in Metro Manila and the major urban centers in the regions. As noted above, Manila and its environs have tended to receive more government resources than other regions. Hence, the need for foreign funding is correspondingly higher. Japanese funding for central Luzon can be explained this way as well, as can funding for regional centers like Cebu, Tacloban and Davao. The regional expenditure patterns exhibited by the Philippine government are complemented by the lack of Japanese aid personnel in the Philippines: in order not to stretch its talent too thin, the Japanese aid program would find it advantageous to undertake projects in the larger, more accessible cities.

One explanation for the fit between the Philippine and Thai governments' development plans and Japanese aid policy is that the three countries' policy makers tend to share complementary views of economic development. They also share views of the role of government in the development process. As noted in the last two chapters, the recipient governments see their role as supporters of private economic development, supplying infrastructure investment to assist that mode of development. Both have held the view that development financed by foreign investment and lending, a view held by the World Bank and other donors, is an appropriate strategy. The Philippine government's interest in investing in infrastructure and capital development is matched by the Japanese aid bureaucracy's view that such investment is an appropriate area for foreign aid funding. In Thailand and the Philippines, then, we see a process of dependent consensus evolving between an aid donor, or set of donors, and a recipient bureaucracy, in which the recipient gets a certain kind of aid from the donor, not because it has no other choice, but because it wants what the donor has to give.[71]

Japan's aid to the Philippines, like its aid to Thailand, has been concentrated in construction and provision of materials and equipment. While this capital bias has no doubt limited the flexibility of Japanese aid, it has also benefitted the recipient. The capital bias of OECF loans to the Philippines, for example, aided their disbursement and reduced the likelihood that loans would be canceled. Compared to other donors, the ability to use OECF loans was relatively high. Thus, Japanese emphasis on loans for procurement of capital goods and services benefitted the Philippines by making it easier to use them.

Japan has been criticized for its emphasis on capital assistance. Yet it is not clear that the recipients are unhappy with it. Japan puts more of its aid into capital projects than any other donor, especially in export-sensitive sectors such as transportation, communications, and power. This type of aid has been given predominantly to middle-income countries where the rates of return on such investments are highest. This has led to criticism by other DAC members, especially the United States, because it reinforces the impression that Japan's aid serves neomercantilist policies.[72]

Note that the locus of criticism is in the DAC. Indeed, the aid literature cited in Chapter One is remarkably free of concern about what recipients think about the issue. Based on the evidence from the development plans set forth by Thailand and the Philippines, we may conclude that these same factors serve recipient development priorities by providing funding for infrastructure projects in priority sectors which the recipients would be unable to fund by themselves. Moreover, Japan's aid has competed with that of the multilaterals, giving the recipients an alternative source of capital aid free of conditionality. The recipients have criticized Japan from time to time about the emphasis on capital aid, but overall it serves their purposes.[73]

Japan established aid niches in Thailand and the Philippines. Those niches were the result of donor competition. Because its bilateral programs began within the context of the consultative groups, Japan found itself adjusting its aid program to a situation dominated by other donors. Its aid for electrification of the Cagayan Valley, for example, probably owed more to the fact that the World Bank and the ADB were already funding power development projects in the more developed parts of Luzon than to any desire to assist the development of the Cagayan Valley itself. The Pan-Philippine Highway offered a way to break into road construction, an area already dominated by the multilaterals. In the Thai case, Thai-USAID pacification strategies in the Northeast meant that Japanese aid went elsewhere, largely to Bangkok. The external constraints imposed by other donors on the bilateral relationship became looser over time as Japan undertook project funding in more regions and sectors in the late 1970s and early 1980s. By the 1980s, Japan was operating in new regions in the Philippines, suggesting that its position as that country's largest bilateral donor gave it more choices for project funding. Ironically, the Third Indochina War led Japan to reorient its grant program toward Northeast Thailand in the early 1980s as the United States pressured it to support political stability in Thailand. In the 1980s Japan became the dominant donor in the Eastern Seaboard.

External constraints reappeared in the Philippine case in the late 1980s as Japan undertook cofinancing with the World Bank and the ADB. MAI revived the consortium style of aid giving seen in the 1970s. Unlike the situation in the early 1970s, however, Japan willingly reimposed those constraints on the bilateral relationship, a process clearly evident in its insistence on World Bank and IMF participation in the MAI. In this case, the invocation of external constraints gave Japan leverage to make the Philippines follow up on its promises to introduce structural adjustment, leverage it could not apply as a bilateral donor. For the Philippines, the effect was to make the external constraints on its bilateral relationship with Japan more onerous in the 1980s and early 1990s than it had been in the early 1970s: while in the earlier period it added a new bilateral donor to its list of funding choices, in the latter period it found that donor forming a united front with donors willing and capable of applying strings to the aid they gave.

External constraints also affected the terms of Japanese aid. Japan's aid terms have usually been set within the parameters expected by the Philippine government. By the 1990s, Japan was providing the Philippines with the softest loan terms possible within its overall aid program, terms more concessional than those offered to Thailand. Moreover, its aid has been more concessional than other major donors' because it has not applied conditionality and has been lenient in cancelling unused loans. Yet, there were clearly constraints on the concessionality of Japan's aid. First, Japan's aid terms to Thailand and the Philippines are within the framework of OECD lending to recipients in middle-income countries. Changes in its tying policy, for example, have occurred largely in response to OECD pressure.

Second, rivalries within ASEAN act as a check on Japan's lending within the region. Japan is aware that the ASEAN recipients watch one another's aid programs, and are likely to ask for terms and amounts of aid similar to their peers'. As a result, Japanese aid programs to the ASEAN countries have developed a rough balance, in which aid increases and term policies are changed for one recipient in proportion to the others. Thus, we have seen that aid terms to Thailand and the Philippines over time have tended to be less concessional than those given to Indonesia but more concessional than those given to Malaysia. Individual recipients simply find that they cannot effect permanent changes in their aid terms from Japan by themselves.

5

Accommodation of Interests in the Aid Relationships

Introduction

We saw in the previous two chapters that Japan's aid generally conforms to Thai and Philippine priorities. This is true particularly in terms of their sectoral and regional priorities and less so with aid terms. We saw in Chapter Four that terms of aid are largely beyond the control of individual recipients. How does this play out at the project level? Does the provision of aid that meets recipient priorities at the economic planning level translate into the provision of aid that meets their priorities at the project level? In this chapter I argue that recipients get what they want at the planning level because their requests can accommodate the various interests of the actors involved in the aid program at the project level.

How do Thailand and the Philippines get the aid they want from Japan? As we have seen already, they get a large part of what they want because they agree with the Japanese government about what governmental activities are appropriate for foreign aid. This convergence of donor and recipient policies is due in part to the fact that they agree that capital aid for infrastructure development of an export-oriented economy is a proper form of economic development. Translating a developmental predisposition into an economic program, however, is not an automatic process. Agreement between donor and recipient that provision of public services is an appropriate governmental activity for the recipient does not necessarily mean that the donor will be willing to fund a particular set of projects that the recipient claims will provide those services. Japan's aid to Thailand and the Philippines, as with any other case of foreign aid, contains instances in which donor and recipient disagree about the implementation of particular projects within a broadly defined area of agreement. The recipient government does not always get what it originally asks for, but often it does.

This chapter argues that the Thai and Philippine governments get what they want because the projects their planners request and the way they request them accommodate the interests of the major actors, defined here as the Japanese, Thai and Philippine bureaucracies, as well as Japanese companies, in the bilateral aid game. Accommodation can be defined as the process whereby the major actors adjust their expectations and actions to allow the other major actors in the relationship to attain their goals in order to maintain the ability to continue to cooperate with one another in the future.

The aid relationship, as it has developed, can be understood as a two-dimensional principal-agent problem. Aid policymaking in all three governments is characterized by interagency competition for aid project proposals. Policymaking in Thailand has generally been dominated by the bureaucracy in tandem with the military, both of which resist encroachment on their policymaking abilities by other domestic actors.[1] In the Philippines during the Marcos period, policymaking was limited to the bureaucracy and Malacanang Palace. The structure of the Philippine government did not change markedly under Aquino, despite its preference for a return to pluralistic participation.[2] The typical interaction between donor and recipient is therefore dominated by bureaucratic politics.

Let us consider the framework of accommodation that makes the aid relationships possible. First, accommodation of interests takes place because the aid relationship is conducted between two sets of autonomous actors, the Japanese and recipient aid bureaucracies. It is possible for either to act in isolation from the other without threatening its own existence. For example, Japan could give aid to Indonesia instead of Thailand or the Philippines and the latter could get aid from the World Bank instead of Japan. No overriding principle of the foreign aid regime requires interaction between them. The aid regime, in fact, denies that recipients have either a moral or legal right to aid. Second, Japan's insistence on the request principle places the formal responsibility for setting the agenda for annual aid negotiations on the recipient government. Third, recipients must accept the autonomy of the Japanese aid bureaucracy. There is little a recipient can do to change the organizational character of the donor's aid agencies. Each principal must respect and live with the institutional arrangements of the other.

Japan interacts with these two recipients repeatedly and continually. Over time, patterns of behavior adapted to the requirements of the aid relationship are likely to develop because the principal actors must find some way to work with one another in order to achieve a desired benefit. Accommodation is the process whereby the major actors in the aid relationship interact to achieve their particular goals, the achievement of which depends upon the other major actors, whose interests are only partially compatible to their own. Accommodation has two separate but interrelated components. The first is the principal-agent relationship between donor agencies and recipient planning agencies. The second is a principal-agent game played between recipient planning agencies and the other parts of their countries' bureaucracies. The two are related first because the same set of actors, the planning agencies, appear in both games. They act as the pivotal point between domestic bureaucracies and others actors and the Japanese aid bureaucracy. On one level, they play an anticipatory bargaining game with the Japanese aid bureaucracy. On another, they play a principal-agent game with the ministries in their home governments. In the first game, they have to find proposals that will appeal to the Japanese so that the Japanese government will fund them. In the second game, the planners must channel the project planning activities of their governments' bureaucracies if they are to ensure that fundable projects are available for request to the Japanese government.

Players in the Aid Game

How do Thailand and the Philippines get the aid they want from Japan? If the recipient governments could plan their development programs perfectly, the answer to the question would be simple. The planners could enforce policy decisions on the implementing ministries and exercise policy control over the sectoral plans within the five-year plans. The planners would get what they want because only those projects that met their development priorities would be presented to Japan for funding.

The reality is a great deal different. The aid planners in each country find themselves in a classic situation of principals attempting to enforce their priorities on their agents in the other ministries. The NESDB and NEDA sit atop bureaucracies that are functionally autonomous from them. This section deals with the NESDB first.

The NESDB is attached to the Office of the Prime Minister. It coordinates the sectoral development budgets proposed by the implementing agencies and advises the agencies on the priorities of the five-year plans. While the NESDB is responsible for coordinating and planning development projects, the Ministry of Finance has the tasks of choosing which projects are to be funded and presenting them to donors. A separate Department of Technical and Economic Cooperation (DTEC) oversees the grant aid program.[3] Loan aid is also screened by a cabinet-level Debt Policy Committee. The NESDB is also responsible to the cabinet, and its policy influence has fluctuated as different political forces have occupied the executive. NESDB influence in project programming in Thailand has been highest when technocratic leadership has dominated the cabinet, such as during the Prem administration (1980-88), and has waned during democratic periods when the maneuvering between political parties in coalition governments has competed with planning considerations in project selection, such as during the Chatichai administration (1988-1991.)[4]

The division of labor between the NESDB and the Finance Ministry caused problems in early attempts to coordinate the aid program. Through the 1970s the ministries did not know how much money the Budget Bureau in the Ministry of Finance would allocate to them when they had to present capital expenditure estimates to the NESDB. As a result, the implementing ministries often ignored NESDB policies and recommendations, and would attempt to bargain directly with the Budget Bureau.[5] Moreover, project managers whose projects had not received approval for national budget funding would often seek foreign funding on their own, with the result that up to one-third of all aid receipts went unreported.[6] The problem persisted until 1981, when the central government required NESDB approval of projects prior to their submission to the cabinet.[7] The division between budget and project authorities persists, and coordination between them is still incomplete.[8]

Through the 1970s, NESDB ability to coordinate even high-priority projects and actual aid disbursements was limited. The five-year plans tended to be collections of sectoral plans promoted by the individual ministries. This had important consequences for borrowing from abroad because that borrowing was likely to favor projects which, for whatever reason, were ready for funding. In the mid-1970s, despite the Thai government's commitment to alleviating rural poverty, the United States government found a shortage of fundable rural development project proposals; the aid program still focussed on infrastructure projects.[9] Likewise, external borrowing in the Fourth Plan favored power and transportation projects because they had better absorptive capacity for foreign funding than other sectors' projects, such as those for agriculture and rural development.[10] While Thai planners may have a good idea about where Japanese aid would be used most effectively, they have not always been in a position to enforce consequent decisions.

In the 1980s, the NESDB undertook measures to improve project and aid planning. Beginning with the Fifth Plan it began preparing the external borrowing program on a long-term basis as well as annually. Moreover, in conjunction with the Budget Bureau, it issued guidelines to the implementing agencies concerning preparation of foreign-financed projects. In that plan it also split the external borrowing budget almost evenly between projects proposed by the ministries and its own priority projects in the ESDP. It also required the agencies to provide projects for screening earlier than they had previously in order to improve its appraisal of projects in terms of plan needs.[11] In the Sixth Plan, it restricted feasibility studies to high-priority projects endorsed in the Plan. Since ministry-proposed projects were to receive second priority to those projects specified in the plan,[12] the effect was to extend NESDB control over the foreign loan aid program.

Problems of principal control remain, however. The late 1980s witnessed the emergence of renewed democracy during the prime ministership of Chatichai Choonhavan. While this may have been salutary for representative government, it also complicated NESDB's planning efforts, since cabinet decisions on projects were often based on partisan alliances and made without the Board's input.[13] With the entrenchment of civilian coalition government since 1992, political priorities are likely to continue to compete with technocratic considerations of development planning. Second, the grant aid program not only remains separate from loan programming, DTEC's programming abilities remain weak as well: it does not fund feasibility studies. The process of project proposal is decentralized, and because many agencies see grant aid as free, they are not careful about considering the quality, usefulness, or impact of their projects on overall development goals when they formulate proposals.[14] One Japanese aid administrator opined that DTEC has no ability to program grant aid, meaning that JICA has to approach the various counterpart agencies to determine which of their projects have priority.[15]

The lack of good projects, however defined, is a recurrent theme in the aid relationship. By itself, the Thai bureaucracy cannot formulate enough projects to meet rising Japanese aid allocations. The Japanese aid bureaucracy does not design its own projects. The gap is filled by other actors who play an informal role in the aid system. While many actors generate project proposals for aid funding, three groups—Japanese officials, other donors, and Japanese companies—show up most frequently in the data on Japan's aid to Thailand.

Japanese government actors can play a role in project creation. It is a curious phenomenon of aid that the supplier of the good often has to create demand for it as well.[16] Japanese aid officials can and do make suggestions about appropriate projects. Japanese embassy personnel who have cultivated good relations with recipient governments can act as sources of projects. Embassy personnel often have a good idea of what kinds of projects have gotten funding, and can therefore suggest possible areas that need development. One Japanese official noted that such suggestions are about project ideas. Japanese companies are a more active source of concrete proposals but, as he stated flatly, "if we didn't suggest projects we wouldn't get any requests."[17]

Other donors have also initiated projects for which Japan provides funding. The World Bank carried out the feasibility studies for the ESDP, and other donors carried out design studies for component projects later funded with Japanese loan aid. Similarly, in 1979, Japan provided an equipment grant for the restoration of the old Thai capital of Sukhotai, the original feasibility studies for which were carried out by UNESCO.

Japanese companies are widely held to be the most important source of project generation in Thailand and other Southeast Asian countries. The companies play a role in the aid process because they fulfill a function that neither the Japanese government, the Thai government, nor the Thai private sector can. The Japanese aid bureaucracy suffers from understaffing and lack of expertise. The Thai bureaucracy is at least as understaffed and lacking in expertise as its Japanese counterpart. The Thai line ministries find it difficult to generate project proposals themselves because their people lack the time and skills required to do so.[18] Japanese companies act as intermediaries between governments because they operate in both environments. They understand Japanese aid procedures better than most Thai implementing agencies and can therefore advise the agencies about how to go about formulating fundable requests.[19] They also operate in Thailand with a facility the Japanese aid bureaucracy lacks. Therefore, they have access to both worlds, placing them in a unique position of influence in relation to each government and to their private sector rivals.

In that role, Japanese companies present a unique principal-agent problem for recipient planners. On the one hand, they are the enabling agents that help formulate projects for Japanese aid funding. They would seem to help the recipient bureaucrats come up with proposals acceptable to the planners. They have the technical expertise to design and promote projects that will meet planning guidelines as well as have access to the Japanese aid bureaucracy. Therefore, they understand the kinds of projects the Japanese negotiators favor.[20] On the other hand, they compete with domestic contractors for project implementation, and who may indeed subvert the recipient's development objectives by substituting their own goals for those of the agencies they purport to help.

It is possible that the projects proposed by Japanese companies may meet neither Thailand's development needs nor the priorities of the Thai government as a whole. As noted in Chapter Three, priority projects listed in the five-year plans get funding from Japan. This suggests that NESDB and the ministries are aware of which projects meet their priorities, and that the government of Japan is aware of them, too. It also suggests that the Japanese companies are aware of them. Only the NESDB and DTEC can make formal aid requests, without which Japan will not accept projects for funding. NESDB and DTEC will accept project proposals only from the line agencies. Moreover, due to the Thai government's fear in the 1980s of incurring a heavy debt burden, projects proposed for external financing have come under strict scrutiny for technical and financial feasibility. This has been the case in particular with loan projects, since they incur external debt that must be repaid.

Other constraints exist as well. Acceptance of project proposals is not automatic; in fact, the Thai government has been known to refuse them. In 1983, for example, the government turned down a Thai shipping industry request for foreign aid to purchase new ships.[21] The government has also changed project design specifications during the implementation phase and, in some cases, changed the amount of funding. A 1984 Thai evaluation cites examples of grant and technical assistance projects suspended or whose funding was diverted by decisions in the Budget Bureau or the cabinet.[22] It has also cancelled project loans already committed. The most notable example occurred in 1992 when it finally cancelled an OECF loan for the National Fertilizer Corporation, a key element of the ESDP and a project for which Japanese contractors had already been selected. Even if a loan is available, there is no guarantee that it will be implemented.

It is probable, therefore, that the general preferences stated in the sectoral plans act as a constraint on Japanese companies' project searches. A project out of line with sectoral preferences is unlikely to be funded, meaning that the company will not make a profit. The Japanese private sector is candid about its interest in profit more than economic cooperation, but the pursuit of profit in the case of project-finding endeavors must create a powerful incentive to locate projects likely to gain approval. For the trading companies, simply identifying the projects themselves is not enough; implementing the ODA portions of them is most important because the profits at that stage are large.[23] Meeting recipient priorities helps project proposals reach the stage at which they become profitable.

The Japanese companies understand the incentives. The trading companies have several employees each in the major recipient countries who are concerned specifically with identifying possible projects. These employees regularly consult informally with officials in the recipient government ministries about ministry priorities, help the recipients make their project proposals conform to Japanese aid requirements, then carry out the project findings.[24]

Companies maintain their importance as intermediaries because tied aid allows them to dominate a closed game. Data from the Overseas Construction Association of Japan, Incorporated (OCAJI), a federation of the largest Japanese construction companies operating overseas, suggests that while private sector projects constituted the major portion of their business in Thailand in 1970s and early 1980s, aid projects represented an important source of contracts as well. Grant aid, particularly in the early 1980s, was a major buttress to their business: in some years Japanese grant aid projects represented half of all new large-scale projects undertaken by OCAJI members.[25] In a closed system of aid tying, lobbying for projects strengthens Japanese companies' chances of winning contracts because competition from foreign firms is reduced.

There is evidence that competition for project contracts in the aid program in Thailand has been increasing recently. Beginning in 1984, competition among Japanese contractors for aid projects in Thailand increased, although OCAJI members continued to dominate projects.[26] In the late 1980s, formal untying of loan aid to Thailand, including the consultancy phase in 1990, increased the number of participants. Examination of the OECF's contractors' lists in its annual reports since 1988 show some diversity in contract awardees. While Japanese companies and Thai-Japanese joint ventures have been well represented, European, Korean, Chinese and Thai firms also won bids. Consortia of Japanese, Japanese-Thai joint venture, and European firms were the norm in telecommunications projects both in the construction and consultancy phases, suggesting that no one country's firms dominate that sector.[27] Japan continues to tie its grant aid, but the declining proportion of grant aid in the overall bilateral program means that opportunities there are decreasing, too. With the 1993 graduation of Thailand from eligibility for Japanese grant aid, that virtual guarantee of business for Japanese contractors has been closed off. Overall, it appears that the decline in participation of Japanese companies in Japanese aid projects worldwide is occurring in Thailand as well.[28]

This suggests two things about the role of Japanese companies in Japan's aid to Thailand. First, untying has opened the system to competition, so the level of uncertainty for Japanese firms operating in the system has increased. Second, as a consequence of greater competition, the cost of lobbying has gone up for individual companies while the payoff in terms of contracts has gone down. The cost of lobbying has increased also because the Thai government in the 1980s has been more capable and willing to push its own priority policies and projects; large commitments of resources to priority projects in the ESDP, for example, squeezed other projects proposed by non-central government actors including Japanese companies. Between them, better Thai government planning and programming capacity in the 1980s and increased competition for aid contracts from foreign and Thai companies meant that Japanese companies in the 1980s were less central to the aid process than they had been in the 1970s.

Accommodating Interests:
Learning and Anticipatory Bargaining

Learning is crucial to the way the Thai and Japanese governments interact in the aid relationship. Thailand gets what it wants from Japan because it has learned what Japan will give aid for. We can observe the learning process in the aid relationship by examining the progress of project requests and project implementation over time. The divergence of project requests and accepted projects lessened in the 1970s. Of nine projects Thailand originally requested for OECF funding under the First Yen Loan package in 1968, one remained at the end of negotiations, and even it had been modified.[29] By the early 1980s, the success rate for Thai project requests had improved, with the majority accepted for funding. By the late 1980s, virtually all projects requested were accepted. Commenting on the negotiations for the 1990 loan package, one OECF officer noted that Thailand had presented a short list of ten projects, and that Japan would fund them.[30]

The time lag between project commitment and implementation has decreased over time, as well. While the time lag between commitment and the commencement of implementation of some projects in the first two yen loan packages was up to two years, by the early 1980s the time lag was considerably shorter, down to a few months in some cases.[31]

The concentration of loan aid undoubtedly fostered learning as recipient agencies had repeated contact with donor agencies. Of nineteen Thai agencies receiving project loans to 1983, three accounted for one-third of all projects worth 36 percent of total loans. Six had received more than five loans apiece.[32] Similarly, six of nine agencies receiving OECF loans for the

ESDP since then have had prior experience with the donor agency.[33] The State Railway of Thailand and the Industrial Finance Corporation of Thailand have experience with Japanese aid going all the way back to the economic agreement that settled Japan's wartime debt.

The learning process has been aided by communications at the policy levels. Discussions about Thai development strategies and Japanese aid policy help each side understand what the other wants. In 1981 and 1986 representatives of the two countries engaged in policy dialogues on Thai economic development and Japan's role in it. The two countries also conducted annual consultations on aid policy throughout the 1980s.[34] Japan has dispatched specialists to help the government of Thailand use Japanese foreign aid more efficiently.[35] By the late 1980s, then, Thai economic planners had a good idea of the kinds of projects Japan is likely to fund, and could pass that information onto the implementing ministries in the form of guidelines for priority projects to be requested in loan packages. In 1988, for example, the Ministry of Finance advised the line agencies of project criteria to be met in order to qualify for inclusion in that year's aid package.[36]

Thailand gets the kind of aid it wants because it anticipates donor aid preferences. As a result, it targets donors. We may call this anticipatory bargaining. Essentially, anticipatory bargaining is a structuring activity, in which an actor attempts to define the elements of a bargaining process in order to expand or limit the range of possible outcomes.[37] As such, anticipatory bargaining attempts to set the agenda for an anticipated course of project negotiations by defining which projects will come up for discussion.

Anticipatory bargaining may be formal or informal. In the Thai case, it has become more formal as the NESDB has asserted its control over the development plans. In the 1970s the implementing agencies tended to submit projects to the NESDB after receiving project appraisal reports from external lenders. This process continued into the mid-1980s: In the Fifth Plan the NESDB simply required Thai agencies and aid donors to coordinate their feasibility studies better. The five-year plans themselves and the documents accompanying them contain forecasts of expected funding from external donors. Often, the forecasts include particular projects for which negotiations are already underway by the time the plans are printed.

This is a logical consequence of learning in aid negotiations. One Japanese aid official noted that the Thai government decides it priorities, then makes its project requests according to donor budgets. He noted that that had not happened in the early loan negotiations because the communication between donor and recipient was poor.[38] That would explain why the first yen package differed so much from the original Thai requests. Yet it is clear that a process of anticipatory bargaining was underway. Each five-year plan since the Third has contained some forecast of the aid Thailand expects from Japan, and the accuracy of these expectations has improved over the course of plan formulation. Over time, the gap between recipient expectations of donor aid and the donor's actual aid have diminished.

Anticipatory bargaining occurs at two levels. The first is the level of macroeconomic planning. When the NESDB makes up its five-year plans based on calculations of donor budgets and project preferences, it engages in anticipatory bargaining of one sort. Although it is not directly negotiating with the aid donor, in this case Japan, it is formulating policies that it hopes will maximize the benefits it can gain from specific negotiations at the aid package level. Policy dialogues, which took place in 1981 and 1986, and the 1989 country study, are negotiations about the overall fit between Japan's aid priorities and Thailand's development priorities. No aid money changes hands, but the outcomes of these negotiations condition later transactions. Such negotiations also help alleviate uncertainty about donor and recipient expectations.

Anticipatory bargaining also takes place in the form of prebargaining before official requests are made. This is the level at which the principal-agent game is played. In the prebargaining phase, as in the planning phase, no aid money changes hands and no binding agreements are reached. Rather, the recipient actors, either the ministries or the consultants engaged in project finding activities, engage in informal communication about the priorities and project criteria of those actors which have formal authority to make or accept project requests. The prebargaining phase is defined as the period of informal negotiation before the recipient government makes its formal project requests to the donor.

Prebargaining is important because getting a proposal on the agenda is the first step in any negotiation process. Getting on the agenda, or in this case, the long list, involves meeting what John Kingdon calls the criteria for survival of a policy idea: technical feasibility, value acceptability (defined in this case as the principles and ideological predispositions of the Thai ministries, Thai planners, and Japan's aid policymakers), and anticipation of constraints.[39] Prebargaining is the process whereby ideas for aid projects are rejected as unworkable, refined to meet official and unofficial criteria of the specialists in the aid or sectoral bureaucracies, and in a few cases passed on to planning authorities in Thailand for serious consideration.

In the case of Japanese aid, getting on the agenda means getting aid negotiators to include one's project proposal in the list of projects for a feasibility study. Prebargaining occurs as project proposers try to maximize their chances of getting their proposals to the feasibility study phase. The companies contact the recipient ministries to see if their proposals meet ministry guidelines because it saves them time and money to do so. One trading company official noted that ODA projects take up to five years from initial conception to implementation, and are thus an expensive risk.[40] The risk increases because the prebargaining environment is competitive. Japanese companies compete among themselves as well as with Thai politicians and contractors to present candidate projects, and only those projects that succeed in receiving ministry approval will go to the planning authorities. Once that stage is reached, Japanese companies, and presumably other project entrepreneurs, no longer have a role in the process.[41]

The Japanese government also engages in prebargaining when it suggests possible projects. Its activities at this level largely perform gatekeeping functions. The Japanese embassy and the Bangkok OECF and JICA offices maintain unofficial contact with the Thai government's agencies. The field offices sometimes ask which projects the ministries are working on, and suggest those that Japan would be able to fund, as well as advise project entrepreneurs about how they can revise their proposals to meet aid specifications. However, final decisions about whether to request aid for a project and from whom to request it are up to the Thai authorities.[42] In the case of grant aid, the JICA official cited above pointed out the importance of these functions. JICA performs the screening of projects that DTEC does not. Thai ministries also talk to the companies about how to approach the Japanese government because intergovernmental communication at the line agency level is not good and there is a great deal of competition.[43] The result is to weed out bad projects and those that are not ready for funding.

Prebargaining is common because the feasibility study teams will almost always approve a project. JICA feasibility study teams are dispatched not to decide whether projects are feasible, but to show that they are. In the case of yen loans, while the four ministries in Tokyo review every project proposal, the time they have to do so together is limited to one or two hours per project.[44] Since the feasibility studies are the major documents by which decisions about loans are made, the important bargaining about projects must take place before the studies. All parties are therefore likely to know whether a project is eligible for funding at an early stage. One study of the grant program in Thailand, for example, noted that a formal feasibility study was required for the National Institute of Coastal Aquaculture project, but that Japan informally had indicated its willingness to fund the project before the study's completion. By the time the feasibility study team had made its report, the negotiations had largely been completed.[45]

Accommodation of interests among the actors involved is possible because their interests intersect. While limits to Japanese private sector activity in aid to Thailand exist, structural features of the way Japanese aid is given allow private sector interests to mesh with those of the governments involved. It has been argued that the resources a Japanese ministry can mobilize to implement its policy include, among other things, the fiscal funds allocated to it and available for public expenditure in the interest of constituents.[46] Ministries in Japan compete for budgetary resources to enhance their own power, and the ODA budget is no different. Larger ministry resources means greater ability to service constituents, in particular the consulting firms that rely upon them for subsidies. The emphasis on budgetary augmentation leads to the situation found in USAID in the late 1960s and early 1970s: the basic unit of analysis for the effectiveness of the aid program is how much money gets spent because that can be used as concrete proof of agency performance in annual budgetary battles.[47] With the exception of the finance ministries, it is reasonable to assume that all the players in the ministries want to see the aid budget rise, even if for different reasons.

The capital bias in Japan's aid reinforces the tendency to measure aid use efficiency in terms of amount of money moved. For the implementing agencies, OECF and JICA, big projects help them circumvent the institutional limitations with which they are saddled. As Tendler points out in USAID's case, a large project that can absorb a lot of funding makes supervision of that funding easier for the implementing agency.[48] Truer words about the Japanese aid bureaucracy were never written.

In general, this tendency dovetails with the interests of the counterpart ministries in the recipient countries. One study found a pronounced bias toward capital projects in both the Thai and Philippine governments.[49] Generally speaking, more aid allows the recipient agency to engage in more development projects, and to therefore claim a bigger share in the development budget. Capital aid will tend to carry a higher price tag than other forms of aid and, in terms of work expended for the ministry, will look more efficient because that aid can be allocated more rapidly. From the recipient ministry's viewpoint, the existence of Japanese companies or anybody else flogging projects is not necessarily a bad thing if those companies can provide it with fundable projects. In Thailand, as in other developing countries, because the local engineering industry does not possess the technical capacity and organizational skills of its Japanese counterpart, it is less capable of servicing the Thai ministries' needs in this manner. The capital bias evident in Japan's aid to Thailand can therefore be explained in part by the internal dynamics of the Thai project development process.

The JICA grant for the Chiang Mai University Hospital mentioned in the introduction illustrates the intersection of recipient and donor interests in capital aid. Seen from the project administrators' viewpoint, the grant also meets recipient priorities. Cancer had become a major cause of death in Thailand, and the number of cancer patients at the hospital was rising. Chiang Mai University's hospital is one of four main regional hospitals in Thailand, and while it had one radiology machine it was insufficient to meet cancer patient demand.[50] The grant helped meet that demand. Japanese aid officials could argue, with justification, that provision of the equipment satisfied a need. From JICA's viewpoint, equipment was disbursed and it had therefore done its job. The equipment also benefitted the grant's immediate recipients, the administrators of the hospital. The hospital received equipment it did not have previously. In addition to increasing its capacity to treat cancer patients, it could also augment its training of medical students with the new equipment. From the official viewpoint, then, the grant was desirable and justified despite the equipment's cost and the subsequent problems of maintenance.

Japan's aid relationship with the Philippines includes the processes of learning and anticipatory bargaining that permit accommodation of Thai and Japanese aid interests. The process of accommodation in the Philippine case is more complex because the recipients' priorities have not been as straightforward, nor have learning and its related processes evolved as uniformly.

Players in the Aid Game

The martial law period (1972-1981) witnessed the centralization of power in the Philippines. The technocratic elements of the bureaucracy were strengthened, and the "New Society" under Marcos came to reflect the development perspectives of the technocrats as well as the Marcoses and their associates. The creation of the National Economic and Development Authority (NEDA) was one result of the economic reforms undertaken during the martial law period. On paper, NEDA during the Marcos period was stronger than the NESDB in Thailand. NEDA was charged with the responsibility of planning economic development in the Philippines, including preparation of the medium-term development plans and programming government activity to complement it. It was also given the responsibility of providing planning guidelines to the sectoral and macroeconomic agencies, and then reviewing those agencies' proposals before the final drafts of the development plans were completed.[51]

Under Marcos, NEDA gained increasing control over foreign aid policy. All projects proposed for the infrastructure development program that were to receive foreign funding were to be evaluated by NEDA, although the foreign financing aspects were also reviewed by the Ministry of Finance.[52] Economic agreements, including foreign aid, were monitored by an Interagency Committee on Trade, Tariffs and Related Matters attached to NEDA. As a result, NEDA gained control of planning and negotiation of all parts of the aid program.

NEDA's ability to control the quality of projects was limited in two ways. First, NEDA, like the NESDB in Thailand, is a planning agency. As such, it is not responsible for formulation of specific projects; that function is fulfilled by the individual ministries. While, in theory, the martial law era reforms established closer coordination of plans and projects, the sectoral plans in the development plans were composed of projects formulated by the ministries.[53]

Second, NEDA could be overridden by the president. The president chaired the NEDA, thereby assuming "responsibility and control in the formulation and implementation of plans, policies, programs, and projects."[54] Presidential activity in development planning could cut two ways. While the support of the president could facilitate prompt decisionmaking and policy implementation, his formal participation in the planning process could and did lead to attempts to subvert developmental activities to support the interests of favored friends and agencies. While the economic decisionmaking machinery of the Marcos administration was in place by the 1970s, it has been argued that Marcos' absolute decree-making power encouraged the president's cronies to bypass that machinery.[55]

The result was that NEDA's development priorities in the aid relationship with Japan were often subverted by presidential interference. Marcos approved all projects for yen loan financing, without which NEDA could not request projects.[56] Marcos also established the office of the implementing officer for the Japanese aid program. The implementing officer negotiated with the OECF and private contractors for loan contract bids, and reported directly to Marcos without consulting NEDA. The implementing officer exercised a great deal of control over the awarding of project contracts, resulting in favoritism toward certain companies.[57]

Some aid projects clearly reflect Marcos' priorities. The San Roque Dam project request is one example. It was included as the highest priority request for the Twelfth Yen Loan package in 1984 by Marcos himself after the completion of NEDA's short list. The request pushed two other projects off the short list.[58] Some JICA grants, such as the grant for agricultural extension at the Don Mariano Marcos Agricultural University in Ilocos Norte, are clearly pork barrel projects.

The discussion of Marcos' role in the aid relationship is clouded by the fact that first lady Imelda Marcos could act as an independent source of patronage and influence. Her role as Minister of Human Settlements allowed her to encroach on policy areas administered by other agencies, making coordination of economic programs in the government more difficult as budgetary resources flowed into the new ministry. Japanese aid was not spared such encroachment: JICA funded a number of projects identified with Imelda, including the Philippine Heart Center, the Philippine General Hospital, the National Maritime Polytechnic, the Tongonan Geothermal Power Plant in Leyte, and the Human Resources Development Center, part of which was administered by the University of Life, an ill-defined enterprise run by the Marcos' daughter Imee.[59] According to one Japanese newspaper, most of the Eighth Yen Loan package in 1980 was composed of projects initiated by Imelda or her cronies.[60] If this is true, the abilities of her cronies to affect Japan's aid policy was remarkable.

It is possible that Marcos projects were acceptable to NEDA, especially in the infrastructure sectors. The Marcos' interest in the Japanese aid program probably stemmed from their interest in augmenting their wealth and distributing patronage to their cronies. While specific projects might catch their eye, it is hard to imagine them initiating projects solely to get Japanese aid. Available information suggests that interference from Malacanang occurred most often at the project implementation stage. This makes sense if we assume that the Marcoses were interested in the pecuniary aspects of aid projects, an assumption consistent with descriptions of their private sector activities. If cronies were awarded the contracts for projects, or if the Marcoses received kickbacks from contractors, they probably did not care whether the project in question was regarded by NEDA as a priority project or whether it was a pet project initiated by the Marcoses themselves. It is likely that they exercised their "initiative" in favor of projects, generated elsewhere in the aid system, that they perceived as furthering their interests as well.

Interference from Malacanang Palace occurred, but we must be careful not to understate the role of NEDA in the aid relationship. The implementing officer for the Japanese aid program, who answered directly to Marcos, did not select, program, or request projects; such tasks were undertaken by the Investment Coordinating Committee within NEDA. The latter had the legal authority to review projects within the sectoral plans, and to negotiate with Japan and other donors for those projects. As noted in Chapter Four, large-scale projects funded by Japan tended to be included in the project annexes attached to the medium-term plans. The experience of the Twelfth Yen Loan request preparation suggests that NEDA decided most projects. NEDA could alter aid packages, as well as cancel projects.

The Philippine case highlights the difficulties planning authorities face in forcing independent agents to meet their priorities. Japanese companies in the aid relationship with the Philippines operate in much the same way as they do in Thailand, formulating projects and then implementing them. During the Marcos administration, Japanese firms, or at least some of them, enjoyed an especially cozy relationship with Malacanang Palace. That relationship resulted in favoritism, which benefitted the companies and Marcos in informal ways. As noted above, the implementing officer was charged with coordinating and monitoring OECF projects and preparing tender documents. He also coordinated what amounted to a bribery scheme through the collection of kickbacks from Japanese companies awarded aid contracts. Documents seized after the Marcos' departure in early 1986 suggest that Marcos' bribery attempts were widespread and systematic.[61] Here, companies were accommodated in the aid relationship because they paid for the privilege.

Japanese companies dominated the early yen loans because the loans were tied. Moreover, the companies were organized to take advantage of political conditions in the Philippines. The relationship of dependence between Japanese consultants and trading firms found in Thailand exists in the Philippines as well. One consequence of this relationship is that consultants tend to write project design specifications tailored to Japanese suppliers' specializations, so Japanese firms are favored in the qualification stages of the bidding process and therefore gain an advantage in procuring contracts.[62] In other words, they have operated in a closed game to their own advantage. The feeling among Japanese firms, especially the larger ones, that they must live down their reputations from the Marcos period has made them less sanguine about engaging in politically sensitive behavior.[63] Despite their new sensitivity, Japanese firms continue to dominate project contracts.[64]

Japanese companies have also organized in other ways to ensure access to contracts. Japanese firms have engaged in *dango,* bid fixing by prior agreement among cooperating companies. At least two cases of *dango* in the aid relationship, one in 1977 and one in 1989, have come to public light.[65] Collusion reinforces the legal instruments of the aid program that give Japanese companies their competitive edge.

Japanese companies are not the only project sources in the Philippines. Proposals from other sources have also been included in the aid program.

For example, the Tongonan and Palimpinon Geothermal Power Plant projects were originally developed by consultants from New Zealand. Japan ended up funding the projects because the government of New Zealand gave only technical assistance, thereby forcing the Philippine government to look for loan funding elsewhere.[66] During the Aquino administration, members of Congress reemerged as sources of project proposals. As one representative put it, the incentive to find projects in one's home district is the result of the real fact of poverty in members' districts coupled with the equally real urge to provide benefits to constituents to secure reelection.[67] While some members undoubtedly rely on project entrepreneurs already in the field, the emergence of two hundred new centers of entrepreneurship must have acted to dilute the position of those preexisting entrepreneurs.

Accommodating Interests:
Learning and Anticipatory Bargaining

We find in the Philippine case a learning process similar to that found in the Thai case. Learning has proved to be crucial in determining the Philippines' ability to get the aid projects it wants. A major difference in the learning between Thailand and the Philippines was that Japan's aid relationship with the Philippines grew out of the reparations program. The early aid relationship involved the dual processes of learning in the aid program and unlearning the experience of the reparations program. We can see this duality in the initial aid negotiations between Japan and the Philippines in the late 1960s. Learning was complicated further by the transition from the Marcos to the Aquino administration.

Initial requests for OECF lending in the late 1960s were made by the Philippine Reparations Mission, which saw such lending as an augmentation of anticipated reparations disbursements. The tone of Philippine demands for new lending was reminiscent of its arguments about why Japan should provide reparations: at one point the Mission's chairman argued that Japan's failure to provide loan aid to the Philippines would be interpreted as discrimination by Japan.[68] For its part, Japan's decision in 1968 to fund equipment and capital expenses for the Pan-Philippine Highway, but to leave decisions about how to use that capital up to the Philippine authorities, was greatly influenced by the pattern of the reparations program.[69]

In 1966, Filipino negotiators presented Japan with a "shopping list" of projects for which they requested $100 million in OECF loans. They also asked for terms better than or equal to those offered to Thailand and

Malaysia. As with Japan's first aid negotiations with Thailand, the Philippines' initial project list and terms were quite different by the time Japan had committed its first yen loan package in 1971. The length of time it took to negotiate the loan package reflected, among other things, Japan's reluctance to lend to the Philippines. The reparations program had not succeeded in helping the Philippines as a whole develop, and Japan was not keen to compound the error by extending additional concessional loans.[70]

Over time, the gap between expectations narrowed. As noted in the previous chapter, in the 1970s Japan funded projects included in the NEDA priority project lists attached to the medium-term plans. By the early 1980s, NEDA presented sets of projects the value of which was close to estimated aid for the year.[71] Most projects requested for OECF funding were accepted and the lag time between project commitment and implementation had decreased. The degree to which Philippine officials could estimate future Japanese aid allocations is exemplified in NEDA's short list preparation of the Twelfth Yen Loan. NEDA calculated that Japanese funding would be incrementally higher than that of the Eleventh Yen Loan, and therefore shortened to 16 the long list of 42 projects requested by the implementing agencies. Thence, it ranked the short listed projects in order of priority. Marcos subsequently modified the list to include the San Roque Dam as first priority, but NEDA's culling process demonstrated that it understood what it could expect from Japan.[72]

Learning in Japan's aid relationship with the Philippines was abetted by repeated contacts between donor and recipient agencies. Three agencies, the National Power Corporation, the National Electrification Administration, and the Ministry of Public Works and Highways (MPWH) accounted for more than half of all OECF project loans between 1971 and 1983. The MPWH alone accounted for 37 percent of all project loans through 1983, more than any other Philippine agency, and accounted for 23 percent of total Japanese project loan funding. It accounted for three times more projects than the National Power Corporation, the second largest recipient of OECF project loans.[73] Despite reorientation of the aid program under the Aquino administration, the MPWH continues to receive an important share of Japan's loan aid.[74]

The concentration of bilateral interactions facilitated learning between donor and recipient agencies. Prior experience of an implementing agency with a particular donor has been positively correlated with that agency's ability to use aid loans. Likewise, there is a negative correlation between previous experience and cancellation of OECF loans. For example, the project with the highest availment rate dated from the late 1970s in a sector with which the Japanese aid bureaucracy and Japanese contractors had previous experience.[75] In other words, the longer an implementing agency worked with the OECF, the more efficiently it could avail of and process committed loans. This suggests that the creation of sectoral and regional niches for aid donors benefitted the Philippines because it fostered working relationships between the OECF and certain line agencies. Learning reduced uncertainty as donor and recipient agencies gained knowledge of each other's needs and operating procedures.

The Aquino administration's aid negotiations with Japan suggest that it has had to undergo a period of relearning as the government adjusted to new priorities and new actors entered the aid policy arena. Aid project programming had suffered during the crises that led to Marcos' ouster, and personnel and structural changes in the bureaucracy after the transition added to the confusion early on.[76] Initial requests by the Aquino administration tended to be for large amounts of money without providing enough project proposals to back those amounts up, or to lump separate annual aid packages into a single request.[77] Ironically, the reforms enacted in the Philippine aid bureaucracy made the learning process harder. The creation of the new executive agencies to handle aid coordination led to confusion in the implementing agencies about who was to do what.[78] This hampered the administration's ability to use Japanese aid to promote its development priorities, and throughout its tenure less than full availment of committed loans was a constant point of discussion between donor and recipient.

The Japanese aid bureaucracy engaged in some efforts to augment Philippine understanding of its aid procedures during the Aquino period. The OECF undertook seminars and other activities designed to increase recipient knowledge of its procedures in the Philippines. In 1987 it provided a loan to finance engineering services for priority projects.[79] A few Japanese officials were seconded to the Philippine government "on a highly selective basis," to give advice on policy formulation, administrative procedures, finding candidate projects and considering projects for Japanese aid funding.[80] Overall, these efforts were limited, and certain aspects of Japan's aid procedures remain unclear to Philippine government counterparts.[81]

The Philippines, like Thailand, gets the aid it wants because it anticipates donor aid preferences. The ability to engage in anticipatory bargaining at the planning level was undoubtedly helped by the creation of the Consultative Group for the Philippines. The informal division of labor worked out among the donors helped the Philippines target donors for specific projects; as noted in Chapter Four, Japan's aid for geothermal power development in the Visayas was preconditioned by the fact that the

ADB and the World Bank had already claimed the Luzon power grid for funding. The niche Japan created for itself in the 1970s reduced the scope of possibilities for Japanese aid, but it also reduced the uncertainty for the recipient about what to request by fostering repeated communication between relevant implementing agencies. Repeated interactions enabled NEDA planners to refine their predictions of Japanese responses to aid requests. As the Twelfth Yen Loan preparations demonstrate, NEDA could base its request lists on reasonably accurate appraisals of the volume and nature of Japanese aid. One NEDA official commented that by looking at which donors funded which projects from the MTPIP one had a good idea of what they would fund in the future. The creation of the MTPIP itself helps NEDA forecast which loan projects Japan will fund because it delimits those projects that will be considered at all.

Prebargaining in the aid relationship is a critical stage in the process of accommodation. Again, no aid money changes hands and no binding agreements are reached at this stage. But the important process of agenda setting, whereby proposals are refined into requestable projects or discarded, determines which projects will be considered seriously by Tokyo. According to one Philippine official, project negotiations are just a formality by the time the bilateral consultations take place in the spring. This phenomenon, already witnessed in the Thai case, involves the same kinds of actors.

A great deal of effort is expended by Japanese officials on weeding out projects that are not ready for funding. The Japanese government also sends signals to project entrepreneurs and the Philippine government. In the case of a JICA grant for the Palawan Crocodile Farming Institute, Japan expressed initial reluctance to fund the project. Two years later, it expressed its willingness to fund the project, upon which NEDA acted with a formal request.[82] Officials seconded from the Japanese government can help proposals through the early stages of the process. A project management officer at one agency reported that a JICA official seconded to her department had lobbied the local Japanese aid offices for the inclusion of a department priority project in the upcoming grant aid package.[83]

NEDA also communicates informally with the Japanese bureaucracy about project status. Although official communications are made to the embassy through the Department of Foreign Affairs, at the technical level, NEDA talks to the embassy, JICA and OECF offices. Occasionally, it will discuss an especially important project directly with the aid policymakers in Tokyo, but, for the most part, its greatest contact is with the Japanese embassy and field offices.[84] The implementing agencies can also use the local Japanese aid agencies as filters; the project management officer cited above observed that she often calls the OECF and JICA offices to check the information given her by Japanese project entrepreneurs.

Japanese companies are active in the prebargaining process because they can operate in both recipient and donor environments. Many of the Philippine implementing agencies rely on the consultants for project formulation and information about the Japanese aid system. Some agencies are completely dependent on consultants, and their project designs rely on consultant specifications. Consequently, the trading companies act as informal intermediaries between recipients and the Japanese government, a role that allows them to push their own projects.[85] That role was important in the 1970s because Japanese aid procedures were not well publicized or understood in the Philippines. Despite Japanese promises to untie the various portions of the aid program in the Philippines, that role persisted in the Aquino administration because new agencies with little experience with Japan's aid process had to deal with it. Given the increase in aid funding from Japan after 1986, the Japanese companies were in a good position to provide projects with the criteria necessary to ensure yen loans and grants.

Yet, there is competition among consulting firms, as well as with other project entrepreneurs, and only the successful proposals go to NEDA for review. The uncertainty whence prebargaining stems leads the companies, as it does other project entrepreneurs, to further reinforce their proposals by seeking support outside of the implementing agencies. Often, they give their proposals to the agencies along with a letter of introduction from a local political official.[86] They also get indications from NEDA about whether a project is likely to be requested by an agency.[87]

After 1986 NEDA was faced with a difficult principal-agent dilemma. On the one hand, the amount of Japanese aid increased dramatically. On the other, institutional restructuring and the relearning process hampered the recipient's ability to use higher volumes of aid. NEDA resolved its principal-agent problem in two ways. First, it structured the competition for project proposals. The planning levels assume that projects proposed by the implementing agencies are their own, regardless of which actors actually formulated them. That assumption does not prevent the ministries themselves from lobbying for projects or allowing consultants or others to do it for them. Until 1987, it was common practice for agencies to submit new project proposals a few days before the annual consultations with the OECF. The MTPIP was designed to reduce the interference from project entrepreneurs by forcing the agencies to set their own priorities. Since the MTPIP's inception, NEDA has refused to request any projects not included in the list, and any new agency proposals must be substituted for their projects already on it.[88] MTPIP helped reduce the lobbying for projects from outside, and thus delimited the project agenda for the Aquino administration.

Second, NEDA abdicated many of its programming functions, and thereby formalized agency slack. It placed the responsibility for setting priorities among projects on the implementing agencies and Japan, reserving for itself a "postal" role in the aid programming process.[89] During the Aquino administration Japan was able to accommodate Philippine priorities because the Philippine government had many priority projects it wished to undertake. The increase in Japan's aid was more than matched by the increase in yen loan requests as implementing agencies competed in a less stringent programming system. At the beginning of the Aquino administration, for example, NEDA supervised a "shopping list" of more than 1,000 capital and technical assistance projects to be included in the overall aid program.[90] Similarly, the second MTPIP, programmed for 1990-94, contained over 1,700 projects to be implemented during that time period. Of that, it presented a "short list" of 207 high-priority projects to the donors at the second MAI pledging session in February 1991.[91] JICA and the OECF asked NEDA for the long list of projects during the annual consultations, allowing the Japanese agencies to select those projects that most suited their priorities and capabilities. A MITI official who had participated in the ministerial review of the Seventeenth Yen Loan package, pledged at the 1991 MAI session, said that the Philippine project requests for that yen loan package had exceeded the final commitment by three times.

Chapter Four showed that Japanese aid contains a bias toward provision of capital goods. That bias is also apparent in the interests of the other actors in the aid system. Active lobbying by Japanese firms and the dependence of Japanese consultants on the trading companies fostered the bias toward capital aid, which the trading companies and their allied suppliers provided.[92] Large-scale construction projects were typical of the Marcos administration's development plans. Individual agencies also perceived benefits from capital aid since it would allow them access to goods not otherwise available to them. It also gave them access to funds for facilities they wanted.[93] The capital bias of OECF loans also facilitated their disbursement. Higher proportions of foreign currency costs in OECF loans were negatively correlated with loan delays and cancellation because they reduce the requirement of counterpart funding. Compared to other donors, the availment rates of OECF loans were relatively high.[94] As a result, OECF loans were easier to use.

The Aquino administration reoriented its priorities away from large-scale projects. Japan responded in two ways. Provision of program loans and local cost financing reduced the direct capital content of Japanese aid. The two governments also agreed to reduce large-scale construction under JICA funding.[95] Since 1988, the Philippine government has also promoted small-scale rural development. One OECF officer noted that in 1990 there were twenty candidate projects all of which were for small-scale rural development, which placed a great burden on that understaffed agency. It was unclear, moreover, whether the Philippines could handle such projects; availment rates during the Aquino period remained at about 75 percent of committed funds, leading Japan to threaten to cut off future aid if funds already committed were not used more efficiently.

Conclusion

Thailand and the Philippines get what they want from Japan because their priorities and how they try to achieve them can accommodate the interests of the other actors in the system. Over time, Thai and Philippine planning officials have learned how to play the aid game with Japan. They have learned what kinds of aid Japan is capable of giving, and how to get them. Recipients engage in anticipatory bargaining because it improves their chances of getting aid at all from Japan. Project entrepreneurs engage in prebargaining at the micro level for the same reason: prebargaining helps them better their chances of getting their project proposals funded. While the recipients' ability to program aid from Japan is imperfect, it appears that over time the planners' priorities have been increasingly met as a result.

Yet, differences exist between the two cases. For one, those differences are attributable to differences in aid programming style. The Philippine government's ability to get what it wants is imperfect partly because it has had to relearn the aid game under the Aquino administration, and because the sheer volume of requests led it to increase agency slack in order to cope. For another, the mix of power in the aid program within each recipient government leads to different principal-agent relationships. While the NESDB in Thailand was undoubtedly subject to pressures from executive actors, the influence Marcos exercised over the aid program gave him special power over aid decisions. The Philippine government's ability to get the aid it wanted under the Marcos administration was imperfect because it was not clear whose needs were considered to be priorities.

The short answer to the question of to whose priorities, Marcos' or NEDA's, did Japan respond is that it responded to both. Japan could accommodate the project priorities of Marcos and NEDA simultaneously because it relied on the request principle. The request principle allows Japan to place the onus of project formulation and request, and therefore the establishment of priorities, on the recipient. Fragmentation within the Japanese aid bureaucracy reinforces this by preventing strategic thinking about the purposes of its aid. As one ADB official noted, "OECF has no brains, but it is able to adjust to any request."[96] From Japan's perspective, a request from anywhere in the Philippine government was a request from the Philippine government as a whole.

Anticipatory bargaining happens because recipients are willing to forgo ideal conceptions of their economic preferences in exchange for tangible types of aid that are reasonably close to their ideals. The willingness to accept a reasonable alternative instead of an ideal is reinforced by the fact that there is room in the development plans for accommodation of donor interests in sectors or aid styles because the recipient has a variety of needs in a variety of areas that it wants satisfied. We cannot say a priori that Japan's preference for infrastructure aid meets recipient needs less than it would if it gave more basic human needs aid, because from the recipients' perspective they need both. Therefore, there is room for the recipient to tailor its aid requests to the donor's preferences or area strengths.

6

Case Studies in the Accommodation of Interests

Introduction

Chapter Five outlined the idea of accommodation as it occurs in the Japanese aid relationship with Thailand and the Philippines. But what does accommodation mean for individual projects? This chapter examines specific cases from each recipient country to shed light on this topic. In particular, it examines three aspects of accommodation: the importance of learning, the number of major actors and the relationships between them, and the degree of success of recipients in renegotiating projects. In the latter two aspects, it highlights the importance key actors attach to maintaining the stability of the long-term aid relationship.

Accommodation works best in an uncrowded field. Despite the political nature of aid, few outside actors can affect the aid relationships for any length of time. For one thing, aid is usually less salient an issue than trade or investment policy, so fewer actors are likely to be as interested in aid as in other kinds of external economic issues. The executive and legislative authorities in the three countries are generally concerned with Japanese aid only when specific problems or policy issues arise, and, even then, their attention is limited. The limitations outside actors face is well illustrated in two cases. One is the Ayutthaya case. The second involves the efforts of Marcos opponents in 1983.

Learning and Accommodation:
Japanese Aid for Land Reform

Chapter Five also made the point that a process of learning has gone on in both of the aid relationships considered here. In the Philippine case, the ability of that government to accurately forecast the kinds and amounts of aid it could expect from Japan was interrupted by the change of government in 1986. A process of relearning occurred in the first years of the new administration, the mechanics of which are well illustrated in the relationship between the Japanese aid bureaucracy and the Department of Agrarian Reform (DAR).

The Aquino administration was inaugurated during a period of widespread revulsion against the excesses of its predecessor. In the first two years of her administration, President Aquino was perceived to have a mandate to reform the Philippine political system to make it more democratic. Land reform was seen to be a key component of democratization, and it was widely believed early on that land reform was not only desirable but possible. Japan was one of the first donor countries to express an interest in supporting land reform efforts. The 1987 country study expressed a desire to use aid for land reform efforts, and Prime Minister Takeshita pledged support for the program in December of that year.[1] Japan dispatched a high-level mission led by elder statesman Okita Saburo in 1988, followed by a working-level team that fall. Japanese aid for the program would appear to be a natural policy outcome since Japan had experience with a successful land reform and the DAR had set its sights on foreign aid to help cover its expenditures. Yet, subsequent progress on commitment and disbursement of Japanese aid was slow. As of mid-1993 only four projects were in the implementation phase, and only one had made it to the basic design phase.[2] A second JICA country study carried out that same year advocated continued support for land reform, but put it well down the list of priority areas for Japanese aid.[3] The process by which Japanese aid largely failed to meet recipient expectations illustrates the importance of learning in developing a relationship of accommodation.

Japan's initial enthusiasm for the program was dampened by the Aquino administration's lack of progress in implementing it. Early progress was promising, with land reform provisions covering all agricultural lands regardless of tenure or crops included in the new 1987 constitution. The president's initiative in the program waned quickly, however. Early land reform program drafts were diluted as sugar and coconut landowners entered the debate in early 1987. Their interests became dominant when

President Aquino ceded decisionmaking power on key components such as retention limits and program timing to the new congress. The Comprehensive Agrarian Reform Law (CARL), passed in June 1988, reflected the interests of the landowning elite who dominated the House of Representatives. In particular, the phasing of the ten-year Comprehensive Agrarian Reform Program (CARP) left the politically difficult issue of transfer of private lands to the final phase of the program, after the 1992 presidential elections, and the alternative of distribution of stock to tenants in lieu of land title left open the question of whether landowners would ever turn over lands to which they held title.[4] Aquino's widely publicized use of the latter option on her home estate reinforced the image that the government was not serious about land reform.

Lack of continuity at DAR hurt its ability to get aid from Japan. DAR had a high turnover of secretaries under the Aquino administration. Three secretaries resigned in one nine-month period; by 1990, it was on its fifth.[5] The chairman of the 1988 Japanese working-level team noted that his mission had negotiated with then-secretary Philip Juico, only to see him resign following disputes over land pricing.[6] The constant turnover limited Japan's ability to set aid policy for land reform because the DAR could not set consistent priorities at the top. A well-publicized fight with the Department of Trade and Industry over conversion of agricultural lands to industrial use did nothing to correct that image.[7]

The upshot of these factors was that the Japanese government took a wait-and-see attitude toward the land reform program. A former NEDA official who had negotiated with the Takahashi mission in 1988 noted that even then Japanese negotiators were suspicious as to whether the Philippine government could carry out agrarian reform.[8] By 1991, Japan was telling the DAR that it was not inclined to commit to CARP with the end of Aquino's administration approaching.[9] Progress under the new Ramos administration remained slow,[10] suggesting that future aid for land reform will be minimal.

A striking aspect of the transition from Marcos to Aquino is that the DAR's bureaucratic structure stayed intact. As a result, DAR had to expand its area of competence to include new activities, even though its personnel had little or no experience with foreign aid. Moreover, whatever experience existed did not apply to Japan, because its aid program before the Aquino administration did not include land reform. The lack of aid expertise in the DAR hampered its efforts to get Japanese funding. Donor involvement in land reform during the Marcos administration had been limited to technical assistance, which was itself a small part of overall DAR activities. For example, although USAID provided technical assistance, its scope of activity was limited to the creation of a largely ineffectual database on which to implement the reforms.[11]

The reverse, incidentally, can be said for Japan. The Ministry of Agriculture, Forestry and Fisheries (MAFF) was especially interested in conveying its experience with land reform in Japan. No one in the ministry, however, had been engaged in land reform work since 1955, and those who had implemented the program during the American Occupation period (1945-1952) had retired. Those bureaucrats resisted coming out of retirement, but played an indirect advisory role. Overall, the MAFF's ability to convey the lessons of Japan's land reform were limited by the lack of available expertise in that field.[12]

The result of this lack of institutional fit led to a considerable amount of fumbling in the first three years of the land reform program. DAR spent a great deal of time in the early phases finding out what Japan would or could give aid for and how much it was willing to spend. One official admitted that DAR and the Japanese aid bureaucrats did not understand each other very well in the early days.[13] Consequently, its requests were not tailored to the Japanese aid system. One Japanese negotiator recalled that he often told the bureaucrats in the DAR that their proposals were unrealistic. They did not know the Japanese aid system, and consequently, made requests for grants containing "huge" amounts of money.[14] In early 1988, for example, the DAR requested a $250 million grant, a sum equivalent to entire yen loan packages in the early 1980s.[15]

Requests did not match Japanese institutional capabilities or policy preferences either. Only one-quarter of CARP's budget was allocated to research and development and infrastructure support, areas in which Japan would find it easiest to provide aid because such support fit its project profile.[16] Early on Japan refused to assist land distribution because of anticipated political difficulty in the Diet.[17] It also shied away from the Fund for External Support of Agrarian Reform (FESAR), a USAID initiative providing program support and foreign exchange for balance of payments support for CARP. Japan told the DAR that it found it difficult to justify putting bilateral aid funds into a common fund. As the DAR respondent noted, "We realized after awhile that we can't deal with them on the broad program level."[18]

DAR also had to learn how to get the aid Japan did agree to. After their initial enthusiasm, DAR officials were disappointed to find that while the government of Japan had declared its support for land reform, it insisted that requests go through the normal aid channels.[19] The slowness of the process was no doubt reinforced by the fact that Japan was entering into a new policy area, and was therefore cautious. As the DAR official observed, "Especially for land reform I think they had a difficult time knowing how to assess the program. They took a wait-and-see attitude . . . . I can't count the number of survey missions."[20] Japanese budgeting added to the problem. Because JICA sets the grant aid budget each year before it receives recipient requests, projects often have to be scaled back. In the case of one DAR request, it found the scope was too big for Japan's budgeting, so the project had to be broken down. The upshot was that DAR found it had projects that could be done in one year, but took eighteen months because of budgeting. Combined with the pace of the survey cycle, projects could not be implemented as fast as DAR bureaucrats would have liked. The respondent noted that a project to improve local water supply required two years before it started: a mapping and agricultural potential project, begun in October, 1990, took a year to negotiate. Overall, DAR found the Japanese aid process frustratingly rigid and slow.

Learning to play the Japanese aid game was critical to DAR because it was a matter of getting onto the agenda of the Philippines' largest donor. DAR was at a disadvantage vis-à-vis other ministries in getting onto the short list of aid projects because it had begun dealing with Japan so recently. As a result, CARP had a short pipeline of aid projects. Japanese aid is focussed on previously requested projects that will often kick around for several years in the prebargaining process before they make it to the short list. As the official stated, "you can't propose new projects. They have to have been in the pipeline for two years or so, so they can comment on it."[21] The aid system's conservatism hurt DAR's chances of making successful requests.

Communication between institutions is a vital component in the establishment of a relationship of accommodation. The evidence suggests that by the end of the Aquino administration DAR and the Japanese aid bureaucracy had not yet reached the point where they could communicate effectively. While DAR engaged in prebargaining, maintaining informal contacts with the embassy and the JICA and OECF offices, it simply had not played the aid game long enough to adjust its expectations and operating procedures to play it well.

Informal Aid Relationships:
Japanese Companies and the Marcos Administration

It has been observed that recipient planners face obstacles to rational aid planning from their political executives as well as from their agents. A great deal of journalistic material that emerged from the transition of power in the Philippines in 1986 makes it clear that the Marcoses and their cronies did not hesitate to subordinate national goals to their own. The Marcos Documents, seized in 1986, shed light on informal relationships between Japanese contractors and Marcos representatives. Japanese aid was no different. A 1977 letter from an employee of a Japanese firm to a company chairman acting as a front man for kickbacks to Marcos highlights the links Japanese companies forged with Marcos. It was the main prop of many discussions of the Marcos scandal in the Japanese press. The letter is interesting, however, for more than its frank admission of illegality. It helps us understand the dynamics of accommodation in Japan's aid relationship to the Philippines under the Marcos administration and the place Japanese companies occupied in it. In particular, it highlights both the vulnerability of Japanese companies operating in the aid system and the extent of potential slack in the administration of the bilateral program.

According to a letter dated October 14 1977, from a Toyo Corporation representative to the Angenit Corporation, the five Japanese manufacturers who won bids for the Cagayan Valley Electrification Project had formed a consortium prior to bidding and elected the C. Itoh Corporation to act as its representative. C. Itoh told the members that based on past practice, the members would be asked by Marcos' representatives to make a "commitment" of 15 percent of project proceeds. As the cartel's representative, C. Itoh resisted the demands for kickbacks and approached the OECF and the Japanese embassy for help. As a result, MITI in Tokyo contacted the members and warned them not to provide the kickbacks. When the bids were opened in May 1977, the evidence of a cartel was clear, and the implementing officer froze the project.[22]

With the project halted, the members of the cartel began to complain about C. Itoh's handling of the kickback issue. C. Itoh felt it had made a mistake in refusing to provide the kickbacks, but also felt it would lose face with the OECF and the embassy if it gave in. Eventually, it approached the implementing officer about a reduced kickback on certain portions of the project, amounting to about 7 percent of the project's total cost, which the implementing officer refused. In the meantime, another member had approached the Angenit Corporation independently and offered a 7.5 percent kickback, which the implementing officer also rejected.

At that point, the author noted that the cartel was becoming weak, and some members were willing to provide a larger commitment to get the contract. Kotake Yoshio, the Toyo representative, suggested that Angenit be patient since the cartel would eventually have to give in. He doubted whether the cartel would agree to the original 15 percent, but thought it would go higher than it had. He also warned the Angenit representative not to press the cartel too hard lest it complain again to the OECF.[23] Negotiations for the contract continued until 1978. One cartel member agreed to pay Angenit 10 percent of its contract price. The others followed suit, although the amount of kickbacks paid is unclear. In April 1979, two members were awarded contracts for transmission line supply. In 1983, C. Itoh won the prime contract, but at a considerably lower price.[24]

The evidence shows that the system of accommodation between Japanese contractors and Marcos was not one of equals. In particular, it illustrates the vulnerability of Japanese companies in the aid relationship. Companies paid bribes because they were the weak link in the aid system. While companies like Toyo depended on aid contracts for a good deal of their business, that business depended on the Japanese and Philippine governments. The companies had no ability to make authoritative decisions in that system. They could not get contracts without the approval of the Philippine government, nor could they unilaterally unfreeze a suspended contract if the implementing officer accused them of unfair bidding practices. In the Philippines, the informal rules included paying off Marcos cronies in return for contracts. The companies had little to protect them from Marcos demands for kickbacks: while the Japanese government could warn the companies not to pay bribes, as MITI did in this case, it was unlikely to follow up the warning with a complaint to Marcos. More likely, as the letter suggests, the companies themselves would suffer, by losing the ability to bid on contracts, if the details of the bribery scheme were disclosed. In short, others made the rules by which the Japanese companies had to play.

Dango was a response to that weakness. Collusion occurred to maximize short-term profit, which is what we would expect. But in the Cagayan Valley case it was also a response to pressures from Marcos to pay for doing business. *Dango* guaranteed some safety from Marcos attempts to extort kickbacks from the companies. Of the cartel members that had won contracts previously, only one had paid bribes to Marcos' front man, and then only once.[25] The cartel's intention to avoid further kickbacks is evident from Kotake's letter, and it succeeded in some measure; while the companies eventually paid, they paid less than Toyo or other companies outside the cartel.

The companies were not completely vulnerable. Marcos was clearly violating Philippine law. His kickback collection system went all the way to members of the cabinet. Not only was the implementing officer involved, but the secretary of the Department of Public Works and Highways from

1966 to 1979 admitted that he had been involved as well. He also confirmed that kickback money from Japanese companies had been salted away in Swiss Bank accounts via Hong Kong on Marcos' behalf, an activity Marcos took great pains to hide.[26] Marcos depended on the Japanese companies for kickbacks. As the cartel case discussed above demonstrates, companies could join together to resist his demands. He was willing to accommodate Japanese companies by favoring them for contracts because they could halt the flow of money if they complained to the Japanese authorities.

The Kotake letter raises a problem about the nature of competition among Japanese companies for contracts. A striking aspect of the Kotake letter is that it was written by an employee of a company outside of the cartel. Toyo and other companies had been excluded because they favored making "commitments" to Marcos front men and would thereby weaken the cartel's internal cohesion in its attempts to resist paying bribes.[27] Yet Kotake's tone in describing the cartel's activities was surprisingly mild. While he urged the Angenit representative to be patient, in the expectation that the cartel would have to agree to a higher commitment, he did not attempt to undercut the cartel. If anything, he told the Angenit representative not to expect the full 15 percent kickback. Why did Toyo take such a mild attitude toward the collusive behavior of a rival cartel?

Toyo took a low posture because it would ensure the continuity of the system of accommodation. Toyo occupied a central place in the circle of Japanese companies favored by the Marcos administration in the construction of aid projects. According to an Angenit document dated October 13 1977, Toyo accounted for just under 40 percent of all contracts awarded for projects in the first five yen loan packages handled for Marcos by an unnamed general. Toyo had participated in every other project that had reached the bidding stage by 1977. In all cases, it had remitted a standard 15 percent of its contract price to that general.[28] Toyo, then, was paying for the privilege of contracts by providing kickbacks to Marcos front men. Kotake's letter makes it clear that Toyo was concerned that the cartel might complain again to the Japanese government, thereby exposing the kickback scheme and Toyo with it.

Toyo's reluctance to undercut the cartel can also be attributed to its expectation that it would have to deal with the cartel's members in the future. According to Angenit's documents, eleven Japanese firms had won yen loan contracts by October 1977. Three of them had worked on projects in which Toyo had participated.[29] Toyo could expect to do business with these companies again; all of them remained active in procuring aid contracts throughout the Marcos period. Toyo could not discount future cooperation with enough certainty to make the short-term payoff of a single contract worth the risk of lost business later.

I suggested above that a feature of accommodation is that the major actors must respect and live with one another's organizational characteristics. This is certainly true with the Japanese aid bureaucracy's treatment of Japanese contractors doing business with Marcos. Brian Woodall argues that coopting or evading government watchdogs is a major prerequisite for the success of collusive action.[30] The particular form of accommodation between Marcos and the Japanese companies could persist because Marcos benefitted and the Japanese government did not act against it. Marcos' reticence is understandable, but the Japanese government's quiescence in matters that clearly contravened the law requires explanation. There are two main reasons the Japanese authorities did not intervene. First, the aid bureaucracy lacked the resources to police the implementation of projects. The JICA and OECF offices in Manila were understaffed and therefore found it difficult to stay abreast of project implementation or carry out evaluations after the work had been completed.[31]

Second, it was politically difficult for Japan to interfere. One legacy of the reparations program was Japan's reluctance to interfere in Philippine government decisions once funds had been disbursed. That attitude carried over into the aid program from the beginning.[32] During the 1986 investigations of alleged misuse of aid funds during the Marcos period, the Japanese government consistently adhered to the position that aid money once disbursed became the sole responsibility of the Philippine government. The aid agencies refused to disclose the names of Japanese contractors or the details of the contracts, arguing that they were private agreements reached between the Philippine government and the individual firms. While the Japanese Ministry of Foreign Affairs dispatched a survey team to the Philippines in March 1986 to evaluate the aid program there, its mission did not include investigation of ODA-related business practices by Japanese companies.[33]

The National Maritime Polytechnic

The National Maritime Polytechnic (NMP) in the Philippines has received a great deal of attention from critics of Japanese aid. Japan's grant aid for the Polytechnic has been presented as a white elephant project, a case of the unsuitability of Japan's aid for Philippine needs and as an example of the Japanese government's willingness to accommodate the Marcoses.[34] The project has these elements, and thereby helps us understand how suboptimal development projects make their way into the aid relationship. The NMP also affords us a view of how the aid environment affects the accommodation of political interests. The decision to fund the project should be considered in the context of the aid process. Removed from its context, the NMP grant suggests that a pushy recipient can make Japan give it what it wants if it knows the Japanese prime minister is going to visit. While this can happen, and it seems to have in the NMP case, this case suggests that this can happen only if certain formal criteria are met.

On paper, the NMP appeared to fill an objective Philippine need. In the 1970s, Filipinos in increasing numbers sought employment abroad, a policy encouraged by the government since their remittances home helped support the domestic economy. Filipino sailors were among those seeking overseas work, and by 1977 about 40,000 of them worked aboard foreign-owned ships.[35] To do so, they required internationally recognized training in seamanship. In order to upgrade the proficiency of Filipino sailors, the Philippine Government created the National Maritime Polytechnic in 1977. The NMP was programmed for Japanese loan aid in the 1978-82 five-year plan.[36]

The project surfaced again in May 1983 during Japanese Prime Minister Nakasone's state visit to the Philippines. In addition to offering the Eleventh Yen Loan package, Nakasone agreed to consider certain grant aid proposals, one of which was a request for grant aid for expansion of the NMP.[37] The Japanese government dispatched a preliminary survey team in August, and a basic design survey team was dispatched in October. The exchange of notes took place in June 1984, with Japan agreeing to construct necessary facilities and provide retraining equipment.[38]

The NMP was a pork barrel project for Imelda Marcos. The facility's site is located in Tacloban, her birthplace. As one Diet member who had attended the groundbreaking ceremony attested, Imelda referred to the project as "my birthday present from Japan."[39] She had repeatedly requested that Japan provide aid for it prior to Nakasone's 1983 visit, and had presented the Japanese embassy in Manila with official request documents, as well as sending verbal notes through the Philippine Foreign Ministry.[40] She had even gone so far as to replace an earlier request for grant aid for the Human Resources Development Center, another pet project, with the NMP well after preliminary survey work on the former had been completed.[41] Political scientist Murai Yoshinori sees the decision to consider the project request as a political maneuver. He argues that the Japanese government had received requests for expansion of the project, but had rejected them because it preferred to fund another facility which carried out maritime training. For Murai, the NMP decision smacks of a political deal between Nakasone and

Imelda resulting in a reversal of prior Japanese policy.[42] The NMP decision should therefore be seen as an example of *omiyage gaiko,* or "gift diplomacy," in which a visiting Japanese official bestows a gift project on the government he is visiting in order to promote better relations.

The political decision to fund the NMP was possible because the project was, at least minimally, feasible at the technical level. One Japanese aid bureaucrat noted that projects suitable for *omiyage gaiko* are those that are nearing completion of negotiations. Therefore the negotiations can be speeded up to be ready in time for the prime minister's trip to the recipient country.[43] In this case, the NMP's utility as a political gesture was made possible by its maturity as a project proposal in the aid pipeline: Imelda could get funding for her project because it was already on the aid agenda. The project had been programmed for Japanese loan aid since the beginning of the 1978-82 plan, so her request for aid was not new. Moreover, its scope had been changed to be more suitable for Japanese funding. The initial plan called for loan aid; by 1983, the request was for grant aid, and therefore appropriate for facilities construction funding.[44] This was an important modification since it lowered the level of funding required and also lowered the project's visibility in the overall aid program. Political gifts in the aid program are almost always grants because their inclusion in an aid package does not alter the package significantly. Finally, the request was for expansion of an existing facility. To the extent the proposal had been scaled down and refined, it would be politically and technically more acceptable to Japan.

The project was also considered feasible from the perspective of the survey teams. Consideration of the way in which the basic design report was written provides a useful insight into how technical feasibility was divorced from political expediency. The survey missions' task was to assess the best way for Japan to contribute to the project. The decision to fund construction of the facilities and equipment provision met the criteria of technical feasibility within the confines of the grant itself. The report confined its impact analysis to noting that the number of Filipinos working overseas was increasing and that training at the NMP would help them do that by providing them with skills necessary for such work. The NMP, moreover, was the only place in the Philippines engaged in retraining activities, which the report viewed as more practical than training. For the design team, building construction and equipment provision would benefit the upgrading of the NMP while remaining within the purview of the Japanese grant program.[45] Provision of the grant was therefore technically feasible, no matter whose project it was or who would benefit politically by it. Whether Imelda used the project as patronage was beyond the scope of the technical assessment.

Despite the inherent narrowness of the technical viewpoint, the NMP would not have been possible politically if it had not met the criteria required by the aid process. Had the project no track record, it is doubtful whether Imelda or Nakasone could have convinced the Japanese ministries to accept the project. Had it been a loan project, and therefore bigger, its visibility might have caused opposition to it. Had it not been judged at least minimally feasible as a grant project, it could not have been funded. In sum, the environment in which projects are requested, reviewed, and then decided upon create constraints on any project proposal no matter how deserving or politically important.

Insulating Aid Policy: The Twelfth Yen Loan to the Philippines

As seen above, the foundations of accommodation had been laid by the early 1980s. Since 1976, Japan and the Philippine government had held annual bilateral aid negotiations. The major actors in the aid system had learned how to deal with one another, if not always successfully or efficiently. In short, a durable aid relationship based on the accommodation of the interests of the different players existed between Japan and the Philippines. The durability of accommodation is well illustrated in the history of the Twelfth Yen Loan, requested in 1983.

This case suggests that accommodation works best with a limited number of actors who have been socialized to the rules of the game. The length of the delay in agreement, and the reasons for it, show how the inclusion of actors outside of the system of aid accommodation can make the decision to accommodate difficult because they can force the consideration of issues outside of the narrow perspective of the aid system.

The early progress of the loan package followed the usual pattern of the Marcos period. NEDA had prepared the short list by late March 1983. Following Marcos' approval and modification, it presented the formal project request to the Japanese embassy in May.[46] The economic crisis in the Philippines in the summer and fall, however, interfered with the loan negotiations. On October 17th the government declared a moratorium on repayment of external debt, signalling the beginning of the "worst balance-of-payments crisis in postwar Philippine history."[47] The crisis caused the Philippines to modify its request for the loan package. In late November the government requested a $230 million commodity loan in place of the project loan package, as well as additional Eximbank lending and export insurance on Japanese exports.[48] The conversion to a commodity loan would allow quick disbursement, clearly a priority for the Philippine government in late 1983.

The Japanese government was inclined to assist the Philippine government. The change from a request for project loans to a request for a commodity loan, however, made a cautious aid bureaucracy even more so because the new request signalled the economic difficulties the Philippines was experiencing. Consequently, the Japanese government looked to the United States and the IMF, making its commitment of aid dependent on agreements between the other two donors and the Philippines.[49] The failure of Philippine-IMF negotiations in November postponed agreement on a yen loan at least until the new year. Despite public attempts by Marcos to disengage the bilateral aid negotiations with Japan from IMF talks in January 1984, Japan continued to state it would wait for the results of an IMF agreement before agreeing to new aid.[50] By mid-month, with no new IMF agreement in sight, Prime Minister Virata admitted that the conversion of the yen loan would have to wait.[51]

In early February, the Japanese government began to finalize plans to extend a commodity loan to the Philippines. Of approximately 55 billion yen anticipated for commitment, just over 30 billion was to be in the form of a commodity loan and 15 billion in the form of debt rescheduling. The Japanese government informed the Philippine government that it awaited the submission of a list of commodities to be imported under the loan, and dispatched a team to help prepare the list.[52] Despite the decision, progress remained slow; by early March, the Philippine government still had not submitted its list of commodities, the four ministries in Tokyo were still in consultations over the commodity loan issue, and final cabinet approval was still pending. In any case, the Philippine government still had not reached final agreement with the IMF.

It is clear that the Japanese aid bureaucracy was inclined to provide a loan package in 1983. Until March 1984 accommodation of Philippine requests was possible within the confines of normal aid negotiation channels. The new request for conversion of the bulk of the project loan to a commodity loan delayed Japanese decisionmaking simply because it forced Japan to redo all of the work it had accomplished to date. Moreover, Japan had not supplied commodity loans to the Philippines since 1978 because the Philippines' level of economic development precluded such concessional lending, and had, in fact, rejected a commodity loan request by Marcos the year before. The insistence on an IMF standby agreement and the three-month delay in deciding to provide the commodity loan were indicators of the Japanese aid bureaucracy's discomfort with the new request. At that stage, however, decisionmaking was still routine.

Despite the delays, the Japanese government appeared ready to enter final negotiations with the Philippines in mid-March. At that point, however, opposition to the loan arose in both the Philippines and Japan. On March 12th, in a press conference in Tokyo, Benigno Aquino's younger brother called on Japan to delay granting the loan until 1985 or at least until after the upcoming Batasan elections in May.[53] Four days later, a small group of supporters demonstrated in front of the Japanese embassy in Manila. In the Japanese Diet, the Socialist Party raised questions about the yen loan during hearings on the government budget, arguing that it should not be committed until the Aquino assassination had been cleared up.[54] In late March, a delegation from the Philippine opposition group Nationalist Alliance for Justice, Freedom and Democracy met with Japanese Diet members opposed to the loan.[55] Despite the opposition, the government argued that it was imperative to help the Philippine economy, and that the Aquino assassination was a separate problem.[56]

The loan became a political issue in March for two reasons. First, the routine phase of the loan decision process was ending, and decisions at the policy level of the Japanese aid bureaucracy were necessary. The end of the relatively opaque stage of loan negotiations allowed the opposition in Japan and the Philippines a target for criticism of Japanese political inaction following the Aquino assassination. Second, the delay in deciding on the commodity loan pushed the anticipated signing date into the period of the Batasan elections, which allowed the opposition to couple the Aquino assassination with the specter of misuse of aid funds by Marcos on the eve of an election.[57] The loan, therefore, became a political issue requiring a political decision, rather than routine ratification.

By late March it was clear that opposition to the loan was growing. Despite suppression of opposition party bids to delay the loan in the House of Representatives, the Budget Committee of the House of Councillors continued hearings on the loan through the end of the month. As a result, the cabinet decision on the loan was delayed until April. By this point the loan had been "kicked upstairs" to the political level of decisionmaking.[58] Nakasone had already expressed his support for aid to the Philippines. The majority of the cabinet agreed with his position that the loan should be committed as soon as possible, but at least two ministers and a number of LDP Diet members opposed Nakasone on the timing of disbursement.

Through April, Japan continued to send positive signals to the Philippine government about the committing of the loan, with the cabinet deciding to approve the exchange of notes before the election, but withholding disbursement of the commodity loan portion until after it.[59] The Japanese government also distanced itself from its position on the IMF agreement, deciding that agreement on a standby credit facility was not a precondition for commitment of the bilateral loan.[60]

As the month drew to a close, the possibility of a final agreement became clear. Japanese officials informed the Philippine Central Bank in the third week of April that only the formal approval of the cabinet remained before completion of the loan agreement, and the signing was tentatively set for the end of the month. On April 27, the cabinet made the formal decision to provide the loan package, and on the 29th the two governments exchanged notes. Reflecting the criticisms of the loan, the agreement contained provisions limiting use of the commodity loan proceeds to development projects mutually agreed upon. It stipulated that the Philippine government report to the Japanese government on the uses for which the funds were spent, and limited the use of the project loan portions strictly to those projects contained in the exchange of notes.[61] The two governments signed the loan agreements for the project portion of the package on May 7th, but the disbursement of the commodity loan was delayed considerably. Despite apprehensions about misuse of commodity loan proceeds, the evidence suggests that the commodity loan was not used for electioneering for the simple reason that it was hardly used at all.[62]

The political decision the Nakasone cabinet made was conditioned by the routine phase that had preceded it. Nakasone's decision to go ahead with the loan commitment kept up the momentum from the lower levels of the aid bureaucracy. The separation of the bilateral negotiations from the IMF standby agreement negotiations allowed Nakasone to set a signing date based on the progress of the commodity loan negotiations alone, the groundwork of which had been laid over the winter. Nakasone's intervention in April, therefore, should be seen as quickening the pace to satisfy a desire within the Japanese aid bureaucracy to accommodate the Marcos administration.

The emergence of external opposition delayed the final loan agreement, but did not succeed in cancelling it. The fact that the decision could be enacted in spite of opposition shows the durability of the relationship of accommodation. In Japan, no opposition actors possessed the legal authority or the political power to countermand a decision to go ahead as planned. While the Diet conducted hearings, in the process delaying decision making on the fiscal 1984 national budget, the funds under discussion had been allocated from the previous year's budget and were therefore out of its hands. The opposition parties could not mount a successful political attack on the loan decision because they were not united.[63] In the Philippines opposition was largely confined to street demonstrations. With opposition excluded from the internal structure of the aid relationship, its impact could be minimized, and progress on negotiations maintained.

Opposition to the Twelfth Yen Loan reminds us that negotiations do not occur in a vacuum. Issues get linked to other issues, and therefore affect negotiators' abilities to reach agreements. Increasing the number of players in a game increases the number of potential issues that impinge on the game.[64] The loan is an example of outsiders trying to get into a closed game. In the process, domestic political games between governments and oppositions became intertwined with intergovernmental negotiations on aid. The case here suggests that outsiders can provoke instability because the game they perceive is not that which the negotiators perceive. Aid negotiators see a set of negotiations as part of a continuous series of interactions. Outsiders, especially in cases like the opponents of the twelfth loan, do not see an iterated game. They see the particular game that presents itself at a specific moment. They discount the future because they are intent on achieving a certain outcome in the current game. As we saw earlier, the aid game is largely confined to bureaucratic interaction. Clearly, the actors in the aid relationships want to keep it that way because it simplifies the number and complexity of issues with which they must deal. From their perspectives, it is wise to do so.

The Ayutthaya Historical Study Center

The Ayutthaya Historical Study Center project is one of the best-known Japanese grant aid projects in Thailand. An extensive literature has developed around it. The extant literature, however, focuses largely on concerns of Japanese cultural insensitivity, Japanese private sector domination of the Thai economy, and political bungling by the Japanese government.[65] While the project's history allows us to observe these factors, it also allows us a chance to observe the process of accommodation in the aid relationship. In particular, it reinforces the conclusion in the Twelfth Yen Loan case that limiting the number of participants makes project negotiation easier.

The impetus for the project originally came from the Bangkok Japanese Chamber of Commerce. In 1984 that organization's tourist bureau began to talk of restoring the site of a seventeenth century Japanese trading community that had existed in the then-capital of Siam at Ayutthaya. The Japanese embassy subsequently adopted the idea as a project to commemorate the upcoming centennial of Thai-Japanese diplomatic relations in 1987, and approached the Ayutthaya provincial government and the Thai Ministry of the Interior. Following negotiations, Japan and Thailand agreed to a grant aid project amounting to 999 million yen. Prime Minister Nakasone was to inaugurate the project during his state visit to Thailand in late September 1987 to celebrate the centennial.[66]

Thai actors subsequently initiated two sets of revisions. The first followed expressions of dissatisfaction from Thai architects. In early September 1987, the Association of Siamese Architects (ASA) submitted a letter to the Thai foreign minister protesting the planned construction of the facility. The ASA argued that Thai nationals should participate in the project's building and landscape design, a responsibility that theretofore rested solely with the Thai-Japanese Association, which owned the land on which the center was to be built. It also argued that Japan's contribution to Thai history in the Ayutthaya period was minimal, and maintained further that employment of Japanese contractors and construction crews at the site was illegal.[67] A week later it demanded in a letter to the foreign ministry that Thai contractors and architects receive a 70 percent share of the project work.[68] The ASA's protest had two results. The first was to derail the diplomatic effect of the center's inauguration. Following the ASA's first letter of protest, the project's chairman, a former minister of finance, cancelled his scheduled trip to Japan in mid-September. In mid-month, the Thai and Japanese governments agreed to cancel Prime Minister Nakasone's inauguration of the Center.[69]

The second result was that Thai architects gained a participatory role in the project design. Initially, JICA had insisted that the design be carried out by Japanese architects, with Thai architects to be consulted on the building specifications.[70] Following the cancellation of Nakasone's visit to the Center, Japan agreed in principle to try to allow Thais a major share in the project's construction and design. It sent a team to Thailand in October to discuss the design with Thai architects. Discussions continued through the winter and spring. In the summer of 1988 the Ministry of Interior's committee delivered an ultimatum that the architectural work be done by Thais, to which the Japanese agreed.[71] The final design was significantly altered to include Thai design elements, and Thai contractors won 70 percent of the project's work.[72] One JICA official commented that it was the first time a JICA basic design study had been radically changed.[73]

The second revision occurred four months after the center's inauguration. In late January 1988 the Ministry of Interior requested that the project site be moved from its original location at the former Japanese village to a location in front of the Ayutthaya provincial office. JICA demurred, arguing that there was no precedent for moving a site following the completion of the basic design, but the move was eventually carried out.[74]

The Ayutthaya case is interesting because it is one of a very few cases in which nongovernmental actors have been able to effect a change in a Japanese aid project that had already been agreed upon.[75] The ASA's effectiveness in convincing Japan to let it participate in the project was undoubtedly due to the political climate in Thailand at the time. ASA's objections to the Ayutthaya project were part of a larger concern about the presence of Japanese companies in Thailand. The provision of the Ayutthaya grant took place in an era of Japanese private sector expansion in the country. Thai companies were dissatisfied with the growing Japanese presence because they saw their foreign counterparts as taking away business from local firms. The suspicion that Japanese companies enjoyed undue influence in gaining aid contracts further reinforced the dissatisfaction. The completion of the Thailand Cultural Center project in early 1897 under a JICA grant particularly galled associations like the ASA, which saw the non-Thai design of the buildings as out of keeping with local aesthetics. By 1987 the major Thai construction and engineering associations, including the ASA, had begun to discuss ways of dealing with the competition from outside.[76]

ASA's position was undoubtedly strengthened by the public nature of the debate over the Ayutthaya project. ASA had already expressed its objections to JICA procurement and contracting procedures earlier in the year in its own journal.[77] The anticipated arrival of the Japanese prime minister for the groundbreaking ceremony created an opportunity for the ASA to take its case to a wider audience. Its objections were carried in Thai newspapers, transforming an industry concern into a foreign policy issue. The wide media coverage of the project created an anticlimax for the centennial ceremonies.[78]

It is important to understand what the Ayutthaya project does *not* represent. The negotiations were about modifying the project, not cancelling it. The ASA succeeded in pressing its demands that the project be reformulated to include meaningful Thai input. Cancelling the project was probably beyond the ASA's reach, although there were fears it might happen.[79] The project's allies in Thailand included the Thai-Japanese Association (under whose auspices the project was originally to have been carried out), the Thai Ministry of Foreign Affairs, and the Ministry of Interior. The latter two were in positions to make authoritative decisions about the project, a position the ASA and its allies in the private sector did not enjoy. Cancellation of the project, moreover, would have risked souring relations between the two governments, a high price for the Thai government to have to pay for the sake of one domestic interest group. We see the shadow of the future constraining unilateral Thai decisions in the aid relationship and limiting the number of effective players.

Resolution of the Ayutthaya grant problem was possible because it was isolated from the rest of the aid program. The Thai construction industry's ire was concentrated on Ayutthaya, and did not spill over into other project negotiations. Indeed, given the furor over Japan's rules for contracting and procurement, it is interesting that the negotiations for the Thirteenth Yen Loan were completed within a week without a hitch. Containment of the issue was undoubtedly helped by the lack of program coordination between JICA and the OECF. The isolation of the Ayutthaya project prevented disagreement from endangering other parts of the aid relationship and, therefore, from threatening bilateral cooperation. Moreover, despite JICA concessions, grant aid procurement practices overall changed little, and there is no evidence that the ASA continues to play an active part in determining Thai priorities in the bilateral aid relationship.

The Laem Chabang Port Loan, 1984

Japan's loan for the Laem Chabang Port in the Eastern Seaboard illustrates the importance of controlling agency slack in the aid relationship. The project is interesting because it was renegotiated at the instigation of the Thai government. Its outcome suggests that the overall aid relationship is more important to Thailand than a single project, and that Thai aid planners are willing to forgo particular benefits in favor of the more general benefit of maintaining the flow of Japanese aid.

The loan for the port project was included in the Eleventh Yen Loan package agreed upon in September 1984. Negotiations for the loan had been concluded 1983, and the design phase had been started by late autumn of that year. Port construction was due to begin in 1984, with completion scheduled for 1988.[80]

Negotiations for the project hit a snag in December 1983. The Minister of Communications, under whose jurisdiction the portworks were to be carried out, asked for a suspension of the Laem Chabang loan, and the Port Authority of Thailand accordingly notified the companies that had been short-listed for the engineering survey to postpone submission of their designs. In early January he notified the NESDB that his ministry intended to cancel the engineering design portion of the Laem Chabang loan already agreed to in the previous loan package and to call for a new port design to triple its capacity to twelve berths. He also proposed cancellation of planned negotiations for the construction phase of the project, due to start in early 1984.[81]

The minister publicly argued that OECF loans hurt the Thai construction industry by favoring Japanese firms. The ministry was also unhappy with Japanese-funded construction of Don Muang Airport in Bangkok, and linked its displeasure over the course of that project with the decision on the Laem Chabang loan.[82] Consequently, it announced it would seek alternative sources for funding the project. The NESDB agreed to suspend the loan negotiations pending official notification to the OECF, and the prime minister called for a meeting in late January to consider the situation.[83]

The Japanese response was firm. Tokyo threatened the Thai Cabinet with the possibility that cancellation of the port loan would endanger future loans. One Japanese official commented that the cancellation would amount to breach of contract. As such, it would be legitimate grounds for cancelling the entire annual loan package.[84]

The dilemma the NESDB faced in the Laem Chabang case illustrates the potential difficulties of playing principal to two separate agents. On the one hand, the Japanese government, represented by the embassy, was concerned that an already-agreed to loan be carried forward. Muscat notes that the donor was adamantly against cancellation of any ESDP project funded by yen loans.[85] On the other hand, the prime minister, who usually supported the NESDB during this period, faced the issue of keeping a coalition government intact. Party rivalries tended to revolve around disputes between military factions and individual party leaders. Such rivalries were clearly present in the cabinet Prem had put together in 1983 and which tackled the Laem Chabang cancellation issue: while Prem was able to appoint technocrats to many cabinet posts, four other parties were represented as well. Nevertheless, the communications minister was a member of a small party (his post was its only portfolio) and a rival military faction.[86]

The minister's argument against the loan was weak, as well. Party leaders were interested primarily in government projects for their pecuniary benefits.[87] Thus, he did not cancel the loan for the obvious reason that the port project was too expensive and not worth the estimated cost of construction, but because it was too small. His alternative plan was to increase the number of berths in the project threefold. Had he argued for cancellation of port construction entirely he might have found allies among opponents of the entire Eastern Seaboard development scheme. That his interest in the loan lay elsewhere meant he could not.

The Japanese position was strengthened by the fact that the Thai Ministry of Finance favored continuation of the project under OECF financing. The ministry had not officially notified the OECF of the proposed cancellation. In fact, in early January it went ahead with its request that a loan for the port's construction be included in the upcoming Eleventh Yen Loan.[88] On January 26 the Eastern Seaboard Development Committee decided to overturn the communications ministry's proposal to cancel the Laem Chabang loan.[89]

The Eastern Seaboard Development Committee's decision to over-rule the communications ministry was conditioned by two factors: Thailand's dependence on Japanese aid for development financing in the Eastern Seaboard and the Thai Ministry of Finance's opposition to cancel-lation. The first conditioned the second. Japan could compel Thai acqui-escence by threatening to cancel future lending if the port loan did not go through, because its threat was credible. By the 1980s Japan supplied up to two-thirds of all bilateral aid to Thailand in any given year. More important, from the Eastern Seaboard Development Committee's point of view, Japan was far and away the largest donor of aid to the Eastern Seaboard. Five projects in the Eastern Seaboard, in addition to the Laem Chabang construction project, were included in the short list for Japanese lending in 1984.[90] If Thailand cancelled the Laem Chabang loan, it ran the risk of endangering the entire Eastern Seaboard program. The NESDB, the Eastern Seaboard Development Committee, and the finance ministry all had stakes in the resolution of the dispute in Japan's favor. The communi-cations ministry's particularistic action, in contrast, ran the risk of cutting off future benefits for other Thai government players. The convergence of interests between the Japanese government and the financial authorities in the Thai government created a powerful alliance that the communications ministry could not oppose successfully. The ministry found itself in a weak position because it was unable to find alternative sources of finance for the project by the January 26th meeting.[91]

The lack of alternative aid sources undoubtedly figured in the finance ministry's calculations to meet the Japanese demand, and weakened the communications ministry's ability to hold out for a better deal. Given the choice between concessional aid terms in a period of increasing external debt and arguments about the impact of Japanese aid on the Thai construction industry in general, it is not surprising that the finance ministry sided with Japan. Accommodation in this case was accomplished by quashing the objections of the dissident ministry.

The Accommodation of Interests: Environmental Aid

The discussion of accommodation in the aid relationship above suggests that the Thai government's ability to have its priorities met stems from its control over which projects will be discussed in the annual aid negotiations. This does not mean, however, that project requests will uniformly meet Thai development priorities or that Thai planners can consistently set priorities. Japan's aid for environmental protection in Thailand provides a good example of the problem. Beginning in the 1980s Japan provided environmental aid to Thailand. In 1989 it provided a grant for the establishment of an environmental research institute, and in 1990 and 1993 it provided small-scale grants for environmental education. In 1993 both governments agreed to increase the environmental project component of annual aid packages substantially, and Japan has offered its lowest interest rates yet on loans for such efforts. In 1981 JICA established a eucalyptus plantation in the northeast to promote field research and training. It has also funded surveys for National Reserve Forest management plans and undertaken a technical training program in logging and log transport. In 1989, the Thai government sought Japanese assistance for reforestation of the northeast over the next five years using eucalyptus as one part of the program, a request to which Japan responded with a grant in 1992.[92]

Aid for reforestation, however, has been criticized by environmentalists as destructive to native fauna and the lifestyles of local inhabitants. Reforestation programs are environmentally suspect for several reasons. First, eucalyptus plantation development, promoted in response to a rise in worldwide demand for wood chips, has encroached on native forests. Plantations have also put pressure on local inhabitants. They are pushed off forest land as large multinational companies have established large-scale private operations there, and forage previously exploited by their domesticated animals has been replaced by eucalyptus. The result has been the displacement of local populations and destruction of rainforest under the guise of afforestation of "marginal" lands.[93] From this perspective, then, the Thai government's support of eucalyptus planting by multinational corporations as well as international donors has led to a suboptimal solution to the problem of deforestation in the north and northeast.

The Thai government's actions become more understandable if we examine its environmental policies. The Thai government has pursued natural resource policies that are often contradictory. Thai planners consistently have subsumed environmental policy under the broader concern of natural resource use. Consequently, there has been a constant tension between exploitation of natural resources for economic development and the protection of natural resources for environmental preservation.[94] The need to preserve native forests has been coupled with export promotion policies, to the detriment of the former. While the Thai government had committed itself in the late 1980s to reforesting 40 percent of the country, mostly through private sector efforts, wood chips from eucalyptus plantations became an increasingly important export commodity. Japanese private sector interests meshed with Thailand's export policy since Japan was a prime market for wood chips and Japanese companies were active investors in eucalyptus production in Thailand. In addition, eucalyptus had the advantage of being fast-growing, and thus appeared to be a good candidate because it could produce quick results on heavily degraded land. This orientation also justified requests for aid to develop eucalyptus, and provided a legitimate rationale for donors like Japan to meet those requests.[95] Aid for natural resources in Thailand is an example of how policy ambiguity can abet the accommodation of interests.

Conclusion

Anticipatory bargaining and prebargaining provide insights into how Thailand and Japan accommodate one another in the aid relationship. These concepts, however, do not tell the whole story. The DAR case suggests how difficult it can be to learn how to develop these techniques. The Laem Chabang and Ayutthaya cases alert us to the fact that prebargaining does not always determine outcomes. The Marcos Documents and the Laem Chabang loan amply illustrate the problem of agency slack, albeit in different ways. Compared to the issues raised by the Marcos Documents, the Laem Chabang incident may seem to be a tempest in a teapot. Yet the ability of even relatively insignificant players to influence projects is clear. The process of accommodation is dynamic and takes place at many points in the aid cycle. It is likely that the majority of projects clear their hurdles through the processes of anticipatory bargaining and prebargaining, but in some cases renegotiation becomes necessary because the recipient demands it.

Accommodation of interests occurs because it helps foster cooperation. It assures the players that they can all derive some benefit out of the aid relationship and smoothes the way for future play. The incentive to cooperate also increases if the players expect to meet again.[96] The aid game Thailand and the Philippines play with Japan is such a game. They have been negotiating annually since 1978, and prebargaining occurs more frequently than that. It is almost certain that the players will engage in a future round. It is therefore in the interests of the actors in the system to accommodate one another—if at different levels and with different degrees of enthusiasm—because the game will continue indefinitely.

Japan accommodated Thailand in the Ayutthaya case because it became politically important to do so. Ayutthaya clearly had a political purpose because it was intended to mark the anniversary of bilateral friendship, so charges of cultural insensitivity had to be answered with a show of Japanese willingness to meet Thai priorities. The Third Yen Loan renegotiation, mentioned in Chapter Three, happened for similar reasons. While the Japanese aid program was nominally unrelated to the anti-Japanese riots, agreeing to aid concessions in the Third Yen Loan package provided a way for Japan to foster better relations with the Thai government. In both cases, Japan accommodated Thai demands because its concessions could help foster a cooperative climate in the aid relationship and in the overall bilateral relationship as well.

Compromise in the Ayutthaya case also served bureaucratic interests. From JICA's perspective, it involved a substantial amount of money. As seen in the case of the Laem Chabang Port loan, moreover, the aid bureaucracy has an aversion to cancelling projects already underway. If this situation made the Japanese government reluctant to cancel the project, it also made possible some sort of compromise with its Thai counterparts. Japan's calculation of the benefits of accommodation thus operated to constrain it. The Thai Foreign Ministry made efforts to mediate between the parties in the months that followed.[97] Agreement for Japan was possible because the dispute was about how to modify an existing design rather than starting completely over.[98] Thus, the distance Japan would have to move on the issue was less than it might have been. While cancellation would be costly, there was room for compromise. Nevertheless, the consensus building process in Tokyo was arduous, lengthening the time it took to reach agreement with the Thai government, and demonstrating the rigidity of the Japanese aid process.[99]

In the Laem Chabang case, however, the Japanese were concerned that a project loan already committed be carried out. This led embassy officials, backed up by communications from Tokyo, to pressure the Thai government into acting to suppress the communications ministry's demands. They were not averse to linking abrogation of the loan to future aid for the entire program. Given the communications minister's minority position in the cabinet and the parliament, the final outcome is not surprising.

The Laem Chabang case is a good instance of Thai and Japanese accommodation to maintain the overall relationship. Japan was clearly the dominant aid donor to Thailand by the early 1980s, and the largest donor of aid to the ESDP. That put it in a nearly monopolistic position for funding the latter. It could therefore afford to threaten to stop funding future development of the whole program if a project loan were canceled, which is what it in fact did with the Laem Chabang loan. While there were other donors available, their resources were simply insufficient for them to act as substitutes for Japanese aid. Moreover, because the ESDP comprised such a large part of Japan's loan aid to Thailand, Japan acquired a stake in the smooth implementation of the project. It would consequently frown on major reversals of policy. Also, given the fact that Thailand is a major recipient of Japan's aid, its desire to cancel a loan would compromise Japan's ability to honor its aid increase pledges to other donors. The aid authorities in the Thai government could use the donor's preference to continue the project to bring a recalcitrant Cabinet minister into line.

Accommodation is imperfect. This chapter has discussed a few examples. For one thing, players in the system change. Bureaucrats who have fostered good relations with counterparts are transferred or retire. Second, the players' capabilities change. The fumbling in the Aquino administration early in its tenure, and the emergence of the neophyte DAR into the bilateral aid relationship, highlight the effect of change in players and capabilities. Third, the players' stakes in the game change. Japanese companies, at least the big trading companies, are now less enthusiastic about aid because they derive fewer benefits. As can be seen from the increasing frequency of Thai complaints in the 1980s about Japanese companies in the system, the Thais are probably not unhappy to see that happen. Accommodation persists because it helps foster a cooperative aid relationship, but there is nothing automatic about it.

The concept of accommodation inherently means that there are potentially divergent interests to accommodate. We must be sure not to ignore the existence of conflict in this discussion of accommodation. Rather, we should understand accommodation and its components as a way to resolve potential or actual conflicts at one level so that cooperation can take place at another level.

One way the recipients have helped to resolve the potential for conflict is by anticipating donor preferences. Another way is by taking what they are offered. This seems to be the case particularly in the grant aid programs, where the possibility of agency slack is greatest. Evidence suggests that actors in the recipient governments look on grant aid in a much more opportunistic light than they do loan aid because there is no direct cost associated with repayment.[100] There are also many more of them because the smaller scale of grant funding means that more agencies can aspire to get it. On the other hand, grant aid is an avowed tool of the Japanese diplomatic tool kit, as the Ayutthaya case demonstrates. It is also an instrument of Japan's industrial policy. Fertilizer grants, for example, help dispose of excess capacity in the Japanese chemical industry. Japan has provided such aid to both recipients even while ASEAN was developing fertilizer project proposals to take advantage of Fukuda Doctrine aid. Indeed, Thailand continued to receive fertilizer through the aid program as it was preparing, and later cancelling, its own plans for a soda ash project in the ESDP. Finally, trends in the international aid regime have affected grant aid. The shift toward agriculture and social development in the early 1980s owes as much to shifts in international aid strategy and a concurrent shift in Japanese aid philosophy as it does to recipient priorities. Indeed, given the bias in both recipient countries toward urban development, the rural component of the Japanese grant program looks like a case of opportunistic substitution of resources the recipient might otherwise have had to provide.[101]

Finally, accommodation is not always optimal because it does not necessarily address certain types of problems. The Philippines is an excellent example of the coincidence of narrow interests between donor and recipient governments. The Marcos Documents make it clear that corruption was tolerated because wider considerations about the aid relationship were ignored.[102] Japanese ODA to the Philippines tended to increase every year regardless of need, absorptive capacity, political situation, economic situation, or availability of good projects. The nominal increase in aid volume also helped mask the need to address the slack created by institutional inadequacies on both sides, such as the lack of personnel, administrative integration, clear goals, executive accountability, and the political will to implement potentially disruptive social programs. The National Maritime Polytechnic and the Twelfth Yen Loan negotiations demonstrate the lack of strategic thinking; in both cases political decisions about the use of aid were subordinated to narrow considerations of meeting specific requests.

The discussion of environmental aid suggests that accommodation can occur at the expense of some ideal conceptions of recipient needs and priorities. As noted above, Thailand is willing to forgo some priorities for the sake of achieving others. The agrarian reform case also illustrates the problem. New ideas, no matter how meritorious, must find vehicles that conform to the requirements of an imperfect system because the system itself does not change to incorporate the new ideas. In this study we have seen the recipients repeatedly accept less than perfect solutions because that is the best they are likely to get, given the structural constraints of the bilateral aid system. The recipients' planners understand this, and the evidence makes it clear that they are willing to make the trade-off.

7

Conclusion

Aid givers are not fairy godmothers.
You must know what you want
and be flexible in your methods of getting it.

—Singaporean aid administrator[1]

This study has examined Japan's aid relationships with Thailand and the Philippines. Broadly, it concludes that the recipients get the kind of aid they want, although there is evidence that they do not get everything they want. There is a surprising degree of uniformity between what recipients include for foreign funding in their development plans and the kind of aid they get. This suggests a broad agreement between donors and recipients about the appropriate role of government in fostering economic development. Japan tends to give aid to those sectors programmed for foreign aid. Moreover, it gives loan aid to those sectors programmed for loan aid, and grants to those programmed for grant aid. Japan has also given aid to projects designated as high priority in the development plans. It also tends to distribute its aid projects to those regions favored by the recipient governments, although it is clear that stated regional development priorities and actual distributions of government resources differ; Japan's aid tends to reflect this contradiction in recipient policy. In neither case do the terms of aid appear amenable to permanent change by the recipients themselves. Aid terms—interest rates, repayment periods, grant/loan ratios—are set in Tokyo for categories of recipients. While aid terms have become more concessional over time, the process is beyond the control of individual recipients.

The evidence that Japan responds to individual recipient priorities is reinforced by the differences in the aid programs in Thailand and the

Philippines. Thailand has taken a more restrictive borrowing strategy, limiting concessional borrowing to individual projects and relending schemes, while the Philippines has used concessional borrowing for both projects and balance of payments recovery. Japan's aid reflects those differences in priorities. Aid to Thailand focuses on project aid and two-step loans, although it has given some program aid since 1989. Its aid to the Philippines is more diverse and includes project aid, program loans, cofinanced loans and commodity loans.

Thailand and the Philippines get the kind of aid they want because they accommodate the interests of the major actors in the aid relationship. The aid relationships should be seen as iterated games in which the major players—the aid bureaucracies in each country and the Japanese consulting and trading firms that provide the requisite technical skills—interact repeatedly in an environment of bureaucratic politics. Over time, the planning authorities and the relevant bureaucrats in the implementing agencies in the recipient governments learn how to play the aid game with Japan. Consequently, they make their aid requests fit the priorities and criteria of the Japanese aid program through the process of anticipatory bargaining. At one level of anticipatory bargaining, the planning authorities assess development projects included in the sectoral plans in terms of their suitability for request in the annual aid negotiations. At another level, the process also goes on at the agency level during the prebargaining phase. At this level, informal communication among project entrepreneurs, including Japanese companies, the recipient ministries and the Japanese aid field offices helps determine which projects are likely to be reviewed for Japanese aid funding by the recipient planning authorities. Anticipatory bargaining is essentially a process of agenda setting.

For the most part, accommodation is implicit in the aid relationship. A major actor probably does not say, "We must accommodate JICA or company X because it enhances the aid relationship in which we operate." More likely he says "company X's proposal is the alternative most likely to get funded this year," or "ministry Y's proposal meets our criteria."

Anticipatory bargaining is not deterministic. Project proposals that survive the prebargaining process do not automatically make the short list for request for aid, nor do short-listed projects automatically survive the annual negotiations with the Japanese government. Chapter Six also makes it clear that projects are subject to renegotiation or cancellation even after the implementation process has begun.

Why do donor and recipient enter this cooperative relationship? The donor has an incentive to cooperate because it has a good (aid) that it wants to give its partner. The good provides no benefits to donor or recipient unless it is given away. Cooperation allows the donor the ability to fulfill the purpose of its aid. The recipient's incentive to cooperate is clearer. The recipient planners calculate that without aid their development objectives would materialize at a slower rate, or might not materialize at all. Getting the donor to give, that is to enter the game, creates the first incentive to cooperate.

Why do donor and recipient continue to cooperate? Once the donor enters into the game, its aid bureaucracy continues to cooperate because doing so allows it to continue to fulfill its functions. That is, the aid bureaucracy, having begun to give aid, will have created a clientele that depends on that aid. It also acquires a stake in the budgetary process at home. The donor also has incentives to cooperate because its aid has purposes that are more than monetary. Since Japan sees Thailand and the Philippines as important foreign policy objects, it uses aid as a way to foster good political relations with them. The recipient's incentive to continue to cooperate stems from the fact that it wants to continue to receive aid. Thailand and the Philippines continue to have development needs which they perceive as requiring foreign aid to resolve.

What does the experience of the Thai and Philippines governments suggest for other potential aid recipients? We can discern five basic rules for getting aid from a donor. First, know the donor. This seems obvious, yet the discussion of learning in previous chapters suggests that this is vital to the success of a recipient's calculations. The institutions that comprise the environment in which aid negotiations take place are governed by routines and standard operating procedures. This situation at once creates the need for accommodation and makes it work. Without more active attempts by the donor to seek out ways to satisfy recipient needs, the recipient is forced to accommodate the rhythms and preferences of the donor's aid system. Set bureaucratic procedures create stability by repeatedly channeling actions through set processes. The recipient learns what the donor's preferences are, and what it can do to make its preferences fit them. This reduces uncertainty because the players come to understand one another's expectations and capabilities.

Institutional adaptation helps the planning authorities in the recipient countries in particular learn how to deal with Japan's aid program. In part, this is due to the fact that key personnel stay longer in their aid-related roles than do their Japanese counterparts.[2] It is also due to the recipients' institutional adaptations to the Japanese aid program. The existence of the implementing officer in the Philippines during the Marcos years represented a response to the importance of Japan as an aid donor. Whatever one may say about the potential for abuse of the authority in that position, its abolition undoubtedly hindered the Aquino government's early attempts to absorb aid after 1986. The new PFC, CODA, and the CCPAP were established to handle the overall aid program, not the Japanese aid program specifically.

Thailand's institutional adjustments to the Japanese foreign aid program have been smoother. DTEC and NESDB operate in the aid relationship as they did in the early 1970s. Although NESDB acquired greater say in the disposition of the development budget in the 1980s, there is no evidence that it changed its organizational structure to take account of the importance of the Japanese aid program. DTEC decisions about Japanese grant aid are made at a different level than for other donors, although this does not seem to have made project coordination any more effective. In sum, accommodation persists because the recipient has made the institutional changes needed to take advantage of the donor's resources.

Cultivation of a donor, especially a large one like Japan, is worth the effort because it reduces transaction costs of looking for aid elsewhere. The MAI experience in the Philippines illustrates this point. Italy joined the initiative as a new donor in 1988. While the Philippine government welcomed its willingness to assist the recipient's economic reconstruction, NEDA found that donor and recipient had to adjust to unfamiliar aid procedures. The result was to slow down disbursements of Italian aid, reducing the utility of its contribution.[3]

A second rule is ask the donor for aid it can give. For idealists, this will be disappointing. For realists, particularly those employed in developing country governments, this is a necessity. Aid relationships are asymmetrical. If we assume that "cooperation occurs when actors adjust their behavior to the actual or anticipated preferences of others, through a process of policy coordination,"[4] this study would conclude that the recipients adjust their behavior to suit the donor's aid program more than the donor adjusts its program to suit recipient aspirations. This is the case for several reasons.

First, the donor has less incentive to adjust its policy for a particular recipient than the recipient does because the number of recipients with which a donor has to deal is greater than the number of donors with which a recipient must deal. Therefore, the resources and attention it can devote to a recipient's specific needs are limited. Second, donor aid policy is subject to factors exogenous to the bilateral aid relationships. OECD pressure on Japan to soften its aid terms is more effective than LDC pressure and, in any case, the combination of the two is more effective than the requests of single recipients. Similarly, the Japanese government's notion that it should balance aid giving among ASEAN members sets limits on its flexibility and willingness to meet individual recipient requests. Third, the share of the donor's aid to a particular recipient in its overall aid budget will likely be smaller than the share of its aid in the recipient's budget. The relative weights of the aid program to donor and recipient favor the donor. As noted above, ODA has accounted for a tiny portion of the total Japanese government budget in the years under study. Thailand and the Philippines, while important recipients, have never accounted individually for more than 12 percent of the ODA budget in any year, and have usually accounted for less than that. Conversely, Japan's aid comprised up to half of the recipients' total aid inflows in the 1970s, and more than that in the 1980s. We saw above that certain sectors and development programs relied heavily on Japan's aid. Because the addition or subtraction of any increment of aid is more important to recipient than donor, the recipient is in a weak bargaining position. Recipients do not possess the power to demand or coerce the Japanese government into giving them aid, nor do they have the ability to influence the decisions of the Japanese aid bureaucracy, except at the margins. Therefore, they bargain within the limits of an environment major parts of which they cannot control.

Thailand and the Philippines accommodate Japan because they have to. International efforts to better the lot of aid recipients, such as calls for a New International Economic Order, have not been successful. In the absence of overarching institutions to improve recipients' positions, they are forced to deal with individual donors. Those donors' capabilities vary. In general, those that provide the most favorable aid terms have small budgets,[5] limiting their usefulness to recipients with large projects or development plans in mind. As we saw with the failure of the sources of funds approach in Thailand during the Second Plan period, the Laem Chabang port loan, and the replacement of the United States by Japan as the Philippines' primary aid donor, there are very few donors with which these recipients can interact on a large scale. If anything, the dependence on Japanese aid has increased as the United States has withdrawn its military presence from the region. As a result, the incentives to find common ground with their primary donor is great while the incentives to stand fast in opposition to the donor on any specific item is small. The payoff for insisting on a particular priority is not worth the risk of jeopardizing many others.

We see this in the 1983 Marcos request for a commodity loan to support the copper industry, cited in the introduction. The amount requested was in the hundreds of millions of dollars, as large as any annual loan package at the time, and would have required extensive revision of ongoing project negotiations. The Japanese prime minister told him so, and he dropped the request.

A third rule is that it helps to be an important recipient. The incentive to give, on Japan's part, helps equalize what otherwise looks like a relationship in which one side acts as supplicant and the other as benefactor. Japan has good reason to give aid to the Philippines and Thailand each year besides the desire to maintain good relations with the recipient governments. Since the late 1970s, Japan's aid budget has risen consistently in response to its promises to the international community to increase its ODA within specific periods of time. Since Thailand and the Philippines are among the top ten aid recipients, Japan's ability to disburse aid to them, and so live up to its international responsibilities, becomes critical. As one observer noted, Japan's reluctance to cut loan funding to Thailand in the late 1980s was due partly to the trouble Indonesia and the Philippines had in absorbing the aid Japan had committed to them; if Thailand significantly reduced its OECF borrowing, Japan's ability to meet annual aid targets would suffer.[6]

The insulation of aid from other policy areas reinforces the push to disburse funds. Political conditions in the recipient country are weakly correlated with overall Japanese aid policy. For the recipient government this would seem to be an advantage. Neither a major change of government coupled with aid scandal in the Philippines nor recurrent coups d'états in Thailand have provoked Japan into suspending its aid. In the wake of the 1991 coup in Thailand, for example, Japan announced it would suspend negotiations on "new aid" only, which simply delayed agreement on the annual aid package by a few months. In other words, bureaucratic pressures reinforced foreign policy considerations in the provision of larger annual aid packages.

Being a major recipient has other advantages. In particular, being an annual aid recipient provides the opportunity to learn, and therefore anticipate, donor preferences and capabilities. This allows the recipient to adjust the potential power imbalance in the bilateral program. The conventional view of asymmetrical cooperation is that the weaker player will cooperate because the stronger player can coerce it into doing so.[7] The slack built into the donor's role seems to confirm this. Yet, there are instances in which the supposedly weaker power obtains better terms than we would expect from the stronger.[8] Clearly, there are ways in which weaker players get what they want from stronger players. There are strategies within the framework of accommodation that allow them to do so. Anticipatory bargaining allows the recipient to strengthen what appears to be a weak position. Anticipatory bargaining and prebargaining are critical in the aid relationship because in a repetitive game the recipient can forecast donor behavior and therefore modify its demands to better meet mutually satisfactory solutions. Anticipatory bargaining and prebargaining help the negotiators define and simplify the negotiation process by determining what to negotiate. These activities are agenda-setting devices, and because of the request principle in Japan's aid policy, the recipient takes the lead in setting the agenda for specific sets of negotiations.

The recipient's bargaining position is strengthened by the fact that Japan is reluctant to link economic aid with the recipient's political performance. It is clear from the aid relationship with the Marcos administration that accommodation was possible because the Japanese government turned a blind eye to the political consequences for the Philippines of its aid. It has also reacted mildly to repeated coups d'états and coup attempts, and the Japanese government, particularly the Ministry of Foreign Affairs, is reluctant to suspend aid negotiations or agreements. Specific project implementation may be delayed by political instability in a certain region of Thailand or the Philippines, but the aid program as a whole will continue. While policy ambiguity can lead to suboptimal outcomes, which are inherent to the accommodation of interests, it can also act as the grease that keeps the aid relationships running.

Fourth, the recipient planners must channel the slack in their aid programs. For reasons outlined above, it is impossible to eliminate agency slack completely. The organization process model alerts us to the fact that bureaucracies rarely establish clear priorities. Much less can we expect clarity of priorities in the interactions of complex organizations which are autonomous from one another. Accommodation occurs in an environment of institutional weakness. The donor has its own interests. Moreover, for all its recent pronouncements, Japan's aid bureaucracy still operates on the request principle, and its people in the field are still few in number. The policymaking ministries in Tokyo still rotate their policy-level personnel every two or three years, so that just as bureaucrats become expert at the aid process they are transferred elsewhere.

On the recipient side, aid is subject to conflicting demands. Agency slack in the recipient governments reinforces the difficulty of establishing hierarchies of clear priorities. The aid planners still tend to see aid in terms of the two-gap model, as a way to cover the difference between domestic savings and public expenditure. Implementing agencies, on the other hand, are more concerned with the gap between their own budgets and the projects they wish to undertake. Even enterprising university professors, albeit on a much lower level in the grant program, see aid as a way to get new facilities or to fund research projects. Indeed, we may say of the grant programs that agency slack is dealt with by being ignored.

Limiting the number of players enhances the possibility of channeling slack. A small number of players limits competition, making interactions more predictable. The point of prebargaining is to reduce competition, and therefore disagreement, at the formal negotiating table. The aid bureaucrats in Japan and the planning authorities in the recipient government are the most important promoters of accommodation because they limit the competition for serious funding consideration to a few proposals. They also deal with one another repeatedly. This is particularly important on the recipient side because the planning authorities, acting as negotiators at the annual bilateral negotiations, will almost certainly negotiate with Japan more often than any other recipient actors. Their expectations about what the Japanese aid program can do and how it works are more accurate than any other actors' on the recipient side.

Consider also that renegotiation or delay of agreed aid projects is forced by actors other than the planning authorities. Simply put, the line agencies in the recipient governments are likely to be less habituated to the accommodation process and therefore more likely to try to force cancellation or modification of projects. The literature on cooperation so far deals with the importance of the number of players in a negotiation in terms of the ability to cooperate.[9] This study suggests that limiting the range of players is as important as simply limiting the number of them.

Fifth, tolerate ambiguity. We began by asking whether two developing countries have gotten what they want from one donor country's aid. The existence of two levels of agency slack facing the recipient principals suggests not only that they must accommodate donor interests and conditions, but that "recipient interest" itself is not monolithic. Rather, developing country governments are subject to competing internal pressures for aid, some of which are met while others are not. The sum of agencies receiving assistance may or may not add up to the "national interest."

Despite obvious drawbacks, ambiguity has its utility. Policy ambiguity abets accommodation. We saw this in the case of environmental aid to Thailand. It occurs on a broader level because Japan has no basic aid law delineating policy objectives. Policy therefore gets made on a case-by-case basis. Because aid decisions are confined largely to the aid bureaucracy, they will tend to be made on administrative grounds. This style of decisionmaking allows Japan's aid policy makers to avoid the thorny problems of political acceptability. It also allows recipient and donor, and their agents, to find projects that meet their multifarious interests.

It was noted above that Japan gives aid for several reasons. Ambiguity in aid philosophy can work to the recipient's advantage. The New Village Development Program in Thailand, discussed in Chapter Three, provides a good example of how ambiguity can smooth over politically difficult issues. Whatever political and security considerations the Thai government may have applied to the program, Japan could justify its provision of aid based on the argument that it was making the grant to promote rural economic development. Ambiguity allowed donor and recipient to view the program from the perspective of their own criteria.

Why is the idea of accommodation important? It helps us explain a broader range of activities in Japan's foreign aid than is found in the usual research on that topic. Accommodation alerts us to recipient aspirations and how they affect Japan's behavior in the aid field. While accommodation allows for donor interest, it helps us account for situations in which particular Japanese interests, such as resource diplomacy or private sector profit, cannot explain outcomes. For example, Japan's aid for the Eastern Seaboard of Thailand was intended to promote the industrial development of that country. Martin Rudner suggests that no specific Japanese interest would be served by funding that scheme.[10] While Japan, or perhaps observers of its aid program, may see aid the ESDP as a way to coordinate Japanese aid with other economic activities,[11] its origins lie elsewhere as do the Thai government's interests in planning and developing it. Similarly, it helps us explain outcomes that appear to satisfy recipient priorities less than fully because it acknowledges the fact that recipients must make trade-offs. Studying the accommodation of interests makes us take recipient government interests seriously, a viewpoint heretofore lacking in the foreign aid literature.

Notes

Introduction

1. Ministry of Foreign Affairs, *Keizai Kyoryoku Hyoka Hokokusho* (Economic Cooperation Evaluation Reports) (Tokyo: Gaimusho, March 1988): 54-55.
2. Robert M. Orr, *The Emergence of Japan's Foreign Aid Power* (New York: Columbia University Press, 1990); Alan Rix, *Japan's Economic Aid* (New York: St. Martin's Press, 1980); Alan Rix, *Japan's Foreign Aid Challenge: Policy Reform and Aid Leadership* (London: Routledge, 1993.)
3. Rix, 1980; Okita Saburo, *Japan's High Dependence on Natural Resource Imports and its Policy Implications* (Canberra: Australia-Japan Economic Relations Research Project, 1976.)
4. Dennis Yasutomo, *The Manner of Giving: Strategic Aid and Japanese Foreign Policy* (Lexington, MA: Lexington Books, 1986); Orr, 1990; Robert M. Orr, "Nihon no Atarashii Buki, ODA" (Japan's New Weapon, ODA), *Seiron* (January 1989); Shafiqul Islam, ed., *Yen for Development* (New York: Council on Foreign Relations, 1991); Dennis Yasutomo, *The New Multilateralism in Japan's Foreign Policy* (New York: St. Martin's Press, 1995).
5. See Igarashi Takeshi, ed., *Nihon no ODA to Kokusai Chitsujo* (Japan's ODA and the International Order) (Tokyo: Association for the Promotion of International Cooperation, 1990); Kusano Atsushi, *ODA Itcho Ni Sen Oku En no Yukue* (The Direction of One Trillion Two Hundred Billion Yen of ODA) (Tokyo: Toyo Keizai Shinposha, 1993); Susan Pharr, "Japanese Aid in the New World Order," in Craig Garby and Mary Brown Bullock, eds., *Japan: A New Kind of Superpower?* (Washington, DC: Woodrow Wilson Center Press, 1994); Alan Rix, "Japan's Foreign Aid Policy: A Capacity for Leadership?" *Pacific Affairs* 62 (winter 1989-90): 461-75; Rix, 1993; Inada Juichi, "Jinken, Minshuka to Enjo Seisaku" (Human Rights, Democratization and Aid Policy) *Kokusai Mondai* (May 1995): 2-17.
6. Orr, 1990; John Sewell and W. Patrick Murphy, *The United States and Japan in Southeast Asia: Is a Shared Development Agenda Possible?* (Washington, DC: Overseas Development Council, May 1991); Julia Chang Bloch, "A US-Japan Aid Alliance?" in Islam, ed., pp. 70-87; Robert Orr, "Collaboration or Conflict? Foreign Aid and U.S.-Japan Relations," *Pacific Affairs* 62 (winter 1989-90): 476-89.
7. Hasegawa Sukehiro, *Japanese Foreign Aid* (New York: Praeger Publishers, 1975); Margee Ensign, *Doing Good or Doing Well?* (New York: Columbia University Press, 1992); David Arase, "Public-Private Sector Interest Coordination in Japan's ODA," *Pacific Affairs* 67 (summer 1994): 171-99; David Arase, *Buying Power: the Political Economy of Japan's Foreign Aid* (Boulder, Colorado: Lynne Rienner, 1995).

8. See, for example, Doi Takako, et al, *ODA Kakumei* (ODA Revolution) (Tokyo: Shakai Sozosha, 1990); Mainichi Shinbun Shakaibu, *Kokusai Enjo Bijinesu* (The International Aid Business) (Tokyo: Mainichi Shinbunsha, 1990); Murai Yoshinori et al., *Musekinin Enjo Taikoku Nippon* (Japan, the Irresponsible Aid Great Power) (Tokyo: JICC Shuppankyoku, 1989); Murai Yoshinori, ed., *Kensho: Nippon no ODA* (Testimony: Japan's ODA) (Tokyo: Gakuyo Shobo, 1992); Sumi Kazuo, *ODA: Enjo no Genjitsu* (ODA: The Reality of Aid) (Tokyo: Iwanami Shoten, 1989). For a rare comprehensive study of Japan's aid to a particular recipient, see Yokoyama Masaki, *Fuiripin Enjo to Jiriki Koseiron* (Philippine Aid and Self-Help) (Tokyo: Akashi Shoten, 1990).

9. John White, *The Politics of Foreign Aid* (New York: St. Martin's Press, 1974); Teresa Hayter and Catherine Watson, *Aid: Rhetoric and Reality* (London: Pluto Press, 1985); Paul Mosley, *Foreign Aid: Its Defense and Reform*. (Lexington, KY: University Press of Kentucky, 1987); Robert Cassen et al., *Does Aid Work?* (Oxford, England: Clarendon Press, 1986).

10. Gun Kut, *Foreign Economic Assistance and Third World Development: Assessment of the Effects of a Global Policy* (PhD. Diss., State University of New York at Binghamton, 1987); David Lumsdaine, *Moral Vision in International Politics: the Foreign Aid Regime, 1949-1989* (Princeton, NJ: Princeton University Press, 1993).

11. Leon Gordenker, *International Aid and National Decisions* (Princeton, NJ: Princeton University Press, 1976).

12. Mosley, pp. 93-95.

13. Cassen et al., p. 89; Anne O. Kreuger, Constantin Michalopoulos, and Vernon Ruttan, *Aid and Development* (Baltimore: Johns Hopkins University Press, 1989), p. 98.

14. White, esp. pp. 88-97; Keith Jay and Constantin Michalopoulos, "Interactions Between Donors and Recipients," in Kreuger, Michalopoulos, and Ruttan, p. 91.

15. Paul Mosley, Jane Harrigan, and John Toye, *Aid and Power: The World Bank and Policy-Based Lending* vol. 1 (London: Routledge, 1991); Howard Lehman, *Indebted Development* (New York: St. Martin's Press, 1993).

16. *Compendium of Aid Procedures* (Paris: Organization for Economic Cooperation and Development, 1981), pp. 71-72.

17. White, pp. 89-90.

18. Ibid., pp. 78-88.

19. Naomi Caiden and Aaron Wildavsky, *Planning and Budgeting in Poor Countries* (New York: John Wiley and Sons, 1974); Dennis Rondinelli, "The Dilemma of Development Administration: Complexity and Uncertainty in Control-Oriented Bureaucracies," *World Politics* (October 1982): 43-72.

20. Terry Moe, "The New Economics of Organization," *American Journal of Political Science* 28 (September 1984): 739-77; Jonathan Bendor, Serge Taylor, and Roland Van Gaalen, "Stacking the Deck: Bureaucratic Missions and Policy Design," *American Political Science Review* 81 (September 1987): 873-96; Mark Ramseyer and Frances Rosenbluth, *Japan's Political Marketplace* (Cambridge, MA: Harvard University Press, 1993).

21. Peter Bachrach and Morton Baratz, "The Two Faces of Power," *American Political Science Review* 61 (December 1962): 947-52.

22. Ibid., 952n.

23. For Japan's perceptions of its interests in Southeast Asia see Charles Morrison, "Japan and the ASEAN Countries: The Evolution of Japan's Regional Role," in Takashi Inoguchi and Daniel Okimoto, eds., *The Political Economy of Japan* vol. 2 (Stanford, CA: Stanford University Press, 1998), pp. 414-15. For discussions of Japan's aid to Southeast Asia see Bruce Koppel and Robert Orr, eds., *Japan's Foreign Aid: Power and Policy in a New Era* (Boulder, Colorado: Westview Press, 1993); Rix, 1993, pp. 134-60.

Chapter 1

1. John White, *The Politics of Foreign Aid* (New York: St. Martin's Press, 1974), p. 75.
2. Bruce Koppel and Robert M. Orr, "A Donor of Consequence: Japan as a Foreign Aid Power," in Bruce Koppel and Robert M. Orr, eds., *Japan's Foreign Aid: Power and Policy in a New Era* (Boulder, Colorado: Westview Press, 1993), pp. 1-18.
3. Robert Wood, *From Marshall Plan to Debt Crisis* (Berkeley and Los Angeles: University of California Press, 1986), pp. 94-137, passim.
4. Wolfgang G. Friedman, George Kalmanoff, and Robert Meagher, *International Financial Aid* (New York: Columbia University Press, 1966), pp. 234-35.
5. In the 1950s Japan negotiated reparations agreements with Indonesia, the Philippines, Burma, and South Vietnam, and economic cooperation agreements with Cambodia, Laos, Malaysia, South Korea, Singapore, and Thailand. Payments ranged from $39 million to South Vietnam over five years to $550 million to the Philippines over twenty years. Payments were made in private sector goods and services, loans, cash grants, and technical assistance.
6. Alan Rix, *Japan's Economic Aid* (New York: St. Martin's Press, 1980).
7. Hasegawa Sukehiro, *Japanese Foreign Aid* (New York: Praeger, 1975), pp. 26-27; Ministry of International Trade and Industry, *Keizai Kyoryoku no Genjo to Mondaiten* (Current Situation and Problems of Japan's Economic Cooperation) (Tokyo: Tsusho Sangyosho, selected years).
8. Organization for Economic Cooperation and Development, *Development Cooperation* (Paris: Organization for Economic Cooperation and Development, 1975), pp. 106-09.
9. Toru Yanagihara and Anne Emig, "An Overview of Japan's Foreign Aid," in Shafiqul Islam, ed., *Yen for Development* (New York: Council on Foreign Relations Press, 1991), pp. 41-42.
10. Ministry of Foreign Affairs, *Japan's Official Development Assistance* (Tokyo: Association for the Promotion of International Cooperation, 1994) p. 17.
11. Dennis Yasutomo, *The Manner of Giving* (Lexington, MA: Lexington Books, 1986), pp. 1-2.
12. *Japan's Official Development Assistance,* (1993), p. 20.
13. *Japan's Official Development Assistance* (1987), p. 106; *Waga Kuni no Seifu Kaihatsu Enjo* vol. 1, (Tokyo: Association for the Promotion of International Cooperation, 1994), p. 32.
14. Juichi Inada, "Japan's Aid Diplomacy: Increasing Role for Global Security," *Japan Review of International Affairs* (spring/summer 1988): 108.

15. Dennis Yasutomo, *Japan and the Asian Development Bank* (New York: Praeger, 1983); Dennis Yasutomo, "Japan and the Asian Development Bank: International Management or Mismanagement?" in Michael Blaker, ed., *Development Assistance to Southeast Asia* (New York: Columbia University Press, 1984); Dennis Yasutomo, "Japan and the Asian Development Bank," in Koppel and Orr, pp. 303-43.

16. *Japan's Official Development Assistance,* (1987), p. 120.

17. Catrinus Jepma, *The Tying of Aid* (Paris: OECD, 1991), p. 37.

18. See *Development Cooperation,* various years; *Japan's Official Development Assistance,* (1992), p. 18.

19. See *Nihon Keizai Shinbun,* June 8, 1995, p. 5.

20. *Far Eastern Economic Review* (March 10, 1988): 65; *Japan's Official Development Assistance* (1992), p. 26.

21. *Sankei Shinbun,* June 8, 1995, p. 11.

22. *Development Assistance for Southeast Asia* (Tokyo: Keizai Doyukai, 1970), p. 53.

23. Hasegawa, pp. 61-64.

24. William Brooks and Robert Orr, "Japan's Foreign Economic Assistance," *Asian Survey* 25 (March 1985): 329.

25. Shoko Tanaka, *Post-War Japanese Resource Policies and Strategies: The Case of Southeast Asia* (Ithaca, NY: Cornell University, 1986), p. 80.

26. Robert M. Orr, "The Rising Sun: Japan's Aid to ASEAN, the Pacific Basin, and the Republic of Korea," *Journal of International Affairs* (April 1987): 49. For a thorough discussion of the ASEAN response to the Fukuda proposal see Marjorie Suriyamongkol, *The Politics of ASEAN Economic Cooperation* (Singapore and New York: Oxford University Press, 1988).

27. Rix, 1980, p. 126.

28. Robert Orr, *The Emergence of Japan's Foreign Aid Power* (New York: Columbia University Press, 1990), pp. 39-40.

29. Rix, 1980, p. 223.

30. Ibid., p. 173.

31. Yasutomo, 1986, p. 71. One Japanese official commented that countries like India with well-established bureaucracies occasion more confidence than other LDCs.

32. Brooks and Orr, pp. 335-36; Rix, 1980, p. 151.

33. Rix, 1980, pp. 151-83. The ministry's International Finance Bureau has only fifteen people.

34. Author's interviews with an Overseas Economic Cooperation Fund official, Tokyo, November 27, 1990, and a JICA official, Tokyo, March 26, 1991.

35. Hassan Selim, *Development Assistance Policies and the Performance of Aid Agencies* (London: MacMillan Press, 1983), pp. 124-31.

36. Brooks and Orr, p. 338.

37. Selim, pp. 131-37.

38. *Japan's Official Development Assistance* (1987), p. 85.

39. *Business Week,* (January 18, 1988): 41; Overseas Economic Cooperation Fund, *Nenji Hokokusho* (Annual Report) (Tokyo: Overseas Economic Cooperation Fund, 1989), p. 1.

40. Overseas Economic Cooperation Fund, *Annual Report* (Tokyo: Overseas Economic Cooperation Fund, 1992), p. 1; *Japan's Official Development Assistance* (1992), p. 65.

41. Rix, 1980, pp. 265-67.
42. Ibid.
43. Robert Orr, "The Aid Factor in US-Japan Relations," *Asian Survey* 28 (July 1988): 743; Yasutomo (1986), pp. 70-71.
44. Bruce Koppel, "Cooperation or Co-prosperity? Asian Perspectives on Japan's Ascendancy as an Aid Power." (Paper presented at the Association for Asian Studies annual meeting, March 18, 1989).
45. Rix, 1980, p. 173.
46. David Arase, "Public-Private Sector Interest Coordination in Japan's ODA," *Asian Survey* 27 (summer 1994): 184-86.
47. Yasutomo, 1986, pp. 70-71; author's interviews with Ministry of Finance and JICA officials, January 23, 1991 and March 26, 1991.
48. Rix, 1980, pp. 205-17.
49. Ibid., pp. 205-08.
50. Author's interview with a Japanese embassy official, Washington, DC, March 22, 1989.
51. Orr, 1990, pp. 25-26.
52. Brooks and Orr, p. 323.
53. Yasutomo, 1986.
54. For a discussion of the limitations and possibilities of Japanese aid leadership see Rix, 1993.
55. Terutomo Ozawa, *Multinationalism, Japanese Style* (Princeton, NJ: Princeton University Press, 1979), pp. 177-78.
56. Hasegawa, pp. 89-94. For a longer-term view of Japan's resource diplomacy since the oil embargo see William Nester and Kweku Ampiah, "Japan's Oil Diplomacy: *Tatemae* and *Honne,*" *Third World Quarterly* 11 (January 1989): 72-88.
57. Yasutomo, 1986, pp. 60-64.
58. Inada, 1989, passim.
59. See *Japan's Official Development Assistance* (1992), pp. 44-67. For an overall assessment of the Charter see Rix, 1993, pp. 99-101. For an assessment of the new emphasis on environmental aid see David Potter, "Assessing Japan's Environmental Aid Policy," *Pacific Affairs* 27 (summer 1994): 200-15.
60. Alan Rix, "Japan's Foreign Aid Policy: A Capacity for Leadership?" *Pacific Affairs* 62 (winter 1989-90): 46-75. See also Rix, 1993, pp. 187-89.
61. Leon Gordenker, *International Aid and National Decisions* (Princeton, NJ: Princeton University Press, 1976); Romeo Reyes, *Absorptive Capacity for Foreign Aid: The Case of the Philippines* (Makati: Philippine Institute for Development Studies and International Center for Economic Growth, 1993), pp. 91-93.

Chapter 2

1. Shigeru Sugitani, *Japan's Economic Cooperation to Thailand* (Bangkok: Economic Cooperation Center for the Asian and Pacific Region, 1975), pp. 40-42.
2. In both the Thai and Philippine cases I have included most cultural grant aid commitments in this category. This type of grant is small, generally involving

commitments of a few thousand dollars. Most are given for at least nominally educational purposes, although their intent is to provide *omiyage*, presents that Japanese prime ministers and other cabinet ministers can bestow on host governments during official visits. In any case, some caution must be used in interpreting the significance of the education and manpower figures.

3. Following the Japanese Ministry of Foreign Affairs practice, I include all loan and grant projects involving two or more regions in the national category. This tends to overrepresent the "national" character of the Japanese aid program and underrepresents the actual allocations for some regions.

4. Miura Shumon, *Kore ga Seinen Kaigai Kyoryokutai Da* (This is the Japan Overseas Cooperation Volunteers) (Tokyo: Sanshusha, 1983), p. 1.

5. Ministry of International Trade and Industry, *Keizai Kyoryoku no Genjo to Mondaiten* (Current Situation and Problems of Japan's Economic Cooperation) (Tokyo: Tsusho Sangyosho, 1989) vol. 2, p. 773; Lawrence Olson, *Japan in Postwar Asia* (New York: Praeger, 1970), p. 177. Terms were comparable to the first Overseas Economic Cooperation Fund loans made to Thailand and Malaysia at about the same time.

Chapter 3

1. See International Bank for Reconstruction and Development, *A Public Development Program for Thailand* (Baltimore: Johns Hopkins University Press, 1959).

2. "Tai no Keizai Kaihatsu to Gaikoku Shakkan" (Thai Economic Development and Foreign Loans) *Kokusai Kaihatsu Janaru* (April 1981): 84.

3. Larry Sternstein, "Internal Migration and Regional Development: The Khon Kaen Development Centre of Northeast Thailand," *Journal of Southeast Asian Studies* 8 (March 1977): 107. Krung Thep and Maha Nakhon may be treated as part of metropolitan Bangkok.

4. Bruce London, *Metropolis and Nation in Thailand: The Political Economy of Uneven Development* (Boulder, Colorado: Westview Press, 1980), pp. 86-112.

5. Bruce London and Kristine L. Anderson, "Population Density and the Distribution of Infrastructural Resources in Thailand," *Sociological Quarterly* 26 (summer 1985): 245.

6. London, 1980, pp. 86-112; Robert Muscat, *Thailand and the United States* (New York: Columbia University Press, 1990), pp. 147-84.

7. National Economic and Social Development Board, *Second National Economic and Social Development Plan (1967-1971)* (Bangkok: National Economic and Social Development Board, @ 1967), p. 58.

8. National Economic and Social Development Board, *Summary of the Second Five-Year Plan (1967-1971)* (Bangkok, 1966), pp. 10-11.

9. C.J. Dixon, "Development, Regional Disparity, and Planning: The Experience of Northeast Thailand," *Journal of Southeast Asian Studies* 8 (September 1977): 213.

10. Muscat, 1990, pp. 185-87.

11. Ministry of Foreign Affairs, *Waga Kuni no Seifu Kaihatsu Enjo* vol. 2 (Tokyo: Association for the Promotion of International Cooperation, 1990), p. 277; *Japanese Contribution to the Kingdom of Thailand through OECF Loans* (Tokyo: Overseas Economic Cooperation Fund, 1983), pp. 19-21.

12. National Economic and Social Development Board. *Third National Economic and Social Development Plan (1972-1976)* (Bangkok: International Translations, 1972), pp. 321-23.

13. Lawrence Olson, *Japan in Postwar Asia* (New York: Praeger, 1970), pp. 218-21.

14. General Accounting Office, *Problems in Coordinating Multilateral Assistance to Thailand* (Report to the Congress by the Comptroller General of the United States, August 25, 1975), pp. 9-10; *Summary of the Second Five-Year Plan,* p. 8.

15. *Japanese Contribution to Economic Development of the Kingdom of Thailand through OECF Loans,* pp. 19-22; *Waga Kuni* (1990), vol. 1, p. 83.

16. *Third National Economic and Social Development Plan,* p. 88. No loan aid was programmed for commerce and services.

17. Ibid., pp. 36, 141-60.

18. Ibid., pp. 88-89; Japan External Trade Organization, *Japan's Economic Cooperation* (Tokyo: Japan External Trade Organization, 1980), pp. 68-69; *Japanese Contribution to Economic Development of the Kingdom of Thailand through OECF Loans,* pp. 23-32.

19. *Japanese Economic Contribution to the Kingdom of Thailand through OECF Loans,* pp. 26-31; *Waga Kuni* (1990), vol. 2, pp. 77, 83.

20. *Third National Economic and Social Development Plan,* p. 99.

21. *Japan's Economic Cooperation* (1980), pp. 68-69.

22. Olof Murelius, *An Institutional Approach to Project Analysis in the Developing Countries* (Paris: Organization for Economic Cooperation and Development, 1981), p. 41. Exim Bank lending is consistent with Wood's assertion that aid for industrial projects is not only scarce but expensive.

23. Khien Theeravit et al., *Research Report on Danish, German and Japanese Assistance to Agricultural Development in Thailand: A Comparative Study* (Bangkok: Institute of Asian Studies, Chulalongkorn University, 1984), p. 245.

24. *Waga Kuni no Seifu Kaihatsu Enjo* vol. 2 (Tokyo: Association for the Promotion of International Cooperation, 1990), pp. 77, 80; Theeravit, pp. 60-69, 80-81.

25. *Japanese Contribution to Economic Development of the Kingdom of Thailand through OECF Loans,* pp. 28, 30.

26. *Third National Economic and Social Development Plan,* p. 98.

27. *Waga Kuni* (1990), vol. 1, p. 84.

28. Shigeru Sugitani, *Japan's Economic Assistance to Thailand* (Bangkok: Economic Cooperation Center for the Asian and Pacific Region, 1975), p. 42.

29. Ibid., pp. 41-44.

30. Sudo Sueo, "The Politics of Thai-Japanese Trade Relations: A Study of Negotiation Behavior," in Chaiwat Khamchoo and Bruce Reynolds, eds., *Thai-Japanese Relations in Historical Perspective* (Bangkok: Institute of Asian Studies, Chulalongkorn University, 1988), pp. 217-22.

31. Ibid., p. 221.

32. For a summary of the Fukuda Doctrine's implications see Alan Rix, *Japan's Economic Aid* (New York: St. Martin's Press, 1980), pp. 232-33.

33. World Bank, *Thailand: Managing Public Resources for Structural Adjustment* (Washington, DC: World Bank, 1984).

34. National Economic and Social Development Board, *Fourth National Economic and Social Development Plan (1977-1981)* (Bangkok: National Economic and Social Development Board, 1976), p. 79.

35. Ibid., pp. 224-30.

36. Ibid., p. 231.

37. Dennis Yasutomo, *The Manner of Giving* (Lexington, MA: Lexington Books, 1986), pp. 43-44; *Japanese Contribution to Economic Development of the Kingdom of Thailand through OECF Loans,* p. 3.

38. *Fourth National Economic and Social Development Plan,* p. 78; *Japanese Contribution to Economic Development of the Kingdom of Thailand through OECF Loans,* p. 32.

39. *Japanese Contribution to Economic Development of the Kingdom of Thailand through OECF Loans,* pp. 38-42.

40. Ibid.

41. Ibid., pp. 37-38, 47.

42. Ibid.

43. *Japan's Economic Cooperation* (1980), p. 67; *Waga Kuni* (1990), vol. 1, p. 80.

44. Yasutomo, 1986, p. 43. There is some debate about the role of the United States in pressing for greater aid for countries like Thailand during this period. Yet neither Yasutomo nor Muscat (1990), in their respective treatment of the Japanese and American foreign aid programs in Thailand, give the American factor much consideration in this case. The United States government did ask Japan to support countries important to the Western alliance, and the two countries' donor agencies engaged in a largely abortive cooperative agriculture development project in the Northeast, but available evidence suggests that the United States' suggestions that Japan increase its aid to Thailand amounted to preaching to the converted.

45. Japan International Cooperation Agency, Medical Cooperation Department, *A Guide to Medical Cooperation Activities* (Tokyo: Japan International Cooperation Agency, @ 1985), pp. 12-13; *Asahi Shinbun,* October 10, 1980, p. 13.

46. Japan limited its role to provision of materials and equipment. "New Village Development Program: A Bottom-Up Approach in the Rural Development Movement," *News Bulletin* (November-December 1978): 12-13.

47. Ibid.

48. Robert Muscat, *The Fifth Tiger* (Armonk, NY: M. E. Sharpe, 1994), pp. 80-81.

49. National Economic and Social Development Board, *Fifth National Economic and Social Development Plan (1982-1986) and Its External Assistance Requirements* (Bangkok: National Economic and Social Development Board, @ 1981), p. 37.

50. National Economic and Social Development Board, *Fifth National Economic and Social Development Plan (1982-1986)* (Bangkok: National Economic and Social Development Board, 1981), pp. 125-58. For an assessment of the rural development planning effort see Muscat, 1994, pp. 181-82.

51. Yasutomo, 1986, p. 95.

52. *Waga Kuni* (1990), vol. 1, pp. 74, 79-80.

53. Ibid., pp. 74, 79-81.

54. Phisit Pakkasem, *Leading Issues in Thailand's Development Transformation, 1960-1990* (Bangkok: National Economic and Social Development Board, Office of the Prime Minister, 1988), p. 23.

55. *Third National Economic and Social Development Plan,* p. 147.

56. National Economic and Social Development Board, *Sixth National Economic and Social Development Plan (1987-1991)* (Bangkok: National Economic and Social Development Board, 1986), p. 275. See also *Bangkok Post,* January 25, 1983, p. 21.

57. *Waga Kuni* (1990), vol. 1, pp. 74, 79-80.

58. Ibid.

59. *Fifth National Economic and Social Development Plan* (1981), p. 292.

60. *Waga Kuni* (1990), vol. 1, p. 74, 79-80.

61. *Fifth National Economic and Social Development Plan* (1981), p. 109.

62. *Asahi Shinbun,* June 5, 1981, p. 9.

63. *Waga Kuni* (1990), vol.1, pp. 74, 79-80; Ministry of International Trade and Industry, *Keizai Kyoryoku no Genjo to Mondaiten* (Current Situation and Problems of Japan's Economic Cooperation) (Tokyo: Tsusansho, 1984), p. 436.

64. Bank of Thailand, *Annual Economic Report* (Bangkok: Bank of Thailand, 1982-1988).

65. *Bangkok Post* January 5, 1984, p. 21; *Waga Kuni* (1985), p. 52.

66. Ino Tadatoshi, *Kokusai Gijutsu Kyoryoku no Michi* (The Path on International Technical Cooperation) (Tokyo: NHK Books, 1989), pp. 173-75.

67. *Sixth National Economic and Social Development Plan* (1986), p. 64. The ceiling was raised to $1.2 billion in 1989, then to $1.5 billion in 1990.

68. Ministry of Foreign Affairs, *Japan's Official Development Assistance* (Tokyo: Association for the Promotion of International Cooperation, 1987), p. 116.

69. *Technical Assistance Under the Sixth National Economic and Social Development Plan* (Bangkok: Department of Technical and Economic Cooperation, 1987), Part 1, p. 9.

70. Author's interview with a Japanese Ministry of Foreign Affairs official, Tokyo, January 23, 1991.

71. Author's interview with a JICA official, Tokyo, March 26, 1991. See, for example, Thavan Vorathepputipong et al., *Administration of Thai Export Promotion Policies and Japan's Cooperation* (Tokyo: Institute for Developing Economies, 1989), p. 62.

72. Kevin Hewison, "National Interests and Economic Downturn: Thailand," in Richard Robison, Kevin Hewison and Richard Higgott, eds., *Southeast Asia in the 1980s* (Sydney, London, and Boston: Allen and Unwin, 1987), pp. 73-75. See also Narongchai Akransee, "Foreign Aid and Economic Development in Thailand," in Uma Lele and Ijaz Nabi, eds., *Transitions in Development: The Role of Aid and Commercial Flows* (San Francisco: ICS Press, 1991), p. 86.

73. Hewison, in Robison, Hewison and Higgott, 1987, pp. 75-76.

74. Varakorn Samakose, "Thailand's White Paper: a Suggested Trade Relationship with Japan," *Thai–Japanese Studies* (August 1988): 34-38; Anucha Chintakanond, "Progress and Problems in Thai–Japanese Relations and Cooperation," in Pasuk Phongpaichit, Busaba Kunasirin, and Buddhagarn Rutchtorn, eds., *The Lion and the Mouse? Japan, Asia, and Thailand* (Proceedings of an International Conference on Thai-Japan Relations. Bangkok: Chulalongkorn University, 1986), pp. 230, 236-37.

75. See Japan International Cooperation Agency, *Country Study for Development Assistance to the Kingdom of Thailand* (Tokyo: Japan International Cooperation Agency, January, 1989).

76. Suzuki Nagatoshi, *Nihon no Keizai Kyoryoku* (Japan's Economic Cooperation) (Tokyo: Ajia Keizai Kenkyusho, 1990), pp. 219-21.

77. *Sixth National Economic and Social Development Plan* (1986), pp. 68-69, 277.

78. National Statistics Office, *Statistical Yearbook* (Bangkok: National Statistics Office, 1989), p. 352; *Statistical Yearbook* (1990), p. 344.

79. Pakkasem, pp. 80-81; *Sixth National Economic and Social Development Plan* (1986), p. 290.

80. *Technical Assistance Under the Sixth Economic and Development Plan (1987-1991)* (1987), Part 1, pp. 15-16.

81. *Waga Kuni* (1994), pp. 84-85, 90-91.

82. Author's interview with a JICA official, Tokyo, March 26, 1991.

83. *Country Study for Development Assistance to the Kingdom of Thailand* (1989), pp. 5-6, 17. See also Okita Saburo, *Approaching the Twenty-first Century: Japan's Role* (Tokyo: Japan Times, 1990), p. 70.

84. *Country Study for Development Assistance to the Kingdom of Thailand,* (1989), pp. 18, 50.

85. Overseas Economic Cooperation Fund, *Annual Report* (Tokyo: Overseas Economic Cooperation Fund, 1988), pp. 95-96. The loan provided for equipment and the cost of civil works and consultants.

86. *Bangkok Post* March 16, 1991, p. 3.

87. *Annual Report* (1988), p. 94; *Annual Report* (1990), p. 106.

88. *Waga Kuni* (1990), vol. 1, pp. 75-76; *Annual Report* (1988), pp. 95-96; *Annual Report* (1989), p. 99.

89. *Waga Kuni* (1990), vol. 1, pp. 75-76.

90. See *Nihon Keizai Shinbun* January 12, 1991, p. 13; *Nihon Keizai Shinbun* February 16, 1991, p. 13.

91. *Japan Economic Journal* February 27, 1988, p. 8.

92. See *Keizai Kyoryoku no Genjo to Mondaiten* (1990), p. 8.

93. See, for example, *Bangkok Post* September 9, 1987, p. 1.

94. *Nihon Keizai Shinbun* April 1, 1988, p. 7.

95. Suzuki, 1990, p. 121.

96. *Far Eastern Economic Review* (May 30, 1990), p. 52.

97. "New Village Development Programme: A Bottom-Up Approach in the Rural Development Movement," p. 12.

98. Shimao Yasuhiko, "Yotsu no Dankai ni Ojita Keizai Kyoryoku no Jidai: Tai o jirei toshite," *Gaiko Forum* (December 1988), p. 50.

99. Muscat, 1990, passim.

100. *Problems in Coordinating Multilateral Assistance to Thailand,* pp. 13-14.

101. Author's interviews with Ministry of International Trade and Industry officials, March 25, 1991.

102. *Asahi Shinbun,* April 1, 1993, p. 2.

Chapter 4

1. Rosario Manasan, *An Analysis of Public Sector Expenditures, 1975-1985* (Manila: Philippine Institute for Development Studies Working Paper 87-05, 1987), pp. 11, 13.

2. Evangeline P. Javier, "Economic, Demographic and Political Determinants of the Regional Allocation of Government Infrastructure Expenditures in the Philippines," *Journal of Philippine Development* 2 (1976): 281.

3. Mohammed A. Nanawi, "Political Participation During the First Five Years of the New Society in the Philippines," *Journal of Southeast Asian Studies* 13 (September 1982): 271-72.

4. Cayetano Paderanga and Ernesto M. Pernia, "Economic Policies and Spacial Urban Development," *Regional Development Dialogue* 4 (autumn 1983): 80-83.

5. CPA Study Team, "Report and Recommendations on NEDA and Regional Development," *Philippine Journal of Public Administration* 33 (July 1989): 256-57; UPLB Rural Development Study Team, *Philippine Rural Development: Problems, Issues and Directions* (Los Banos: University of the Philippines Los Banos, 1991), pp. 30, 34.

6. World Bank, *The Philippines: Priorities and Prospects for Development.* (Washington, DC: World Bank, 1976), p. 451.

7. Ibid., p. 467; "Sources and Uses of Foreign Assistance to the Philippines, 1972-1976," *Journal of Philippine Development* 4:1 (1977), p. 104.

8. National Economic and Development Authority, *Four-Year Development Plan, FY 1974-77* (Manila, National Economic and Development Authority, 1973), p. 99; Gerardo Sicat, *New Economic Directions in the Philippines* (Manila: National Economic and Development Authority, 1974), p. 222.

9. Tsuda Mamoru and Leo Deocadiz, *RP-Japan Relations and ADB: In Search of a New Horizon* (Manila: National Book Store, 1986), p. 56.

10. National Economic and Development Authority, *Four-Year Development Plan,* FY 1971-74 (Manila, National Economic and Development Authority, 1970), pp. 22-31.

11. Jose D. Ingles, *Philippine Foreign Policy* (Manila: Lyceum of the Philippines, 1982), esp. pp. 39-60.

12. James K. Boyce, *The Political Economy of External Indebtedness: A Case Study of the Philippines* (Manila: Philippine Institute for Development Studies, Monograph No. 12, 1990), pp. 8-10.

13. National Economic and Development Authority, *Four-Year Development Plan, FY 1972-75* (Manila: National Economic and Development Authority, 1971), pp. 60, 95.

14. *The Philippines: Priorities and Prospects for Development* (1976), pp. 468-69.

15. Sicat, 1974, pp. 26-27.

16. Ibid., p. 226.

17. Overseas Economic Cooperation Fund, *Japan's Contribution to Economic Development in the Republic of the Philippines through OECF Loans* (Tokyo: Overseas Economic Cooperation Fund, April 1984), p. 8.

18. *Four-Year Development Plan, FY 1971-74,* (1970), p. 140.

19. *The Philippines: Priorities and Prospects for Development* (1976), p. 83.

20. *Four-Year Development Plan, FY 1974-77* (1973), pp. 236-37.

21. See National Economic and Development Authority, *Regional Development Projects: Supplement to the Four-Year Development Plan, 1974-77* (Manila: National Economic and Development Authority, 1973), p. 69, passim.

22. *Japan's Contribution to Economic Development in the Republic of the Philippines through OECF Loans,* (1984), pp. 8-9.

23. National Economic and Development Authority, *Five-Year Philippine Development Plan, 1978-1982: Profile of Selected Development Projects* (Manila: National Economic and Development Authority, 1977), p. 135.

24. *Five-Year Philippine Development Plan, 1978-1982* (1977), pp. 64-70.

25. *Four-Year Development Plan, FY 1974-77* (1973), p. 253; *Four-Year Development Plan,* FY 1972-75, (1971), pp. 178, 183.

26. See *Four-Year Development Plan, FY 1974-77* (1973), pp. 99-100, 247-53.

27. National Economic and Development Authority, *Official Development Assistance Flows to the Philippines, 1970-79* (Manila: National Economic and Development Authority, December, 1980), p. 3.

28. See *Japan's Contribution to Economic Development in the Republic of the Philippines through OECF Loans,* (1984), pp. 41-8; Ministry of Foreign Affairs, *Waga Kuni no Seifu Kaihatsu Enjo* vol 1. (Tokyo: Association for the Promotion of International Cooperation, 1990), p. 107; "RP-Japan Relations," *Philippine Development* 5 (May 31, 1977), p. 3.

29. *Four-Year Development Plan, 1974-1977,* p. 127.

30. Ministry of International Trade and Industry, *Keizai Kyoryoku no Genjo to Mondaiten* (Current Situation and Problems of Japan's Economic Cooperation) vol. 2 (Tokyo: Tsusho Sangyosho, 1989), p. 211.

31. *Five-Year Philippine Development Plan, 1978-1982* (1977), pp. 251-343.

32. Ibid., pp. 251, 289, 311, 335. Specific data for the 1978-82 period was not included in the plan.

33. Ibid., p. 404.

34. Romeo Reyes, *Official Development Assistance to the Philippines: A Study of Administrative Performance and Capacity* (Manila: National Economic and Development Authority, 1985), pp. 25-26.

35. *Japan's Contribution to Economic Development in the Republic of the Philippines through OECF Loans,* (1984), passim; *Waga Kuni* (1990), vol. 1, p. 108.

36. See *Five-Year Philippine Development Plan, 1978-1982* (1977), pp. 337, 352; *Japan's Contribution to Economic Development of the Republic of the Philippines through OECF Loans,* pp. 69, 73, 77, 87.

37. "Japan Extends $35 M for Power Barge Project," *Philippine Development* 6 (January 15, 1979), p. 5; Author's interview with a *Nihon Keizai Shinbun* reporter, January 23, 1991.

38. See *Five-Year Philippine Development Plan, 1978-1982* (1977), pp. 253, 264, 272; *Japan's Contribution to Economic Development in the Republic of the Philippines through OECF Loans,* (1984), pp. 9-11.

39. *Five-Year Philippine Development Plan, 1978-1982* (1977), pp. 59-60.

40. Ingles, 1982, p. 61.

41. Reyes, 1985, p. 189. The availment rate is defined as the ratio of loans actually drawn to loans committed during a given period.

42.   Ibid., p. 205.

43.   Ibid., pp. 200, 205.

44.   *Five-Year Philippine Development Plan, 1983-1987: Technical Annex* (Manila: National Economic and Development Authority, 1982), pp. 26-45. The Plan specifically identified Cebu, Iloilo, Bacolod, Davao, and Cagayan de Oro for infrastructure investment.

45.   Ibid., p. 149.

46.   *Waga Kuni* (1985), vol. 2, p. 17; *Waga Kuni* (1989), vol. 2, p. 95.

47.   This analysis covers the Eleventh through Thirteenth Yen Loans. Although the Aquino administration actually signed the exchange of notes for the latter, it was negotiated during the Marcos administration. Despite some modifications to that package resulting from the change of government in the spring of 1986, the package was substantially the same. I also include the special yen loan for the Calaca II power facility, agreed to in June 1987.

48.   *Waga Kuni,* various years. The Ministry of Foreign Affair's *Japan's Official Development Assistance* (1987) lists a yen loan for the Iligan Integrated Steel Mill as part of the Eleventh Yen Loan, but the loan appears in no other source and apparently was canceled.

49.   Boyce, 1990, pp. 10-17.

50.   *Keizai Kyoryoku no Genjo to Mondaiten* (1989), p. 211.

51.   Tsuda and Deocadiz, 1986, pp. 63-69.

52.   *Nihon Keizai Shinbun* August 22, 1987, p. 1.

53.   David Timberman, *A Guide to Philippine Economic and Business Information Sources* (Manila: Joint Forum for Philippine Progress, 1990), pp. E-4, E-5; Romeo Reyes, *Absorptive Capacity for Foreign Aid: The Case of the Philippines* (Manila: Philippine Institute for Development Studies and the International Center for Economic Development, 1993), pp. 80-81.

54.   National Economic and Development Authority, *Medium-Term Public Investment Program, 1989-1992* (Manila: National Economic and Development Authority, 1990), p. vii; National Economic and Development Authority, *Medium-Term Philippine Development Plan,* 1987-1992 (Manila: National Economic and Development Authority, 1986), p. 48.

55.   Author's interview with a NEDA official, Manila, February 6, 1991.

56.   *Medium-Term Philippine Development Plan, 1987-1992* (1986), p. 45.

57.   Ibid., pp. 45-46, 49; Romeo Reyes and Filologo Pante, *Japanese and U.S. Development Assistance to the Philippines: A Philippine Perspective* (Manila: Philippine Institute for Development Studies Working Paper No. 89-07, 1989), p. 13.

58.   *Medium-Term Philippine Development Plan, 1987-1992* (1986), pp. 383-84.

59.   Country Study Group for Development Assistance to the Republic of the Philippines, *Country Study for Development Assistance to the Republic of the Philippines* (Tokyo: Japan International Cooperation Agency, April, 1987.)

60.   See *Waga Kuni* (1994), vol. 2, pp. 129-30; Overseas Economic Cooperation Fund, *Annual Report* (Tokyo: Overseas Economic Cooperation Fund, 1992), pp. 101-2; *Far Eastern Economic Review* (February 10, 1994): 45. The CALABARZON plan was controversial because it pitted the agroindustrial export thrust of the CAIDs against land reform efforts.

61. *Manila Chronicle* December 8, 1988, p. 13.
62. Program lending and cofinancing have benefitted Japan as well. Japan treats the disbursement of program loans as it does commodity loans; once the funds are released they become the recipient government's responsibility. The workload for program loans is correspondingly lower than for project loans at a time when loan funding levels have increased. Cofinancing has helped Japan make up for its lack of expertise in program financing because it can follow the multilateral lender's lead. Author's interviews with an Export-Import Bank of Japan official, Manila, February 4, 1991, and an Overseas Economic Cooperation Fund official, Washington, D.C., August 29, 1991.
63. Author's interview with a Philippine embassy official, Tokyo, October 12, 1990.
64. Boyce, 1990, p. 29.
65. Fukami Hiroaki, "The International Debt Problem and Japan's Response," *Japan Review of International Affairs* 3 (fall/winter 1989): 210-11; Author's interview with an Export-Import Bank of Japan official, Manila, February 4, 1991.
66. David F. Lambertson, "Future Prospects for the Philippines," *Department of State Bulletin* (May, 1989), p. 47. A former United States embassy official in Tokyo observed more tartly that MAI was a good example of the United States trying to flog a policy it could not afford.
67. See *Business World* (October 2, 1990): 1.
68. See *Far Eastern Economic Review* (August 3, 1989), p. 8.
69. *Far Eastern Economic Review* (August 4, 1994), p. 63.
70. See *Far Eastern Economic Review* (August 20, 1992), p. 64; *Philippine Daily Inquirer* June 24, 1992, p. 17.
71. See Bruce E. Moon, "Consensus or Compliance? Foreign-Policy Change and External Dependence," *International Organization* 39 (spring 1985): 297-329.
72. Julia Chang Bloch, "A US–Japan Aid Alliance?" in Shafiqul Islam, ed., *Yen for Development* (New York: Council on Foreign Relations Press, 1989), p. 75.
73. Reyes (1993) states the pros and cons nicely when he notes that capital aid tends to distort project formulation in favor of expensive foreign exchange components, no small consideration in an indebted country like the Philippines. On the other hand, he notes that Japan is the only donor that provides construction funds under its grant program, a boon to projects in the social and agriculture sectors. See pp. 33-34, 98.

Chapter 5

1. See William Siffin, *The Thai Bureaucracy: Institutional Change and Development* (Honolulu, Hawaii: East-West Center, 1966), pp. 158-59; David Morell and Chai-anan Samudavanija, *Political Conflict in Thailand: Reform, Reaction, and Revolution* (Cambridge, MA: Oelgeschlager, Gunn, and Hain, 1981), pp. 41-50.
2. Ledevina Carino, "The Philippines," in V. Subravanium, ed., *Public Administration in the Third World* (New York: Greenwood Press, 1990), pp. 102-27.
3. Prasert Chittawatanapong, "Japan's ODA Relations with Thailand," in Bruce Koppel and Robert Orr, eds., *Japan's Foreign Aid* (Boulder, Colorado: Westview Press, 1993), p. 99.

4. Muscat, 1994, pp. 171-222.

5. Naomi Caiden and Aaron Wildavsky, *Planning and Budgeting in Poor Countries* (New York: John Wiley and Sons, 1974), pp. 195, 245, 249-53.

6. Priya Osthananda, "Financial and Technical Assistance to Thailand," in *Southeast Asian Perceptions of Foreign Assistance. Papers and Proceedings of a Workshop Organized by the Institute of Southeast Asian Studies, Singapore and the Institute of Asian Studies, Chulalongkorn University, Bangkok* (Singapore: Institute of Southeast Asian Studies, 1977), p. 33.

7. National Economic and Social Development Board, *Fifth National Economic and Social Development Plan* (Bangkok: National Economic and Social Development Board, 1981), pp. 323, 337.

8. Suzuki Nagatoshi, *Nihon no Keizai Kyoryoku* (Japan's Economic Cooperation) (Tokyo: Ajia Keizai Kenkyusho, 1990), p. 218.

9. General Accounting Office, *Problems in Coordinating Multilateral Assistance to Thailand* (Report to the Congress by the Comptroller General of the United States, August 26, 1975), pp. 9-10.

10. Department of Technical and Economic Cooperation, *Outline of the Fifth National Economic and Social Development Plan and Its External Assistance Requirements* (Bangkok: Department of Technical and Economic Cooperation, @ 1981), p. 34.

11. Ibid; *Fifth National Economic and Social Development Plan (1982-1986)* (1981), pp. 322-24.

12. National Economic and Social Development Board, *Sixth National Economic and Social Development Plan (1987-1991)* (Bangkok: National Economic and Social Development Board, 1986), p. 65.

13. Muscat, 1994, p. 179.

14. Likhit Dhiravegin, "The Politics of Japan's Economic Success and Its Relations with Asia," in Pasuk Phongpaichit, Busaba Kunasirin, and Buddhagarn Rutchatorn, eds., *The Lion and the Mouse? Japan, Asia and Thailand. Proceedings of an International Conference on Thai–Japan Relations* (Bangkok: Chulalongkorn University, April 1986), p. 326; Khien Theeravit et al., *Research Report on Danish, German, and Japanese Assistance to Agricultural Development in Thailand* (Bangkok: Institute of Asian Studies, Chulalongkorn University, 1984), pp. 231-37.

15. Author's interview with a JICA official, Tokyo, March 26, 1991.

16. Judith Tendler, *Inside Foreign Aid* (Baltimore, Maryland: Johns Hopkins University Press, 1975), pp. 86-87.

17. Author's interview with a Ministry of Finance official, Tokyo, January 23, 1991.

18. One respondent who had worked at the Asian Development Bank noted that both the Philippines and Thailand had fewer people handling sectoral administration than other countries in the region.

19. Suthy Prasartsert and Kongsak Sonteperkswong, "Structural Forces behind Japan's Economic Expansion and the Case of Japanese-Thai Economic Relations," in Phongpaichit, Kunasirin, and Rutchatorn, eds., pp. 162-63.

20. They thus meet Kingdon's requirement of value acceptability, and they augment the planners' ability to argue the technical merits of aid requests, a tactic Odell found to be successful when Latin American governments negotiated with the United States

over trade issues. See John Odell, "Latin American Trade Negotiations with the United States," *International Organization* 34 (spring 1980), pp. 207-28.

21. *Bangkok Post,* January 6, 1983, p. 15.

22. Theeravit et al., pp. 196, 204.

23. Interview with Igarashi Takeshi, Tokyo University, March 25, 1991.

24. Ibid.

25. Kaigai Kensetsu Kyokai, *Sanju-nen no Ayumi* (Thirty Years of Progress) (Tokyo: Kaigai Kensetsu Kyokai, 1985). Large-scale projects were those worth more than 1 billion yen.

26. Prasert Chittiwatanapong et al., *Japanese Official Development Assistance to Thailand: Impact on the Construction Industry* (Tokyo: Institute of Developing Economies Joint Research Program Series No. 80. 1989), pp. 24-26. See also Prasartsert and Sonteperkswong, in Phongpaichit, Kunasirin, and Rutchatorn, 1986, pp. 193-94.

27. Overseas Economic Cooperation Fund, *Annual Report* (Tokyo: Overseas Economic Cooperation Fund, selected years). For a critical analysis of the accuracy of Overseas Economic Cooperation Fund data, see Margee Ensign, *Doing Good or Doing Well?* (New York: Columbia University Press, 1992), pp. 49-71.

28. See Overseas Construction Association of Japan, Inc., *Facts about the Construction Industry in Japan* (Tokyo, November 1989), p. 10; Robert Orr, *The Rise of Japan's Foreign Aid Power* (New York: Columbia University Press, 1990), pp. 65-68.

29. Shigeru Sugitani, *Japan's Economic Assistance to Thailand* (Bangkok: Economic Cooperation Center for the Asian and Pacific Region, 1975), p. 42.

30. Author's interview with an Overseas Economic Cooperation Fund official, Tokyo, November 27, 1990.

31. See Overseas Economic Cooperation Fund, *Japanese Contribution to Economic Development of the Kingdom of Thailand through OECF Loans* (Tokyo: Overseas Economic Cooperation Fund, 1983), passim.

32. Ibid., pp. 13-17.

33. See Watanabe Toshio and Kusano Atsushi, *Nihon no ODA o Do Suru ka* (What Is to Be Done with Japan's ODA?) (Tokyo: NHK Books, 1991), p. 125; *Annual Report* (1992), pp. 104-05.

34. Ministry of Foreign Affiars, *Japan's Official Development Assistance* (Tokyo: Association for the Promotion of International Cooperation, 1987), p. 77.

35. For different perspectives on the role of Japan International Cooperation Agency specialists see David Arase, *Buying Power* (Boulder, Colorado: Lynne Rienner, 1995), p. 106; Theeravit et al., 1984, passim.

36. See *Japan Economic Journal* February 27, 1988, p. 8.

37. See Brian Tracy, "Bargaining as Trial and Error: The Case of the Spanish Base Negotiations," in William Zartman, ed., *The Negotiation Process* (Beverly Hills, CA: Sage, 1978), p. 196.

38. Author's interview with an Overseas Economic Cooperation Fund official, Tokyo, November 27, 1990.

39. John W. Kingdon, *Agendas, Alternatives and Public Policies* (Boston: Little, Brown and Company, 1984), pp. 138-46.

40. Author's interview with a trading company official, Tokyo, November 27, 1990.

41. Author's interviews with Taniguchi Koji, Institute of Developing Economies, Tokyo, November 26, 1990, and an Overseas Economic Cooperation Fund official, Tokyo, November 27, 1990.

42. Author's interviews with a JICA official, Tokyo, November 20, 1990, and an Overseas Economic Cooperation Fund official, Tokyo, November 27, 1990.

43. Interview with Taniguchi Koji; Likhit Dhiravegin, "The Politics of Japan's Economic Success and Its Relations with Asia," in Phongpaichit, Kunasirin, and Rutchatorn, 1986, p. 326.

44. Author's interview with a JICA official, Tokyo, March 26, 1991.

45. Theeravit et al., 1984, p. 56.

46. Masahiko Aoki, "The Japanese Bureaucracy in Economic Administration: A Rational Regulator or Pluralist Agent?" in John B. Shoven, ed., *Government Policy toward Industry in the United States and Japan* (New York: Cambridge University Press, 1988), pp. 272-73.

47. Tendler, 1975, pp. 88-94.

48. Ibid., p. 56; see also Susan Pharr, "Japanese Aid in the New World Order," in Craig Garby and Mary Brown Bullock, eds., *Japan: A New Kind of Superpower* (Washington, DC: Woodrow Wilson Center Press, 1994), p. 175.

49. Olof Murelius, *An Institutional Approach to Project Analysis in the Developing Countries* (Paris: OECD, 1981), pp. 12-13.

50. Ibid., p. 54.

51. Lela Garner Noble, "Emergency Politics in the Philippines," *Asian Survey* 18 (April 1978): 334; Robin Broad, *Unequal Alliance: The World Bank,* the International Monetary Fund and the Philippines (Berkeley, CA: University of California Press, 1988); Emeline S. Huang and Alfonso Naanep, "Development Planning and Management under the New Society," *Philippine Journal of Public Administration* 26 (April 1982): 128-52.

52. Juanita Amatong, "Financing Government-(2)," *Philippine Journal of Public Administration* 30 (October 1986): 358; Richard Kessler, "'Development Diplomacy': The Role of the Ministry of Foreign Affairs in the Philippines," *Philippine Journal of Public Administration* 24 (January 1980): 40.

53. Huang and Naanep, p. 151.

54. Ibid., p. 150.

55. Gerardo Sicat, "A Historical and Current Perspective on Philippine Economic Problems," *Social Science Information* 12 (January-March, 1985).

56. Author's interviews with NEDA officials, Manila, February 6 and 7, 1991.

57. Doi Takako, the head of the Japan Socialist Party, following the party's independent investigation of the aid program in 1986, noted that she had found no case in which Marcos overturned a recommendation by the implementing office in the award of a contract. See "Japanese Government Playing Down the Marcos Scandal: Interview with Diet Member Doi Takako," *Japan-Asia Quarterly Review* 18: 1 (1987): 61.

58. Tsuda Mamoru and Leo Deocadiz, *RP-Japan Relations and ADB: In Search of a New Horizon* (Manila: National Book Store, 1986), pp. 28, 29. The feasibility study was conducted the following year, but the project does not appear in the list of projects in that package.

59. Belinda Aquino, *The Politics of Plunder* (Quezon City: UP College of Public Administration and Great Books Trading Company, 1987), pp. 66-69; *Business Day,* (September 6, 1985): 23; *JICA in the Philippines* (Japan International Cooperation Agency, 1990), pp. 22, 27; Raymond Bonner, *Waltzing with a Dictator* (New York: Vintage Books, 1988), pp. 259-60; Author's interview with a former NEDA official, Manila, February 7, 1991.

60. *Asahi Shinbun,* February 10, 1980, p. 9. The article does not explain how Imelda gained control over the request process.

61. See *Asahi Janaru,* April 4, 1986, pp. 98-103; *Asahi Janaru,* May 2, 1986, p. 17; unpublished documents in the office of the Subcommittee on Asian and Pacific Affairs, Committee on Foreign Relations, United States House of Representatives, United States Congress (hereinafter the "Marcos Documents").

62. Bruce Koppel and Michael Plummer, "Japan's Ascendancy as a Foreign Aid Power," *Asian Survey* 29 (November 1989): 1051.

63. Author's interview with a trading company official, Tokyo, November 27, 1990.

64. See *Annual Report,* selected years.

65. In 1977, the Philippine government announced that Japanese companies had colluded to fix the bidding for contracts in the Cagayan Valley electrification project loan. In 1989, Japanese Diet members informed the Philippine government that Japanese companies had fixed bids for a fisheries refrigeration and storage facilities loans in 1986.

66. Author's interview with a former NEDA official, Manila, February 7, 1991. The project's origin suggests that Imelda's interest was fortuitous.

67. Author's interview with a member of the House of Representatives of the Philippines, Tokyo, October 29, 1990.

68. Lawrence Olson, *Japan in Postwar Asia* (New York: Praeger, 1970), pp. 177-78.

69. Ministry of Foreign Affairs, *Tenki ni Tatsu Nippi Keizai Kyoryoku* (A Turning Point in Japan–Philippine Economic Cooperation) (Tokyo: Gaimusho, 1973), p. 73.

70. Olson, 1970, pp. 177-78.

71. Romeo Reyes, *Absorptive Capacity for Foreign Aid: The Case of the Philippines* (Manila: Philippine Institute of Development Studies and the International Center for Economic Development, 1993), p. 100.

72. See Tsuda and Deocadiz, 1986, p. 28.

73. Overseas Economic Cooperation Fund, Overseas Economic Cooperation Fund, *Japan's Contribution to Economic Development in the Republic of the Philippines through OECF Loans* (Tokyo: Overseas Economic Cooperation Fund, April 1984), pp. 18-21.

74. See for example *Annual Report* (1992), pp. 100-101.

75. Romeo Reyes, *Official Development Assistance to the Philippines: A Study of Administrative Capacity and Performance* (Manila: National Economic and Development Authority, 1985), pp. 211, 214-15, 227.

76. Reyes, 1993, pp. 85, 111-12.

77. See *Nihon Keizai Shinbun,* October 19, 1986, p. 5; *Nihon Keizai Shinbun,* November 4, 1986, p. 1; *Nihon Keizai Shinbun,* April 27, 1987, p. 7; *Nihon Keizai Shinbun,* June 23, 1987, p. 1.

78. Author's interview with a NEDA official, February 5, 1991.

79. See *Annual Report* (1988), p. 39; Overseas Economic Cooperation Fund, *Quarterly Report on OECF Operations for the Second Quarter of FY 1989* (Overseas Economic Cooperation Fund, July-September 1989), p. 4.

80. *Country Study for Development Assistance to the Republic of the Philippines,* (1987), p. 10.

81. Koppel and Plummer, pp. 1051-52; Author's interviews with Department of Agrarian Reform and NEDA officials, February 4, 6, 1991.

82. Author's interview with a NEDA official, February 6, 1991. The respondent noted that this was the "usual pattern."

83. Author's interview with a Department of Agrarian Reform official, Manila, February 4, 1991.

84. Author's interview with a NEDA official, February 6, 1991.

85. Author's interviews with a Department of Agrarian Reform official, Manila, February 4, 1991, and a Bungei Shunju reporter, Tokyo, October 30, 1990.

86. Author's interview with a Bungei Shunju reporter, Tokyo, October 31, 1990.

87. Author's interview with a NEDA official, February 5, 1991.

88. Author's interview with a NEDA official, February 5, 1991.

89. Reyes, 1993, esp. pp. 99-102.

90. *Philippine Development* (January, 1988), p. 26. The "shopping list" analogy is NEDA's.

91. *Business World* (February 19, 1991): 11.

92. Filologo Pante and Romeo Reyes, *Japanese and U.S. Development Assistance to the Philippines: A Philippines Perspective* (Manila: Philippine Institute for Development Studies, Working Paper No. 89-07, 1989), p. 14.

93. One NEDA official specifically mentioned the National Maritime Polytechnic and the Palawan Crocodile Farming Institute in this regard.

94. Reyes, 1985, pp. 223, 227.

95. Author's interviews with a JICA official, Tokyo, March 26, 1991, and a former NEDA official, Manila, February 5, 1991. The latter, newly ensconced in his office at the University of the Philippines, noted somewhat ruefully that his institution might have benefitted from continued JICA construction funding.

96. Author's interview, February 7, 1991.

Chapter 6

1. Japan International Cooperation Agency, *Country Study for Development Assistance to the Republic of the Philippines* (Tokyo: Japan International Cooperation Agency, April, 1987), p. 20; *Asahi Shinbun,* December 11, 1987, p. 2.

2. See JICA's annual reports for 1991, 1992, and 1993. See also Department of Agrarian Reform, *The State of Agrarian Reform after the First Year of the Ramos Administration* (Quezon City: Department of Agrarian Reform, August, 1993), pp. 9-10.

3. Committee on the Country Study for Japan's Official Development Assistance to the Republic of the Philippines, *The Second Country Study for Japan's Official Development Assistance to the Republic of the Philippines* (Tokyo: Japan International Cooperation Agency, 1994), pp. 33-49.

4. Arsenio Balisacan, "Why Do Governments Do What They Do? Agrarian Reform in the Philippines." in Dante Canlas and Sakai Hideyoshi, eds., *Studies in Economic Policy and Institutions: the Philippines* (Tokyo: Institute of Developing Economies, 1990), pp. 90-96.

5. *Newsweek,* Japanese edition, May 3-10, 1990, p. 23; Author's interview with Takahashi Akira, Tokyo University, October 17, 1990.

6. Author's interview with Takahashi Akira. Tokyo University, October 17, 1990.

7. Takahashi Akira, "From Reparations to Katagawari: Japan's ODA to the Philippines," in Bruce Koppel and Robert Orr, eds., *Japan's Foreign Aid Power* (Boulder, CO: Westview Press, 1993), p. 81.

8. Author's interview February 5, 1991, Manila.

9. Author's interview with a Department of Agrarian Reform official, Manila, February 4, 1991.

10. Jeffrey Riedinger, "The Philippines in 1993," *Asian Survey* 34 (February 1994): 144. See also "The MTADP: Failing Farmers by Forgoing Basics," *Farm News and Views* 6 (July-August 1993): 5, 10.

11. Linda K. Richter, *Land Reform and Tourism Development: Policy-Making in the Philippines* (Cambridge, MA: Schenkman Publishing, 1982), pp. 70, 79.

12. Author's interview with Takahashi Akira, October 17, 1990.

13. Interview with a DAR official, Manila, February 4, 1991.

14. Author's interview with Takahashi Akira, October 17, 1990.

15. *Financial Post* March 4, 1988, p. 16.

16. See Sakamoto Nobuo, "Nochi Kaikaku: sono gaiyo to kongo no kadai," *OECF Research Quarterly* 11: 4 (1989): 23-24.

17. Author' interview with a DAR official, February 4, 1991; Balisacan, in Canlas and Sakai, p. 92.

18. Author's interview with a DAR official, Manila, February 4, 1991.

19. Interview with a DAR official, Manila, February 4, 1991.

20. Author's interview with a DAR official, Manila, February 4, 1991.

21. Author's interview with a DAR official, Manila, February 4, 1991.

22. The cartel's members were Kanematsu Gosho, Sumitomo Shoji, C. Itoh, Tomen, and Kawasaki Steel. According to the letter, Toyo was not a member. Angenit Corporation was a Marcos front company run by a crony, Andres Genito, Jr. See Letter from Kotake Yoshio, Toyo Corporation, to Angenit Corporation, October 14, 1977, Marcos Documents, pp. 1060-61; *Asahi Shinbun,* August 1, 1977, p. 7; "Shirazu, Yorokobazu, Yakutatzu" (Unknown, Unsatisfying, Useless), *Asahi Janaru* (April 4, 1986): 100-03.

23. Kotake Letter, pp. 1060-61. See also *Washington Post,* March 22, 1986, pp. A1, A26.

24. Letter from the Office of the Implementing Officer, Philippine–Japan Project Loan Assistance Program, to Ferdinand E. Marcos, April 11, 1979; *Mainichi Shinbun,* April 10, 1986, p. 22.

25. This conclusion is based on evidence in a letter from the Angenit Corporation to an unidentified subject, Marcos Documents, October 13, 1977, pp. 1583-97.

26. *Asahi Shinbun,* April 14, 1989, p. 6. The secretary was also mentioned in the Kotake letter. Marcos' attempts to hide the paper trail from his Swiss banks included the use of pseudonyms and overseas holding companies.

27. See Kotake letter, p. 1600.
28. Angenit letter, pp. 1581-97.
29. Ibid. In fact, Kotake recommended Kanematsu Corporation, a cartel member, to replace Caterpillar Corporation (which refused to pay the 15 percent bribe) as supplier for the Manila South Diversion Road interchange project financed in the Fifth Yen Loan package.
30. Brian Woodall, "The Logic of Collusive Action: The Political Roots of Japan's *Dango* System," *Journal of Comparative Politics* 25 (April 1993): 287-312.
31. See the *Country Study*, p. 32. One *Nihon Keizai Shinbun* reporter who had researched Japanese economic cooperation for the Philippine power sector told me that the Overseas Economic Cooperation Fund officer in charge of the Tongonan geothermal power project loan had never been to the site.
32. Gaimusho, *Tenki ni Tatsu Nippi Keizai Kyoryoku* (A turning point in Japan-Philippines Economic Cooperation) (Tokyo: Gaimusho, 1973), p. 73.
33. *Asahi Shinbun,* March 25, 1986, p. 2. A member of the Philippine Commission on Good Government, the committee set up by President Aquino to investigate the Marcos fortunes, alleged that the Nakasone government had made a less than thorough investigation a quid pro quo for future aid. He averred further that kickbacks from the companies had in some cases been diverted to key LDP politicians, although this has never been proven.
34. See for example, Mainichi Shinbun Shakaibu, *Kokusai Enjo Bijinesu* (Tokyo: Mainichi Shinbun, 1990), pp. 132-39; Murai Yoshinori, *Musekinin Enjo Taikoku Nippon* (Tokyo: JICC Shuppankai, 1989), pp. 47-51.
35. *Annex to the Philippine Development Plan, 1978-1982: Profile of Selected Development Projects* (Manila: NEDA, 1977), p. 92.
36. Ibid.; National Economic and Development Authority, *Five-Year Philippine Development Plan: Profile of Selected Development Projects, 1978-1982,* (Manilla: National Economic and Development Authority), p. 214.
37. *Kokusai Enjo Bijinesu,* (1990), p. 132.
38. Ibid.; Japan International Cooperation Agency, *Basic Design Study Report on the Expansion and Modernization of the National Maritime Polytechnic, Tacloban, in the Republic of the Philippines* (Tokyo: Japan International Cooperation Agency, March 1984).
39. Author's interview with a House of Councillors member, Tokyo, October 12, 1990.
40. Murai, 1989, p. 48.
41. Kuroyanagi Toshiyuki, "Historical Development of the Philippine Human Resource Development Center," *Technology and Development* 7 (1994): 66-67.
42. Murai, 1989, p. 48.
43. Interview with a Finance Ministry official, Tokyo, January 23, 1991.
44. This conclusion was corroborated circumstantially by a NEDA official, February 6, 1991.
45. *Basic Design Study Report on the Expansion and Modernization of the National Maritime Polytechnic,* (1984), pp. 1-3.
46. Tsuda Mamoru and Leo Deocadiz, *RP-Japan Relations and ADB: In Search of a New Horizon* (Manila: National Bookstore, 1986), pp. 28-29.

47. James Boyce, *The Political Economy of External Indebtedness: A Case Study of the Philippines,* Monograph No. 12 (Manila: Philippine Institute of Development Studies, 1990), pp. 15-16.

48. Kyodo News Service, November 22, 1983; *Far Eastern Economic Review* (December 5, 1983); 68.

49. See *Nihon Keizai Shinbun,* November 11, 1983, p. 5; *Far Eastern Economic Review* (December 5, 1983): 68; *Business Day* (January 5, 1984): 2.

50. See *Business Day* (January 3, 1984): 1, 3; *Business Day* (January 5, 1984): 2; *Business Day* (January 16, 1984): 2.

51. *Business Day* (January 16, 1984): 2; *Business Day* (January 17, 1984): 2.

52. See *Nihon Keizai Shinbun,* February 2, 1984, p. 5; *Business Day* (February 9, 1984): 2.

53. *Business Day* (March 12, 1984): 15.

54. *Asahi Shinbun,* March 12, 1984, p. 1.

55. *Business Day* (March 30, 1984): 18.

56. *Asahi Shinbun,* (March 12, 1984): 1; *Business Day* (March 23, 1984): 13.

57. See Yokoyama Masaki, *Fuiripin Enjo to Jiriki Koseiron* (Philippine Aid and Self-Help) (Tokyo: Akashi Shoten, 1990), pp. 153-58; Tsuda and Deocadiz, 1986, pp. 9-10.

58. Robert Orr, *The Emergence of Japan's Foreign Aid Power* (New York: Columbia University Press, 1990), pp. 20-21.

59. *Business Day* (April 9, 1984): 3.

60. *Business Day* (April 5, 1984): 7.

61. *Asahi Shinbun,* April 27, 1984, p. 2, evening edition; *Asahi Shinbun,* April 29, 1984, p. 2; *Business Day* (May 5, 1985): 7.

62. By January 1985 less than 15 percent of the loan had been disbursed. *Business Day* (January 28, 1985): 2.

63. The Socialist Party denounced the disbursement of the loan. The Komeito, however, had no position on the loan until the Philippine government made public its findings about the Aquino assassination, effectively neutralizing itself in the Diet debates.

64. See Robert Axelrod and Robert Keohane, "Achieving Cooperation under Anarchy: Strategies and Institutions," in Kenneth Oye, ed., *Cooperation under Anarchy* (Princeton: Princeton University Press, 1986), pp. 239-43; Robert Axelrod, *The Evolution of Cooperation* (New York: Basic Books, 1984), p. 130.

65. See Prasert Chittiwatanapong et al., *Japanese Official Development Assistance to Thailand: Impact on the Construction Industry* (Tokyo: Institute of Developing Economies Joint Research Program Series No. 80, 1989), pp. 17-18; Prasert Chittiwatanapong, "Japan's Foreign Aid to Thailand," in Koppel and Orr, pp. 91-110; *Kokusai Enjo Bijinesu,* (1990), pp. 90-99; Murai, 1989, pp 72-73; Orr, 1990, p. 64; Kusano Atsushi, *ODA: Itcho Ni-sen Oku En no Yukue* (Tokyo: Toyo Keizai Shinposha, 1993), pp. 83-87.

66. *Kokusai Enjo Bijinesu,* (1990), pp. 91-92.

67. *Bangkok Post,* September 10, 1987, p. 2.

68. *Bangkok Post,* September 15, 1987, p. 3.

69. *Bangkok Post,* September 10, 1987, p. 2; *Bangkok Post,* September 16, 1987, p. 5.

70. Orr, 1990, p. 64.

71. Chittiwatanapong, 1989, p. 34.
72. Author's interview with a JICA official, Tokyo, November 20, 1990.
73. *Kokusai Enjo Bijinesu,* (1990), p. 98.
74. Ibid., pp. 89-92.
75. The Thai government has initiated revisions in projects, for example with the National Institute of Coastal Aquaculture, after work has begun. Khien Theeravit et al., *Research Report on Danish, German, and Japanese Assistance to Agricultural Development in Thailand* (Bangkok: Institute of Asian Studies, Chulalongkorn University, 1984), p. 56.
76. Chittiwatanapong, 1989, pp. 19-36.
77. Ibid., p. 17.
78. Ibid., p. 34.
79. See *Bangkok Post,* September 25, 1987, p. 6.
80. Ministry of International Trade and Industry, *Keizai Kyoryoku no Genjo to Mondaiten* (Current Situation and Problems of Japan's Economic Cooperation) vol. 2 (1989), p. 237; *Far Eastern Economic Review,* (February 2, 1984): 54.
81. *Far Eastern Economic Review* (February 2, 1984): 54-56; *Bangkok Post,* January 12, 1984, p. 1.
82. *Bangkok Post,* January 13, 1984, p. 18; *Far Eastern Economic Review* (February 2, 1984): 18.
83. *Bangkok Post,* January 13, 1984, p. 18; *Bangkok Post,* January 17, 1984, p. 15.
84. *Bangkok Post,* January 26, 1984, p. 1.
85. Robert Muscat, *The Fifth Tiger* (Armonk, NY: M. E. Sharpe, 1994), p. 216.
86. For a description of the complexities Prem faced in establishing that cabinet see Suchitra Punyaratabandhu-Bhakdi, "Thailand in 1983," *Asian Survey* 24 (February 1984): 189-90.
87. Muscat, 1994, p. 178.
88. *Far Eastern Economic Review,* (February 2, 1984), pp. 54-55.
89. *Bangkok Post,* January 27, 1984, p. 1.
90. Ibid.
91. *Far Eastern Economic Review* (February 2, 1984): 54.
92. See *Keizai Kyoryoku no Genjo to Mondaiten* (1993), pp. 263, 270; Overseas Economic Cooperation Fund, *Annual Report* (Tokyo: Overseas Economic Cooperation Fund, 1994), p. 127; Japan International Cooperation Agency, *JICA's Technical Cooperation to Kingdom of Thailand* (internal document, Japan International Cooperation Agency, 1990); Larry Lohmann, "Commercial Tree Plantations in Thailand: Deforestation by Any Other Name," *The Ecologist* 20 (January/February 1990): 13-14.
93. Philip Hirsch and Larry Lohmann, "Contemporary Politics of the Environment in Thailand," *Asian Survey* 29 (April 1989): 449.
94. See, for example, National Economic and Social Development Board, *Summary of the Sixth National Economic and Social Development Plan 1987-1991* (Bangkok: National Economic and Social Development Board, 1986), p. 21; Prapant Svetanant et al., *2000-nen ni Mukete no Tai Keizai* (The Thai Economy Looking to the Year 2000) (Tokyo: Ajia Keizai Kenkyusho, 1995), pp. iii, 78-79.

95. David Potter, "Assessing Japan's Environmental Aid Policy," *Pacific Affairs* 67 (summer 1994): 213-14.
96. Axelrod, 1984, pp. 115-16, 126-30.
97. Chittiwatanapong, 1989, p. 34.
98. Author's interview with a JICA official, Tokyo, November 20, 1990.
99. Chittiwatanapong, 1989, p. 34.
100. See Theeravit et al., 1984, passim; Author's interviews with a NEDA official, February 2, 1991, and a JICA official, March 26, 1991.
101. See Paul Mosley, *Foreign Aid: Its Defense and Reform* (Lexington, Kentucky: University Press of Kentucky, 1987), pp. 93-95 for a fuller discussion.
102. Incidentally, while I know of no publicly revealed corruption in Thailand to match the Marcos scandals, the potential for this kind of slack exists. The Thai term *hua* conveys the same meaning as *dango* in Japan, and its occurrence is widespread. See Nakata Thinapan, "Corruption in the Thai Bureaucracy: Who Gets What, How and Why in its Public Expenditures," *Thai Journal of Development Administration* 18 (January 1978): 102-28.

Chapter 7

1. Quoted in Arun Senkuttuvan, "A Preliminary View of Financial and Technical Assistance to Singapore," in *Southeast Asian Perceptions of Foreign Assistance.* Papers and Proceedings of a Workshop Organized by the Institute of southeast Asian Studies, Singapore, and Chulalongkorn University (Singapore: Institute of Southeast Asian Studies, 1977): 32.
2. In 1991, for example, NEDA's Japan loan desk officer had been employed in that position since 1986, and had served at the grant aid desk for two years before that.
3. Romeo Reyes, *Absorptive Capacity for Foreign Aid: A Case Study of the Philippines* (Philippine Institute for Development Studies and the International Center for Economic Growth, 1993), pp. 91-93.
4. Robert Keohane, *After Hegemony: Cooperation and Discord in the World Political Economy* (Princeton, NJ: Princeton University Press, 1984), p. 51.
5. J. Stephen Hoadley, "Small States as Aid Donors," *International Organization* 34 (winter 1980): 121-37. Recently, Taiwan and South Korea have emerged as regional donors, but their programs remain small.
6. Author's interview with Sakai Hideyoshi, Institute of Developing Economies, Tokyo, November 26, 1990.
7. Keohane, 1984; Charles Lipson, "Bankers' Dilemmas: Private Cooperation in Rescheduling Sovereign Debts," in Kenneth Oye, ed., *Cooperation under Anarchy* (Princeton, NY: Princeton University Press, 1986), pp. 200-25; Helen Milner, "International Theories of Cooperation Among Nations: Weaknesses and Strengths," *World Politics* 44 (April 1992): 480.
8. See Jeffrey LeFebvre, *Arms for the Horn: US Policy in Ethiopia and Somalia, 1953-1991* (Pittsburgh, PA: University of Pittsburgh Press, 1991), pp. 11-30; William Habeeb, *Power and Tactics in International Negotiation* (Baltimore, MD: Johns Hopkins Press, 1988); Milner, 1992, p. 480.

9.   See Robert Axelrod, *The Evolution of Cooperation* (New York: Basic Books, 1984), p. 130: Oye, 1986, passim; Milner, 1992, pp. 473-74.
10. Martin Rudner, "Japan's Official Development Assistance to Southeast Asia," *Modern Asian Studies* 23 (February 1989): 98-101.
11. See David Arase, *Buying Power: The Political Economy of Japan's Foreign Aid* (Boulder, Colorado: Lynne Rienner, 1995), esp. p. 105.

Bibliography

Abiad, Virginia de Guia. *The Impact of Japanese Reparation Payments on the Private Sector of the Philippine Economy.* Quezon City: University of the Philippines School of Economics and the National Council, April, 1972.

Allison, Graham. *Essence of Decision: Explaining the Cuban Missile Crisis.* Boston: Little Brown and Co., 1971.

Amatong, Juanita. "Financing Government-(2)," *Philippine Journal of Public Administration* 30 (October 1986): 354-67.

Aquino, Belinda. *Politics of Plunder.* Quezon City: UP College of Public Administration and Great Books Trading Company, 1987.

Arase, David. *Buying Power: the Political Economy of Japan's Foreign Aid.* Boulder, Colorado: Lynne Rienner, 1995.

———. "Public-Private Sector Interest Coordination in Japan's ODA," *Pacific Affairs* 67 (summer 1994): 171-99.

Asia Yearbook. Hong Kong: Far Eastern Economic Review, selected years.

Asian Development Outlook. Manila: Asian Development Bank, selected years.

Axelrod, Robert. *The Evolution of Cooperation.* NY: Basic Books, 1984.

Bachrach, Peter, and Morton Baratz. "Two Faces of Power," *American Political Science Review* 61 (December 1962): 947-52.

Baldwin, W. Lee, and W. David Maxwell. *The Role of Foreign Financial Assistance to Thailand in the 1980s.* Lexington, MA: Lexington Books, 1975.

Bank of Thailand. *Annual Economic Report.* Bangkok: Bank of Thailand, selected years.

Bello, Walden. "Aquino's Elite Populism," *Third World Quarterly* 8 (July 1986): 1020-30.

Bendor, Jonathan, and Terry Moe. "An Adaptive Model of Bureaucratic Politics," *American Political Science Review* 79 (September 1985): 755-73.

Bendor, Jonathan, Serge Taylor, and Roland Van Gaalen. "Stacking the Deck: Bureaucratic Missions and Policy Design." *American Political Science Review* 81 (September 1987): 873-96.

Blaker, Michael, ed. *Development Assistance to Southeast Asia: the U.S. and Japanese Approaches.* New York: Occasional Papers of the East Asia Institute, Columbia University, 1983.

Bonner, Raymond. *Waltzing with a Dictator.* New York: Times Books, 1987.

Boyce, James. *The Political Economy of External Indebtedness: A Case Study of the Philippines.* Monograph No. 12. Manila: Philippine Institute of Development Studies, 1990.

Broad, Robin. *Unequal Alliance: The World Bank, the International Monetary Fund, and the Philippines.* Berkeley, CA: University of California Press, 1988.

Brooks, William and Robert Orr, Jr. "Japan's Foreign Economic Assistance," *Asian Survey* 25 (March 1985): 322-40.

Bryant, William E. *Japanese Private Economic Diplomacy.* New York: Praeger, 1975.

Caiden, Naomi. "Comparing Budget Systems: Budgeting in ASEAN Countries," *Public Budgeting and Finance* 5 (winter 1985): 23-38.

Caiden, Naomi, and Aaron Wildavsky. *Planning and Budgeting in Poor Countries.* New York: John Wiley and Sons, 1974.

Canlas, Dante and Hideyoshi Sakai, eds. *Studies in Economic Policy and Institutions: the Philippines.* Tokyo: Institute of Developing Economies, 1990.

Carino, Ledevina. "The Philippines," in V. Subravanium, ed. *Public Administration in the Third World.* New York: Greenwood Press, 1990, pp. 41-50.

Cassen, Robert et al. *Does Aid Work?.* Oxford: Clarendon Press, 1986.

Chinwanno, Chulacheeb. "Japan as a Regional Power," *Thai-Japanese Studies* (August 1988): 58-66.

Chittawatanapong, Prasert et al. *Japanese Official Development Assistance to Thailand: Impact on the Construction Industry.* Tokyo: Institute of Developing Economies Joint Research Program Series No. 80, 1989.

Committee for Economic Development. *Development Assistance to Southeast Asia.* New York: Committee for Economic Development, 1970.

Committee on the Country Study for Japan's Official Development Assistance to the Republic of the Philippines. *The Second Country Study for Japan's Official Development Assistance to the Republic of the Philippines.* Tokyo: Japan International Cooperation Agency, 1994.

Compendium of Aid Procedures. Paris: Organization for Economic Cooperation and Development, 1981.

CPA Study Team. "Report and Recommendations on NEDA and Regional Development," *Philippine Journal of Public Administration* 33 (July 1989): 253-77.

De Dios, Aurora. "Japan in the Philippines: Dimensions of Inequality." Quezon City: Miriam College, unpublished, 1989.

De Guzman, Raul, et. al. "The Political/Administrative Aspects of Regionalization and Development in the Philippines: Problems, Issues and Prospects," *Philippine Journal of Public Administration* 21 (July-October 1977): 342-70.

Dixon, C.J. "Development, Regional Disparity and Planning: The Experience of Northeast Thailand," *Journal of Southeast Asian Studies* 8 (September 1977): 210-23.

Doi, Takako, et. al. *ODA Kakumei* (ODA Revolution). Tokyo: Shakai Sozosha, 1990.

Dominguez, Carlos. *Comments on the Proposed Accelerated Land Reform Program.* Memorandum, Department of Agriculture, Government of the Philippines, April 29, 1987.

Drifte, Reinhard. *Japan's Foreign Policy.* London: Routledge, 1990.

Ensign, Margee. *Doing Good or Doing Well?.* New York: Columbia University Press, 1992.

Frances, Lai Fung-Wai. "Without a Vision: Japan's Not Playing a Greater Role in ASEAN's Solidarity and Development," in R. P. Anand, and Purificacion Quisumbing, eds. *ASEAN: Identity, Development and Culture.* University of the Philippines Law Center and East-West Center Culture Learning Center, 1981, pp. 333-55.

Friedman, Wolfgang, George Kalmanoff, and Robert Meagher. *International Financial Aid.* New York: Columbia University Press, 1966.

Fukami, Hiroaki. "The International Debt Problem and Japan's Response," *Japan's Review of International Affairs* 3 (fall/winter 1989): 182-212.

Gordenker, Leon. *International Aid and National Decisions.* Princeton, NJ: Princeton University Press, 1976.

Gorra, Marilyn Noval. "Social Development Alternatives in the Philippines," *Regional Development Dialogue* 7 (spring 1986): 136-60.

Habeeb, William M. *Power and Tactics in Asymmetrical Negotiation.* Baltimore: Johns Hopkins University, 1988.

Hasegawa, Sukehiro. *Japanese Foreign Aid: Policy and Practice.* New York: Praeger, 1975.

Hawes, Gary. *The Philippine State and the Marcos Regime.* Ithaca, NY: Cornell University Press, 1987.

Hayter, Teresa, and Catharine Watson. *Aid: Rhetoric and Reality.* London: Pluto Press, 1985.

Higgott, Richard, and Richard Robison, eds. *Southeast Asia.* London: Routledge and Kegan Paul, 1985.

Hirsch, Philip, and Larry Lohmann. "Contemporary Politics of the Environment in Thailand," *Asian Survey* 29 (April 1989): 439-51.

Ho, Robert, and E.C. Chapman, eds. *Studies in Contemporary Thailand.* Canberra: Australian National University, 1973.

Hoadley, J. Stephen. "Small States as Aid Donors." *International Organization* 34 (winter 1980): 121-37.

Huang, Emeline S., and Alfonso Naanep. "Development Planning and Management under the New Society," *Philippine Journal of Public Administration* 26 (April 1982): 128-52.

Igarashi, Takeshi, ed. *Nihon no ODA to Kokusai Chitsujo* (Japan's ODA and the International Order). Tokyo: Nihon Kokusai Mondai Kenkyujo, 1990.

Inada, Juichi. "Japan's Aid Diplomacy: Increasing Role for Global Security," *Japan Review of International Affairs* (spring/summer 1988): 91-112.

———. "Jinken, Minshuka to Enjo Seisaku," (Human Rights, Democratization, and Aid Policy). *Kokusai Mondai* (May 1995): 2-17.

Ingles, Jose D. *Philippine Foreign Policy.* Intramuros, Manila: Lyceum of the Philippines, 1982.

Ino, Tadatoshi. *Kokusai Gijutsu Kyoryoku no Michi* (The Path of International Technical Cooperation). Tokyo: NHK Books, 1989.

Inoguchi, Takashi, and Daniel Okimoto, eds. *The Political Economy of Japan.* vol 2. Stanford, CA: Stanford University Press, 1988.

International Bank for Reconstruction and Development. *A Public Development Program for Thailand.* Baltimore: Johns Hopkins University Press, 1959.

Islam, Shafiqul, ed. *Yen for Development.* New York: Council of Foreign Relations Press, 1991.

Itoh, Hiroshi, ed. *Japan's Foreign Policy Making.* Buffalo, NY: State University of New York, 1982.

Japan, Ministry of Foreign Affairs. *Highlights of Japan's Foreign Aid.* Tokyo: Ministry of Foreign Affairs, 1969.

———. *Japan's Official Development Assistance.* Tokyo: Association for the Promotion of International Cooperation, annual.

———. *Keizai Kyoryoku Hyoka Hokokusho* (Evaluation Report of Economic Cooperation). Tokyo: Gaimusho, selected years.

———. *Keizai Kyoryoku Sanka e no Tetsuzuki* (Procedures for Participation in Economic Cooperation). Tokyo: Association for the Promotion of International Cooperation, 1990.

————. *Tenki ni Tatsu Nippi Keizai Kyoryoku* (A Turning Point in Japan - Philippines Economic Cooperation). Tokyo: Gaimusho, 1973.

————. *Tenki ni Tatsu Tai Keizai to Waga Kuni no Kyoryoku* (A Turning Point in the Thai Economy and Japan's Cooperation). Tokyo: Gaimusho, 1972.

————. *Waga Kuni no Seifu Kaihatsu Enjo* (Japan's Official Development Assistance). Tokyo: Association for the Promotion of International Cooperation, annual.

Japan, Ministry of International Trade and Industry. *Keizai Kyoryoku no Genjo to Mondaiten* (Current Situation and Problems of Japan's Economic Cooperation). Tokyo: Tsusho Sangyosho, annual.

Japan External Trade Organization. *Japan's Economic Cooperation.* Tokyo: Japan External Trade Organization, 1980.

Japan International Cooperation Agency. *Annual Report.* Tokyo: Japan International Cooperation Agency, selected years.

————. *Basic Design Study Report on the Expansion and Modernization of the National Maritime Polytechnic, Tacloban, in the Republic of the Philippines.* Tokyo: Japan International Cooperation Agency, March, 1984.

————. Country Study Group for Development Assistance to the Kingdom of Thailand. *Country Study for Development Assistance to the Kingdom of Thailand.* Tokyo: Japan International Cooperation Agency, January, 1989.

————. Country Study Group for Development Assistance to the Republic of the Philippines. *Country Study for Development Assistance to the Republic of the Philippines.* Tokyo: Japan International Cooperation Agency, April, 1987.

————. *Fuiripin Kunibetsu Enjo Kenkyukai Hokokusho* (Report of the Study Team on Aid to the Philippines). Tokyo: Japan International Cooperation Agency, May, 1987.

————. *Japan International Cooperation Agency in the Philippines.* Tokyo: Japan International Cooperation Agency, 1990.

————. *JICA's Technical Cooperation to Kingdom of Thailand* (Internal document). Tokyo: Japan International Cooperation Agency, 1990.

————. *Tai Kunibetsu Enjo Kenkyukai Hokokusho* (Report of the Study Team on Aid to Thailand). Tokyo: Japan International Cooperation Agency, January, 1989.

————, Medical Cooperation Department. *A Guide to Medical Cooperation Activities.* Tokyo: Japan International Cooperation Agency, 1985.

Javier, Evangelina P. "Economic, Demographic and Political Determinants of the Regional Allocation of Government Infrastructure Expenditures in the Philippines," *Journal of Philippine Development* 3, no. 2 (1976): 281-311.

Jepma, Catrinus. *The Tying of Aid.* Paris: Organization for Economic Cooperation and Development, 1991.

Johnson, Chalmers. *MITI and the Japanese Miracle.* Stanford, CA: Stanford University Press, 1982.

Jose, Vivencio R. "Philippine External Debt Problem: the Marcos Years," *Journal of Contemporary Asia* 21, no. 2 (1991): 222-45.

Kaigai Kensetsu Kyokai. Sanju-nen Ayumi (Thirty Years' Progress). Tokyo: Kaigai Kensetsu Kyokai, 1985.

Kaneko, Yoshinori. "Issues and Prospects for the Research Institute for Tropical Medicine of the Philippines," *Technology and Development,* no. 3 (January 1990): 100-11.

Kato, Jumpei. "Nihon no Kaihatsu Enjo," (Japan's Development Aid). *Kokusai Seiji,* no. 1 (1980): 40-60.

Keohane, Robert. *After Hegemeony: Cooperation and Discord in the World Political Economy.* Princeton, NJ: Princeton University Press, 1984.

Kesavan, K. V. *Japan's Relations with Southeast Asia: 1952-1960.* Bombay: Somaiya Publications Pvt. Ltd., 1972.

Kessler, Richard. "'Development Diplomacy:' the Role of the Ministry of Foreign Affairs in the Philippines," *Philippine Journal of Public Administration* 24 (January 1980): 39-45.

Khamchoo, Chaiwat, and E. Bruce Reynolds, eds. *Thai-Japanese Relations in Historical Perspective.* Bangkok: Institute of Asian Studies, Chulalongkorn University, 1988.

Kharas, Homi J., and Hisanobu Shishido. *Thailand: An Assessment of Alternative Foreign Borrowing Strategies.* Washington, DC: World Bank Staff Working Paper No. 781. World Bank, 1985.

Kingdon, John. *Agendas, Alternatives and Public Policies.* Boston: Little, Brown and Company, 1984.

Koppel, Bruce, and Michael Plummer. "Japan's Ascendancy as a Foreign Aid Power," *Asian Survey* 29 (November 1989): 1043-56.

Koppel, Bruce, and Robert Orr, eds. *Japan's Foreign Aid Power.* Boulder, Colorado: Westview Press, 1993.

Kreuger, Anne O., Constantin Michalopoulos, and Vernon Ruttan. *Aid and Development.* Baltimore, MD: Johns Hopkins University Press, 1989.

Kuroyanagi, Toshiyuki. "Historical Development of the Philippine Human Resources Development Center," *Technology and Development,* no. 7 (July 1994): 65-75.

Kusano, Atsushi. *ODA Itcho Ni Sen Oku En no Yukue* (The Direction of One Trillion Two Hundred Billion Yen of ODA). Tokyo: Toyo Keizai Shinposha, 1993.

Kut, Gun. *Foreign Economic Assistance and Third World Development: Assessment of the Effects of a Global Policy.* PhD. Dissertation, State University of New York at Binghamton, 1987.

LeFebvre, Jeffrey. *Arms for the Horn: U.S. Policy in Ethiopia and Somalia, 1953-1991.* Pittsburgh, PA: University of Pittsburgh Press, 1991.

Lehman, Howard P. *Indebted Development.* New York: St. Martin's Press, 1993.

Lele, Uma, and Ijaz Nabi, eds. *Transitions in Development: the Role of Aid and Commercial Flows.* San Francisco: ICS Press, 1991.

LePoer, Barbara Leich. *Thailand: a Country Study.* 6th ed. Washington, DC: Library of Congress Federal Research Division, 1989.

Likhit, Dhiravegin. *The Bureaucratic Elite of Thailand.* Bangkok: Thai Khadi Research Institute, Thammasat University, 1978.

Lohmann, Larry. "Commercial Tree Plantations in Thailand: Deforestation by any Other Name," *The Ecologist* 20 (January/February 1990): 9-15.

London, Bruce. *Metropolis and Nation in Thailand: the Political Economy on Uneven Development.* Boulder, Colorado: Westview Press, 1980.

Lopez, Salvador. "Development, Diplomacy, and the Third World," *Studies in Third World Societies* 12 (June 1980): 63-72.

Loutfi, Martha E. *The Net Cost of Japanese Foreign Aid.* New York: Praeger, 1973.

Lumsdaine, David. *Moral Vision in International Politics: The Foreign Aid Regime, 1949-1989.* Princeton: Princeton University Press, 1993.

Magno, Cora P. "Notes on Development Loan Assistance to the Philippines," *Journal of Philippine Development* 3, no. 2 (1976): 313-32.

Mainichi Shinbun Shakaibu. *Kokusai Enjo Bijinesu* (The International Aid Business). Tokyo: Mainichi Shinbun, 1990.

Manasan, Rosario. *An Analysis of Public Sector Expenditures, 1975-1985.* Manila: Philippine Institute for Development Studies Working Paper No. 87-05, September, 1987.

Manglapus, Raul. *Japan in Southeast Asia: Collision Course.* New York: Carnegie Endowment for International Peace, 1975.

Marcos Documents. Unpublished documents in the office of the Subcommittee on Asian and Pacific Affairs, Committee on Foreign Relations, United States House of Representatives, United States Congress.

Matsumoto, S. "Nihon no Tonan Ajia Keizai Enjo to sono Seijiryoku-gaku," (Japan's Foreign Aid and Its Dynamics in Southeast Asian Politics). *Kokusai Seiji* 2 (1978): 111-31.

Matsuzaka, Hideo. "The Future of Japan-ASEAN Relations." *Asia Pacific Community* 21 (summer 1983): 11-22.

Matsuura, Kiochiro. *Enjo Gaiko no Saizensen de Kangaeta Koto* (Thoughts at the Front Line of Aid Foreign Policy). Tokyo: Association for the Promotion of International Cooperation, 1990.

Milner, Helen. "International Theories of Cooperation Among Nations: Strengths and Weaknesses," *World Politics* 44 (April 1992): 466-96.

Minami, Isao. "Small-Scale Integrated Rural Development by Means of *Tameike* [Special Ponds] in Northeast Thailand." *Technology and Development,* no. 2 (January 1989): 63-74.

Miura, Shumon. *Kore ga Seinen Kaigai Kyoryokutai Da* (This is the Japan Overseas Cooperation Volunteers). Tokyo: Sanshusha, 1983.

Moe, Terry. "The New Economics of Organization," *American Journal of Political Science* 28 (September 1984): 739-77.

Moon, Bruce E. "Consensus or Compliance?: Foreign Policy Change and External Dependence," *International Organization* 39 (spring 1985): 297-330.

Morell, David, and Chai-anan Samudavanija. *Political Conflict in Thailand.* Cambridge, MA: Oelschlager, Gunn and Hain, 1981.

Morrison, Charles. *Japan, the United States and a Changing Southeast Asia.* New York: University Press of America, 1985.

Mosley, Paul. *Foreign Aid: Its Defense and Reform.* Lexington, Kentucky: University of Kentucky Press, 1987.

Mosley, Paul, Jane Harrigan, and John Toye. *Aid and Power: the World Bank and Policy-Based Lending.* vol. 1. London: Routledge, 1991.

Murai, Yoshinori. *Musekinin Enjo Taikoku Nippon* (Japan, the Irresponsible Aid Great Power). Tokyo: JICC Shuppankyoku, 1989.

———. *Kensho: Nippon no ODA* (Testimony: Japan's ODA). Tokyo: Gakuyo Shobo, 1992.

Murelius, Olof. *An Institutional Approach to Project Analysis in the Developing Countries.* Paris: Organization for Economic Cooperation and Development, 1981.

Muro, Osamu. "'Enjo Kihon-ho' o Teigen Suru," (I Propose an "Aid Basic Law"). *Sekai.* (November 1986): 287-95.

Muscat, Robert. *Thailand and the United States: Development, Security and Foreign Aid.* New York: Columbia University Press, 1990.

———. *The Fifth Tiger.* Armonk, NY: M.E. Sharpe, 1994.

Nagai, Hiroshi. *Sareru Gawa kara Mita "Enjo"* ("Aid" Seen from the Receiving Side). Tokyo: Keiso Shobo, 1989.

Nakagawa, Nobuyoshi, ed. *Ajia Shin-Kogyoka to Nichibei Keizai* (Asia's New Industrialization and the Japanese and American Economies). Tokyo: Tokyo Daigaku Shuppankai, 1990.

Nakata, Thinapan. "Corruption in the Thai Bureaucracy: Who Gets What, How and Why?" *Thai Journal of Development Administration* 18 (January 1978): 102-28.

Nanawi, Mohammed. "Political Participation During the First Five Years of the New Society in the Philippines," *Journal of Southeast Asian Studies* 13 (September 1982): 270-78.

Nester, William, and Kweku Ampiah. "Japan's Oil Diplomacy: *Tatemae* and *Honne*," *Third World Quarterly* 11 (January 1989): 72-88.

Nishihara, Masashi. *The Japanese and Sukarno's Indonesia*. Honolulu: University of Hawaii Press, 1976.

Noble, Lena Garner. "Emergency Politics in the Philippines," *Asian Survey* 18 (April 1978): 350-62.

Nophaket, Suthin. *The Administrative Requirements of Development Planning in Thailand*. PhD. Dissertation, Clarement Graduate School, 1973.

Odell, John. "Latin American Trade Negotiations with the United States," *International Organization* 34 (spring 1980): 207-28.

Ohno, Takushi. *War Reparations and Peace Settlement*. Manila: Solidaridad, 1986.

Olson, Lawrence. *Japan in Postwar Asia*. New York: Praeger, 1970.

Okita, Saburo. *Approaching the Twenty-first Century: Japan's Role*. Tokyo: Japan Times, 1990.

―――. *Japan's High Dependence on Natural Resource Imports and its Policy Implications*. Canberra: Australia-Japan Economic Relations Research Project, 1975.

Ongoing and Pipelined Official Development Assistance (ODA) to CARP. Philippines, Department of Agrarian Reform, unpublished, February, 1991.

Organization for Economic Cooperation and Development. *Development Cooperation*. Selected Years.

Orr, Robert M. "Collaboration or Conflict? Foreign Aid and U.S. - Japan Relations," *Pacific Affairs* 62 (winter 1989-90): 476-89.

―――. *Japan's Emergence as a Foreign Aid Power*. New York: Columbia University Press, 1990.

―――. "Nihon no Atarashii Buki: ODA," (Japan's New Weapon: ODA) *Seiron* 28 (January 1989): 133-41.

―――. "The Aid Factor in US-Japan Relations," *Asian Survey* 28 (July 1988): 740-56.

―――. "The Rising Sun: Japan's Foreign Aid to ASEAN, the Pacific Basin and the Republic of Korea," *Journal of International Affairs* (April 1987): 39-62.

Overseas Construction Association of Japan, Inc. *Facts about the Construction Industry in Japan*. Tokyo, November 1989.

Overseas Economic Cooperation Fund. *Annual Report*. Tokyo: Overseas Economic Cooperation Fund, selected years.

―――. *Japan's Contribution to Economic Development in the Republic of the Philippines through OECF Loans*. Tokyo: Overseas Economic Cooperation Fund, April 1984.

―――. *Japanese Contribution to Economic Development in the Kingdom of Thailand through OECF Loans*. Tokyo: Overseas Economic Cooperation Fund, June 1983.

────. *Nenji Hokokusho* (Annual Report). Tokyo: Overseas Economic Cooperation Fund, 1989.

────. *Quarterly Report on OECF Operations for the Second Quarter of FY 1989*. Tokyo: Overseas Economic Cooperation Fund, July-September 1989.

Oye, Kenneth, ed. *Cooperation Under Anarchy*. Princeton, NJ: Princeton University Press, 1986.

Ozawa, Terutomo. *Multinationalism, Japanese Style*. Princeton: Princeton University Press, 1978.

Paderanga, Cayetano, and Ernesto Pernia. "Economic Policies and Spacial and Urban Development," *Regional Development Dialogue* 4 (Autumn 1983): 67-86.

Pakkasem, Phisit. *Leading Issues in Thailand's Development Transformation, 1960-1990*. Bangkok: National Economic and Social Development Board, Office of the Prime Minister, 1988.

Pangestu, Mari. *Japanese and Other Foreign Investment in the ASEAN Countries*. Canberra: Australia-Japan Research Centre, 1981.

Pante, Filologo, and Romeo Reyes. *Japanese and U.S. Development Assistance to the Philippines: a Philippines Perspective*. Manila: Philippine Institute for Development Studies, Working Paper No. 89-07, April 1989.

Pharr, Susan. "Japanese Aid in the New World Order," in Craig Garby and Mary Brown Bullock, eds., *Japan: A New Kind of Superpower*. Washington, DC: Woodrow Wilson Center Press, 1994, pp. 159-80.

Philippines, Department of Agrarian Reform, *The State of Agrarian Reform after the First Year of the Ramos Administration*. Quezon City: Department of Agrarian Reform, August 1993.

Philippines, National Economic and Development Authority. *Annex to the Philippines Five-Year Development Plan, 1978-1982: Profiles of Selected Projects*. Manila: National Economic and Development Authority. 1977.

────. *Five-Year Philippine Development Plan: Profile of Selected Development Projects, 1978-1982*. Manila: National Economic and Development Authority. 1977.

────. *Five-Year Philippine Development Plan, 1983-1987: Technical Annex*. Manila: National Economic and Development Authority. 1982.

────. *Four-Year Development Plan, FY 1971-74*. Manila: National Economic and Development Authority. 1970.

────. *Four-Year Development Plan, FY 1972-75*. Manila: National Economic and Development Authority. July 23, 1971.

────. *Four-Year Development Plan, FY 1974-77*. Manila: National Economic and Development Authority. 1973.

────. *Medium-Term Philippine Development Plan, 1987-1992*. Manila: National Economic and Development Authority. 1986.

────. *Medium-Term Public Investment Program, 1989-1992*. Manila: National Economic and Development Authority. September 1989.

────. *Official Development Assistance Flows to the Philippines, 1970-79*. Manila: National Economic and Development Authority. December, 1980.

────. *Regional Development Projects: Supplemental to the Four-Year Development Plan, 1974-77*. Manila. National Economic and Development Authority. 1973.

────. *Updates on the Medium-Term Philippine Development Plan, 1990-1992*. Manila. National Economic and Development Authority. 1990.

Philippines, Office of Foreign Aid Coordination, National Economic Council. *Annual Report of Foreign Aid Programs in the Philippines for FY 1964.* Manila. Office of Foreign Aid Coordination. 1964.

Philippines, *The President's Budget Highlights: Four-Year Infrastructure Program, 1976-1979 and Fiscal Year 1976 Budget.* Manila: Government Printing Office, 1975.

Phongpaichit, Pasuk, Busaba Kunasirin, and Buddhagarn Rutchatorn, eds. *The Lion and the Mouse? Japan, Asia and Thailand.* Proceedings of an International Conference of Thai-Japan Relations. Bangkok: Chulalongkorn University, April, 1986.

Pombhejara, Vichitvong Na, ed. *Readings in Thailand's Political Economy.* Bangkok: Printing Enterprise Co., 1978.

Potter, David. "Assessing Japan's Environmental Aid Policy," *Pacific Affairs* 67 (summer 1994): 200-15.

Puntasen, Apichai, Somboon Siriprachai, and Chaiyuth Punyasavatsut, "Political Economy of Eucalyptus: Business, Bureaucracy and the Thai Government," *Journal of Contemporary Asia* 22, no. 2 (1992): 187-206.

Punyaratabandhu-Bhakdi, Suchitra. "Thailand in 1983," *Asian Survey* 24 (February 1983): 187-93.

Putnam, Robert. "Diplomacy and Domestic Politics: the Logic of Two-level Games," *International Organization* 42 (summer 1988): 427-60.

Ramseyer, Mark, and Frances Rosenbluth. *Japan's Political Marketplace.* Cambridge, MA: Harvard University Press, 1993.

Ray, Jayanta. "Development and US Aid: A Case Study of Thailand," *IDSA Journal.* (July-September 1984): 401-54.

Reyes, Romeo. *Official Development Assistance to the Philippines: A Study of Administrative Capacity and Performance.* Manila: National Economic and Development Administration, 1985.

———. *Absorptive Capacity for Foreign Aid: The Case of the Philippines.* Manila: Philippine Institute of Development Studies and the International Center for Economic Growth, 1993.

Richter, Linda. *Land Reform and Tourism Development: Policy-making in the Philippines.* Cambridge, MA: Schenkman Publishing, 1982.

Riddell, Roger C. *Foreign Aid Reconsidered.* Baltimore: Johns Hopkins University Press, 1987.

Riedinger, Jeffrey. "The Philippines in 1993," *Asian Survey* 34 (February 1994): 139-46.

Rix, Alan. *Japan's Economic Aid.* New York: St. Martin's Press, 1980.

———. *Japan's Aid Program: A New Global Agenda.* Canberra: Australian Government Publishing Service, 1990.

———. "Japan's Foreign Aid Policy: A Capacity for Leadership?" *Pacific Affairs* 62 (winter 1989-90): 46-75.

———. *Japan's Foreign Aid Challenge.* London and New York: Routledge, 1993.

Robinson, David, Yangho Byeon, and Ranjit Teja. *Thailand: Adjusting to Success.* Washington, DC: International Monetary Fund, 1991.

Robinson, Richard, Kevin Hewison, and Richard Higgott, eds. *Southeast Asia in the 1980's.* London and Boston: Allen and Unwin, 1987.

Rudner, Martin. "Japan's Official Development Assistance to Southeast Asia," *Modern Asian Studies* 23 (February 1989): 73-116.

Saasa, O. S. "Public Policy-making in Developing Countries: the Utility of Contemporary Decision-making Models," *Public Administration and Development.* (October-December 1985): 309-22.

Sakamoto, Nobuo. "Nochi Kaikaku: Sono Gaiyo to Kongo no Kadai," (Agrarian Reform: Its Outline and Future Topics). *OECF Research Quarterly* 11 (1989): 22-44.

Samakose, Varakorn. "Thailand's White Paper: A Suggested Trade Relationship with Japan," *Thai-Japanese Studies* (August 1988): 34-38.

Seagrave, Sterling. *The Marcos Dynasty.* New York: Harper and Row, 1988.

Selim, Hassan. *Development Assistance Policies and the Performance of Aid Agencies.* London: Macmillan Press Ltd., 1983.

Sewell, John, and W. Patrick Murphy. *The United States and Japan in Southeast Asia: Is a Shared Development Agenda Possible?* Washington, DC: Overseas Development Council, May, 1991.

Shibuya, Yukio, and Shoichi Yamashita. *Foreign Aid and Economic Growth of Developing Asian States.* Tokyo: Institute of Asian Economic Affairs, 1968.

Shimao, Yasuhiko. "Yotsu no Dankai no Ojita Keizai Kyoryoku no Jidai: Tai o Jirei toshite," (The Era of Four-Level Economic Cooperation: Thailand as a Case). *Gaiko Forum* (December 1988): 48-54.

Shoven, John, ed. *Government Policy toward Industry in the United States and Japan.* New York: Cambridge University Press, 1988.

Sicat, Gerardo. "A Historical and Current Perspective of Philippines Economic Problems, *Social Science Information* 12 (January-March 1985).

———. *New Economic Directions in the Philippines.* Manila: National Economic and Development Authority, 1974.

Siffin, William. *The Thai Bureaucracy: Institutional Change and Development.* Honolulu: East-West Center Press, 1966.

Singer, Marshall R. *Weak States in a World of Powers.* New York: The Free Press, 1972.

Sivaraksa, S. "Rural Poverty and Development in Thailand, Indonesia and the Philippines," *Ecologist* 15 (1985): 266-68.

Solidum, Estrella. "Philippine Perceptions of Crucial Issues Affecting Southeast Asia," *Asian Survery* 22 (June 1982): 536-47.

"Sources and Uses of Foreign Assistance to the Philippine Government, 1972-1976," *Journal of Philippine Development* 4, no. 1 (1977): 104-26.

Southeast Asian Perceptions of Foreign Assistance. Papers and Proceedings of a Workshop Organized by the Institute of Southeast Asian Studies, Singapore, and the Institute of Asian Studies, Chulalongkorn University. Singapore: Institute for Southeast Asian Studies, 1977.

Sternstein, Larry. "Internal Migration and Regional Development: the Khon Kaen Development Centre of Northeast Thailand," *Journal of Southeast Asian Studies* 8 (March 1977): 106-16.

Sudo, Sueo. "The Road to Becoming a Regional Leader: Japanese Attempts in Southeast Asia." *Pacific Affairs* 61 (spring 1988): 27-50.

Sugitani, Shigeru. *Japan's Economic Assistance to Thailand.* Bangkok: Economic Cooperation Center for the Asian and Pacific Region, 1975.

Sumi, Kazuo. *ODA: Enjo no Genjitsu* (ODA: the Reality of Aid). Tokyo: Iwanami Shoten, 1989.

———. "Shin no 'Enjo Neezu' ni Sotta Enjo o" (Aid Which Really Meets "Aid Needs"), *Komei* (June 1990): 108-22.

Suriyamongkol, Marjorie. *The Politics of ASEAN Economic Cooperation.* Oxford: Oxford University Press, 1988.

Svetanant, Prapant et al. *2000-nen ni Mukete no Tai Keizai* (The Thai Economy Looking toward the Year 2000). Tokyo: Ajia Keizai Kenkyusho, 1995.

Suzuki, Nagatoshi. *Nihon no Keizai Kyoryoku* (Japan's Economic Cooperation). Toyko: Ajia Keizai Kenkyusho, 1990.

"Tai no Keizai Kaihatsu to Gaikoku Shakkan" (Thailand's Economic Development and Foreign Loans), *Kokusai Kaihatsu Janaru* (April 1981): 84-87.

Takahashi, Akira. *Japan's ODA to the Philippines.* Tokyo: Tokyo University Research Institute for the Japanese Economy, July, 1990.

——. "Making the Most of Development Aid," *Japan Quarterly* (October-December 1983): 402-5.

——. *The Impacts of Japanese Aid on Beneficiaries: Observations in Southeast Asia.* Tokyo: Tokyo University Research Institute for the Japanese Economy, October, 1987.

Tanaka, Shoko. *Post-War Japanese Resource Policies and Strategies: The Case of Southeast Asia.* Ithaca, NY: Cornell University Center for Southeast Asian Studies, 1986.

Tendler, Judith. *Inside Foreign Aid.* Baltimore: Johns Hopkins University Press, 1975.

Thailand, Department of Technical and Economic Cooperation. *Outline of the Fifth National Economic and Social Development and its External Assistance Requirements.* Bangkok. Department of Technical and Economic Cooperation. @ 1981.

——. *Technical Assistance Under the Sixth National Economic and Social Development Plan, 1987-1991.* Bangkok: Department of Technical and Economic Cooperation. 1987.

Thailand, National Economic Development Board. *Performance Evaluation of Development in Thailand for 1965.* Bangkok: National Economic Development Board. @ 1966.

Thailand, National Economic and Social Development Board. *Fifth National Economic and Social Development Plan (1982-1986).* Bangkok: National Economic and Social Development Board. 1981.

——. *Fifth National Economic and Social Development Plan (1982-1986) and Its External Assistance Requirements.* Bangkok: National Economic and Social Development Board. @ 1981.

——. *Fourth National Economic and Social Development Plan (1977-1981).* Bangkok: National Economic and Social Development Board. 1976.

——. *Second National Economic and Social Development Plan (1967-1971).* Bangkok: National Economic and Social Development Board. @ 1967.

——. *Sixth National Economic and Social Development Plan (1987-1991).* Bangkok: National Economic and Development Board. 1986.

——. *Summary of the Sixth National Economic and Social Development Plan (1977-1981).* Bangkok: National Economic and Development Board. @ 1986.

——. *Third National Economic and Social Development Plan, 1972-1976.* Bangkok: International Translations, 1972.

Thailand, National Statistics Office. *Statistical Yearbook.* Bangkok: National Statistics Office. Selected years.

Theeravit, Khien et al. *Research Report on Danish, German, and Japanese Assistance to Agricultural Development in Thailand.* Bangkok: Chulalongkorn University, Institute of Asian Studies, 1984.

Timberman, David, ed. *A Guide to Philippine Economic and Business Information Sources.* Manila: Joint Forum for Philippine Progress, 1990.

Tinakorn, Pranee. "Japan's Economic Assistance to Thailand, 1969-1986," in Yoshihara Kunio, ed. *Japan in Thailand.* Kuala Lumpur: Falcon Press, 1990: 51-76.

Toba, Reijiro. "ASEAN Development Strategy and Japanese Cooperation," *Asia Pacific Community* 24 (spring 1984): 74-84.

Tracy, Brian. "Bargaining as Trial and Error: the Case of the Spanish Base Negotiations," in William Zartman, ed. *The Negotiating Process.* Beverly Hills, CA: Sage, 1978.

Tsuda, Mamoru, and Leo Deocadiz. *RP-Japan Relations and ADB: in Search of a New Horizon.* Manila: National Book Store, 1986.

United States Agency for International Development. *A Survey of Foreign Economic and Technical Assistance Programs in the Philippines.* Washington, DC: United States Agency for International Development, 1965-66.

United States General Accounting Office. *Problems of Coordinating Multilateral Assistance to Thailand.* Report to the Congress by the Comptroller General of the United States, August 26, 1975.

UPLB Rural Development Study Team. *Philippine Rural Development: Problems, Issues and Directions.* Los Banos: University of the Philippines Los Banos, 1991.

Vellut, J. L. "Japanese Reparations to the Philippines," *Asian Survey.* (October 1962): 496-506.

Vorathepputipong, Thavan, et. al. *Administration of Thai Export Promotion Policies and Japan's Cooperation.* Tokyo: Institute of Developing Economies, 1989.

Warr, Peter, ed. *The Thai Economy in Transition.* Cambridge, UK: Cambridge University Press, 1993.

Watanabe, Toshio, and Kusano Atsushi. *Nihon no ODA o Do Suru ka* (What Is to Be Done About Japan's ODA?). Tokyo: NHK Books, 1991.

White, John. *The Politics of Foreign Aid.* New York: St. Martin's Press, 1974.

Wood, Robert. *From Marshall Plan to Debt Crisis.* Berkeley and Los Angeles: University of California Press, 1986.

Woodall, Brian. "The Logic of Collusive Action: the Political Roots of Japan's *Dango* System," *Comparative Politics* 25 (April 1993): 297-312.

World Bank. *Thailand: Industrial Development Strategy in Thailand.* Washington, DC: World Bank, 1980.

———. *Thailand: Managing Public Resources for Structural Adjustment.* Washington, DC: World Bank, 1984.

———. *The Philippines: Priorities and Prospects for Development.* Washington, DC: World Bank, 1976.

Wurfel, David. *Filipino Politics.* Quezon City: Ateneo de Manila University Press, 1988.

Yamane, Hiroko. "Japan as Asian/Pacific Power," *Asian Survey* 27 (December 1987): 1240-55.

Yasutomo, Dennis T. *Japan and the Asian Development Bank.* New York: Praeger, 1983.

———. *The Manner of Giving: Strategic Aid and Japanese Foreign Policy.* Lexington, MA: Lexington Books, 1986.

———. *The New Multilateralism in Japan's Foreign Policy.* New York: St. Martin's Press, 1995.

———. "Why Aid? Japan as an 'Aid Great Power'" *Pacific Affairs* 62 (winter 1989-90) 490-503.

Yokoyama, Masaki. *Fuiripin Enjo to Jiriki Koseiron* (Philippine Aid and Self-Help.) Tokyo: Akashi Shoten, 1990.

Yoshino, Michael. *Japan's Multinational Enterprises.* Cambridge, MA: Harvard University Press, 1976.

Appendix:
Interviews and Assistance

Kimura Etsuko, Training Coordinator, International Cooperation Service Center, Sendai, Japan.

Nowada Koichi, Managing Director, Japan International Cooperation Agency, Tohoku Branch, Sendai.

Edmund Klamann, Nihon Keizai Shinbun, Tokyo.

Ernesto S. Castro, Under Secretary and Officer-in-charge, Office of the Executive Director, Coordinating Council of the Philippine Assistance Program, Manila.

Robert Orr, Professor, Stanford University Institute of Japanese Studies, Kyoto.

Evan Garcia, First Secretary, Economic Section, Embassy of the Philippines, Tokyo.

Domoto Akiko, House of Councillors, Diet of Japan.

Takahashi Akira, Professor, Tokyo University Faculty of Economics, Tokyo.

Fukushima Mitsuo, Institute of Developing Economies, Tokyo.

Yoshida Mikimasa, Institute of Developing Economies, Tokyo.

R. Byron Sigel, Second Secretary, Economic Section, United States Embassy, Tokyo.

Romy Peralta, Director, Resource Center for Philippine Concerns, Tokyo.

Nishikawa Jun, Professor, Waseda University, Tokyo.

Nikki M. L. Coseteng, House of Representatives, Congress of the Philippines.

Anne Emig, Researcher, Export-Import Bank of Japan.

Michael Mullen, International Affairs Advisor to Hamada Takujiro, House of Representatives, Diet of Japan.

Bonifacio Gillego, House of Representatives, Congress of the Philippines.

Oshima Katsuhiko, Public Relations Division, General Affairs Department, Japan International Cooperation Agency.

Sugishita Tsuneo, Deputy Director, Comment and News Analysis Department, Yomiuri Shinbun.

Kasahara Hideaki, Deputy Director, First Regional Division, Planning Department, Japan International Cooperation Agency.

Hashimoto Goro, Director, Political Division, Yomiuri Shinbun.

Sakai Hideyoshi, Institute of Developing Economies, Tokyo.

Taniguchi Koji, Institute of Developing Economies, Tokyo.

Ogawa Hitoshi, Director, Economic Cooperation Division, Marubeni Corporation.

Ejima Shinya, Manager, First Division, Loan Department 1, Overseas Economic Cooperation Fund.

Aoki Keiichi, First Division, Loan Department 1, Overseas Economic Cooperation Fund.

Akatsuka Yuzo, Professor, Faculty of Engineering, Tokyo University.

Ono Katsushi, Forum for a Liberal Society, Tokyo.

Kato Hiroshi, Correspondent, Shukan Bunshun, Tokyo.

Inoue Toneri, Public Affairs Section, Nihon Kensetsu Rengo, Tokyo.

Aburaya Tsutomu, Overseas Construction Association of Japan, Inc., Tokyo.

Isomata Akio, Loan Aid Division, Economic Cooperation Bureau, Ministry of Foreign Affairs, Tokyo.

Nakamura Morio, Aid Policy Division, Economic Cooperation Bureau, Ministry of Foreign Affairs, Tokyo.

Sato Seizaburo, International Institute for Global Peace, and Tokyo University.

Honda Etsuro, Senior Research Fellow, International Institute for Global Peace, Tokyo.

Matsumoto Hiroshi, Executive Director, Association for the Promotion of International Cooperation, Tokyo.

Harada Yutaka, Postal Ministry Research Institute, Tokyo.

Akabane Ryoya, Tohoku Die-Cast Kogyosha and TDC Philippines Corporation, Sendai.

Motomura Yoshiyuki, Director, Customs Bureau, Ministry of Finance, Tokyo.

Virginia G. Abiad, Visiting Research Fellow, Institute of Developing Economies, Tokyo.

Morisawa Keiko, Visiting Research Associate, University of the Philippines School of Economics, Manila.

Takeuchi Kikuo, Deputy Resident Representative, Philippine Office, Japan International Cooperation Agency, Manila.

Umeda Kazunori, Chief Representative, Export-Import Bank of Japan, Manila.

Florian Alburo, Professor, University of the Philippines School of Economics, Manila.

Mariles Navarro, Japan Officer, Public Investment Staff, National Economic and Development Authority, Manila.

Romeo Reyes, Assistant Director-General, National Economic and Development Authority, Manila.

Floro Adviento, Overseas Economic Cooperation Fund, Manila.

Watanabe Eiichi, Director, Programs Division (East), Asian Development Bank.

Kojima Tomakata, Senior Deputy Director, Development Finance Division, Ministry of Finance, Tokyo.

Igarashi Takeshi, Professor, Tokyo University Faculty of Law.

Maeda Yasuhiro, Economic Cooperation Division, International Trade Policy Bureau, Ministry of International Trade and Industry, Tokyo.

Noguchi Kunio, Economic Cooperation Division, International Trade Policy Bureau, Ministry of International Trade and Industry, Tokyo.

Iwanami Takao, Assistant Chief, Economic Cooperation Coordination Office, International Trade Policy Bureau, Ministry of International Trade and Industry, Tokyo.

Tomimoto Ikufumi, Deputy Director, First Basic Design Study Division, Grant Aid Study and Design Department, Japan International Cooperation Agency, Tokyo.

Prasert Chittawatangpong, Professor, Thammasat University Faculty of Political Science.

Index

accommodation xv-xvi, 102-103, 151,
154-155, 157-159
Afghanistan 18
aid terms
to Thailand 30-32
to the Philippines 37-40
Angenit Corporation 132-133, 182n
anticipatory bargaining xvii, 109-112,
121, 158-160
Aquino assassination 86, 140, 184n
Aquino, Corazon 87, 128, 183n
ASEAN-Japan Development Fund (AJDF)
8, 9
Asian Development Bank (ADB) 6, 44,
49, 66, 68, 73, 78, 80, 81, 83, 93, 94,
99, 121
Asian Industrial Development Plan (AID)
9
Association of Siamese Architects (ASA)
143-144
Association of Southeast Asian Nations
(ASEAN) 8-9, 24, 51, 54, 57, 59,
100, 152
Australia 2, 49
availment rate 83, 174n
Ayutthaya Historical Study Center 127,
142-145, 150

Bangkok Japanese Chamber of Commerce
142
Bank for Agriculture and Agricultural
Cooperatives (BAAC) 49, 50, 54,
57, 67
bilateralism 2, 10
Boyce, James 86
Burma 165n

C. Itoh Corporation 132-133

CALABARZON 93, 175n
Cassen, Robert xii
Chatichai administration 104-105
Chiang Mai University hospital grant ix,
114
China 7, 8, 9
cofinancing 94, 176n
Colombo Plan 2
Committee on Official Development
Assistance 88, 156
commodity loans ix, 35, 38-39, 40, 72-73,
78, 86, 90, 93, 139, 154
companies, Japanese xv, 15-16, 45, 66,
88, 105, 106-109, 112, 117, 122,
123, 132-135, 143, 144, 145
companies, Thai 62, 66, 108, 144, 146
Comprehensive Agrarian Reform Law
(CARL) 129
Comprehensive Agrarian Reform Program
(CARP) 129-130
conditionality xii, xiv, 2, 6, 94, 95, 99, 100
Congress, Philippines 118, 129
Coordinating Committee for the Philippine Assistance Plan (CCPAP) 88,
156
corruption 87, 88, 117, 132-135, 152,
183n, 186n
Country Study for Development Assistance to the Kingdom of Thailand
64, 65
Country Study for Development Assistance to the Republic of the Philippines 90-92, 93
Countryside Agro-industrial Development
program (CAID) 89, 92, 175n
coup d'etat, Thailand 68, 158

dam construction, aid for 45-46, 53

dango 117, 133, 180n, 182n 186n
debt crisis, Philippines 72, 86, 138
debt policy, Philippines 90, 94-95
debt policy, Thailand 60
Debt Policy Committee, Thailand 103
debt rescheduling 12, 35, 39, 94
Department of Agrarian Reform (DAR) 128-131, 151
Department of Technical and Economic Cooperation (DTEC) 60, 62, 63, 104, 105, 107, 112, 156
Department of Trade and Industry 129
Development Assistance Committee (DAC) 3, 5, 7, 21, 48, 68, 98
development plans, Philippines 71-90
development plans, Thailand 24, 43-64
Diet, Japan 11-12, 16, 87, 130, 140-142, 180n, 183n, 184n
disaster relief 26, 27, 34, 35
Doi Takako 179n

Eastern Europe 9
Eastern Seaboard Development Plan (ESDP) 28-29, 58-60, 63, 64, 99, 105, 107, 109, 110, 145-147, 151, 152, 161
Economic Planning Agency x, 11, 20
embassies, Japanese 13-14, 106, 136, 143
England 2
environmental aid 65-66, 148-149, 167n
eucalyptus plantations 148-149
Export-Import Bank of Japan 3, 8, 12, 13, 24, 32, 37, 45, 48, 50, 86, 94, 169n

feasibility studies 105, 106, 112
France 6
Fukuda Doctrine 9, 24, 51, 152, 169n

Germany 2, 6, 7, 13, 49, 61, 81, 83
Gordenker, Leon xi-xii
growth pole strategy 42, 47, 57, 63, 65
implementing officer 83, 8, 117, 133, 155, 179n
Indochina 30, 51, 54, 99
Indonesia 2, 7, 8, 9, 11, 18, 53, 158, 165n
Industrial Finance Corporation of Thailand (IFCT) 45, 50, 65, 67, 110
international aid regime 1-3

International Monetary Fund (IMF) 86, 94, 95, 96, 139, 141
Iran 18
Italy 95, 156

Japan-Asia Industrial Development Organization (JAIDO) 8, 9
Japan International Cooperation Agency (JICA) ix, 5, 12, 13, 14, 15, 65, 91, 105, 112, 113, 114, 115, 121-122, 123, 131, 135, 143-145, 148, 150, 178n
Japan Overseas Cooperation Volunteers (JOCV) 13, 32
Jay, Keith xi

Kingdon, John 111, 177n
Kotake Yoshio 132, 134
Kreuger, Ann xii

Laem Chabang Port loan 145-147, 149, 150-151, 157
land reform 90, 92, 128-131
Latin America 9
Liberal Democratic Party (LDP) 16
loan cancellation 83, 100, 119, 123, 150

Malaysia 9, 100, 119, 165n
Marcos, Ferdinand ix, 19, 88, 115-116, 132, 182n
Marcos, Imelda 93, 116, 136-138, 180n
Marcos Documents 132, 149, 152
martial law, Philippines 69, 114
medium-term development plans 41-99
    as statements of government priority xviii
Medium-Term Public Investment Program (MTPIP) 88, 92, 97, 121, 122-123
Mekong Committee 45-46
Michalopoulis, Constantin xii
Ministry of Agriculture, Forestry and Fisheries (MAFF) 13, 130
Ministry of Communications, Thailand 145-147
Ministry of Finance, Japan x, 3, 11, 12, 20
Ministry of Finance, Philippines 115, 121
Ministry of Finance, Thailand 66, 103, 110, 147

Ministry of Foreign Affairs, Japan x, 3, 7, 9, 11, 12, 19, 97, 135, 159
Ministry of Foreign Affairs, Thailand 67, 144
Ministry of Interior, Thailand 143, 144
Ministry of International Trade and Industry x, 11, 12, 13, 20, 49, 132, 133
Ministry of Public Works and Highways 119, 133
Mosley, Paul xii
Multilateral Assistance Initiative (MAI) xiv, xviii, 9, 12, 91, 95-96, 99, 123, 156, 176n
Murai Yoshinori 136
Muscat, Robert 45, 146, 170n

Nakasone Yasuhiro 87, 136, 140, 143
National Economic and Development Authority (NEDA) 88, 103, 114-117, 119, 121, 122-123, 124, 156, 186n
National Economic and Social Development Board (NESDB) 46, 61, 103-105, 107, 110, 124, 125, 145-147, 156
National Maritime Polytechnic (NMP) 116, 135-138, 152
New Village Development Program 53, 55, 161
New Zealand 118
nongovernmental organizations (NGOs) 20, 91

official development assistance, Japan
    budget process 11-12
    concessionality 6-8, 87
    First Medium-Term Target 4
    geographic distribution 8-9
    grant aid 5
    growth in aid volume 4
    loan aid 5
    media input 16-17
    multilateral aid 6, 12
    ODA Charter 20, 167n
    organization of aid bureaucracy 10-16
    purpose of aid 9, 17-20
    Second Medium-Term Target 4
Ohira Cabinet 18, 54

omiyage gaiko 137
Organization for Economic Cooperation and Development (OECD) 3, 7, 19, 100, 156
Orr, Robert x, 9
Overseas Construction Association of Japan, Inc. (OCAJI) 108
Overseas Economic Cooperation Fund (OECF) 10, 11, 12, 13, 14, 15, 32, 37, 45, 48, 66, 83, 84, 86, 97, 98, 107, 109, 112, 113, 115, 118-119, 120, 121-122, 123, 125, 135, 146-147, 183n
Overseas Technical Cooperation Agency (OTCA) 13, 45, 78

Pakistan 18
Palawan Crocodile Institute 121
Pan-Philippine Highway 32, 36, 74, 77, 78, 82, 92, 93, 118
Paris Club 95
People Power 87
Philippine Commission on Good Government 183n
Philippines, regions 36-37
    Cagayan Valley 77, 79, 82, 99, 132-133, 180n
    Ilocos Norte 82, 93, 116
    Leyte 82, 116
    Luzon 74, 76, 78, 82, 85, 92, 93, 97, 121
    Manila 70, 74, 76, 78, 82, 85, 90
    Mindanao 76-77, 78, 80, 90, 92, 93
    Visayas 77, 78, 80, 81, 82, 85, 90, 92, 93
policy dialogue xi, 111
prebargaining 111-112, 121-122, 124, 149
Prem cabinet 104, 146
principal-agent problem xiii-xv, 102-103, 106, 122
program loans 40, 123, 154, 176n
Project Facilitation Committee (PFC) 88, 156

Ramos administration 96, 129
reforestation projects 148
refugee aid 54-55, 65

reparations program 3, 12, 17, 32, 40, 45,
        118, 135, 165n
request principle xiv, 10, 125
resource diplomacy ix, 18, 167n
Reyes, Romeo 83, 176n
Rix, Alan x, 3, 10, 14, 15, 20
rolling plans 62, 91
Rudner, Martin 161

second face of power xvi
sectoral distribution of Japanese aid
        to Thailand 26, 27-28, 45-46, 48-
                49, 52-55, 57-60, 64-66, 68, 69
        to the Philippines 34-35, 72-74,
                77-79, 81-82, 85-87, 90-92,
                97, 99
Singapore 9, 153, 165n
"sources of funds" approach 49
South Korea 19, 165n, 186n
State Railway of Thailand 110
strategic aid xvii, 18-19, 54-55
studies of Japan's foreign aid x-xi
survey missions 14-15
Suzuki Zenko 57

Takeshita Noboru 128
Tanaka Kakuei 50
technical assistance 4, 5-6, 11, 13, 54, 57,
        62, 63, 67, 107
Tendler, Judith 113
Thailand, regions 28-30
        Bangkok 42, 45, 48, 49, 52, 56, 58,
                63, 65
        Central Plain 42, 54, 65
        North 46, 47, 49, 54-55
        Northeast 43, 44, 46, 47, 49, 54-55
                65, 99
        South 63, 64
Toyo Corporation 132-134, 182n
Twelfth Yen Loan, Philippines 138-142,
        152
two-step loans 40, 154
tying status 6-7, 30-32, 38-39, 50, 51, 62,
        66, 79, 83, 108-109, 122, 146

UNESCO 106
United Nations (UN) xii, 2, 6
United States x, 2, 3, 8, 43, 45, 51, 61, 72,
        80, 85, 91, 95, 96, 98, 104, 139, 157,
        170n
United States Agency for International
        Development (USAID) xv, 2, 68,
        83, 84, 94, 99, 113, 130

Vietnam 18, 30, 51, 165n
Virata, Cesar 139

White, John xii
White Paper on Thai-Japanese Relations
        60, 61-62, 67
Wood, Robert 2, 169n
Woodall, Brian 135
World Bank xii, 2, 5, 20, 24, 35, 38, 44,
        49, 61, 66, 67-68, 70, 73, 78, 80, 81,
        83, 93, 94, 98, 99, 121

Yasutomo, Dennis x, 18, 54, 170n